POPULAR MEDIA
and the
Teaching of English

Edited by
THOMAS R. GIBLIN

University of Colorado
Colorado Springs Center

GOODYEAR PUBLISHING COMPANY, INC.

Pacific Palisades, California

Goodyear Education Series

Theodore W. Hipple, *Editor*
UNIVERSITY OF FLORIDA

Popular Media and the Teaching of English
THOMAS R. GIBLIN

School Counseling: Problems and Methods
ROBERT MYRICK AND JOE WITTMER

Secondary School Teaching: Problems and Methods
THEODORE W. HIPPLE

Copyright © 1972 by

GOODYEAR PUBLISHING COMPANY, INC.
Pacific Palisades, California

Library of Congress Catalog Card Number: 79-164464

ISBN: 0-87620-716-6

Y-7166-5

Current printing (last number):

10 9 8 7 6 5 4 3 2 1

Printed in the United States of America

To My Parents

Contents

Preface

There is a need to rethink the shape and design of learning experiences in our high schools in terms of the meanings which inhabit the personal world of each young person.

This book is a collection of ideas that deal essentially with the *why* and the *how* of popular media study in the secondary English classroom: *why* English teachers need to look more closely at the popular media of communication—television, movies, radio, records, paperbacks, newspapers, magazines—and *how* English teachers might act upon these perceptions. If you are currently contemplating a career in the teaching of English, I hope these ideas will provide an adequate balance between the why and how of media education. If you are already a teacher of English, I hope this book will provide the momentum needed to initiate a media study program or the supportive reinforcement to continue and to expand your present curriculum.

One assumption underlying this book is that these popular media of communication are major sources of information and persuasion that represent a significant influence on the English curriculum. A second assumption is that these media are communication systems worthy of study in their own right as well as useful vehicles in the achievement of instructional goals, such as the improvement of reading through the newspaper. This dual view is important if we are to comprehend fully the media's value and influence.

The English classroom should be an environment wherein the student identifies and learns to use the tools that will assist him in cognitive and affective growth intrinsic to his search for personal meaning. His study of modern media can increase his capacity in creative and critical thinking, his effectiveness of self-expression, and his sensitivity to visual, aural, and tactile perceptions, which is vital to human interaction and communication. The study of the popular media can complement the study of the spoken and written word, which

Norman K. Hamilton and J. Galen Saylor, eds., *Humanizing the Secondary School* (Washington, D.C.: Association for Supervision and Curriculum Development, 1969), p. 10.

dominates today's English programs in most schools. The popular media can evoke emotional response, self-understanding, and concept development unthought of a few years ago. Through television, for example, today's adolescent can see and feel the terror of a war thousands of miles from home, have the best seat in the house for a Shakespearean drama, view the mysteries of the undersea world, or enjoy his major league sports idol in action.

English teachers are discovering that it is better to train young people to understand and to use the media wisely than to have them used by it. They are also learning that the media, unlike many other materials, can be relevant to all students regardless of their social class, cultural background, age, and experience. Some English programs are already alive with exciting media study. Classroom activities include composition with film, propaganda analysis in advertising, speaking/listening improvement through simulated radio and television programing, individualized reading programs facilitated by newspapers, magazines, and paperbacks, a new sensitivity for poetry found in modern music and song lyrics, sharpened perceptions resulting from film study, and *much dialogue!*

These activities provide a bridge between the school and the student's world, assisting each individual in his sometimes desperate struggle for self-identity. The media can generate a climate in which exploratory dialogue evolves naturally and no student has to feel inferior because he can't read a certain book or diagram sentences; each perception about a movie, television program, or song lyric has intrinsic worth. Such a climate will be most beneficial to the high school student who wants to know who he is, what is important, where he is going, and what he is going to be when he "arrives." This struggle is not novel with today's adolescent, but it is a significantly different challenge when one considers the multiple influences serving to help or to hinder his process of becoming.

I would like to express my appreciation for the stimulation and support given me by several individuals. Very sincere thanks are due to my students, each of whom in his or her own way has been influential in the preparation of this book; to the publishers and authors who have made this book possible; to Dr. David Manly for the initial inspiration; to Mr. Gregory Byrne for his support of my media interests; and to Dr. Theodore Hipple for his most helpful guidance throughout the preparation of this book.

Above all, I wish to thank Peggy, my wife, for her invaluable suggestions and the many hours she devoted to this project.

SECTION ONE

Developing a Rationale for Popular Media Study

On Mediacy   **FRANK McLAUGHLIN**

believes "The electronic revolution has created a nongraded world where school is possibly the least powerful force of information and persuasion." He discusses the inadequacy of traditional teaching methods, which do not meet the needs of the modern adolescent "groping to understand the real world."

**Popular Culture
and Negro Education**   **RICHARD L. BEARD**

identifies "a lack of a strong print tradition among Negro students" as the source of many problems of the Negro student in a print-oriented educational system. He believes popular culture, because it is a common medium available to all, is worthy of analysis as a potential aid to students seeking skill in the print tradition.

**Violence and the Mass Media:
Challenge to Education**   **CHARITY M. MANCE**

sees a curriculum "relevant to today's issues and problems" and to experiences important to the adolescent as a key to preparing young adults to deal "more effectively with some of the underlying causes of violence."

**Mass Media Curriculum:
Fantasy or Reality?**   **MARTIN A. McCULLOUGH**

believes that "the mass media do not influence greatly the basic values of the vast majority of young people," and recommends greater involvement

1

in learning or recreational activities for those important *exceptions* who " 'escape' to the fantasy involvement of television and the other media."

Image and Reality   S. I. HAYAKAWA

relates how television created a new "image" for him. He goes on to speculate on the relationship of television and student demonstrations, the drug experience, the democratic process, our materialistic culture, and education.

Film, Television, and Reality   CLIFFORD SOLWAY

asks whether most people in our society use "film as a guide to reality." Is television film generally accepted as being an accurate "picture of the times"? Solway's thesis is that viewing requires an "intelligent presence, someone who knows how to use the film medium without being used by it."

On Mediacy

Frank McLaughlin

A decade ago the image of the teacher presented to the public was in the Mr. Peepers, Our Miss Brooks vein. A lovable bumbler. I suppose today's counterpart would be someone who constantly walks in front of the overhead projector, trips over the legs of the portable screen, or whose abortive demonstrations end with, "Well, you know how it *should* turn out." Ineptness is the unhappy fusion of the wrong attitude and of inadequate techniques. Too often teachers who rant about man being subjugated by machines won't face the fact that they are unable to operate the most simple mechanical devices. Alert students intuitively realize that teachers who never reach beyond books and their own voices and who belabor the "dehumanizing" aspects of technology are reflecting their inability to cope with the present.

The teenager today is no longer insulated from the people who create news and from the problems which beset society. The electronic revolution has created a nongraded world where school is possibly the least powerful force of information and persuasion. Television has particularly intensified this situation. A teacher must know more than "the subject" if he expects to be an effective

From Frank McLaughlin, "On Mediacy," created from two articles that appeared in *Media and Methods.* Reprinted by permission of *Media and Methods* and the author.

contributor to the tapestry of learning experiences confronting the high school student.

Shouldn't we sympathize with the thousands of "psychic dropouts" who numbly endure the legion of irrelevant teachers—the obsolete communicating their obsolescence. Consider: The teachers who endlessly carp about TV. The textbook-forever faction who appraise paperbacks by tear-testing their pages. The reactionaries who wouldn't dream of using available electronic equipment. The "above-it-all" snob who dismisses the folk-rock transistorized adolescent subculture. Such "educators" would profit by examining their grasp of the present. Too often the "good old days," "I won't sell out attitude" is a reflection of being oblivious to the media which shape us.

Who we are and how we communicate are inextricably bound to the material we organize and present. The efficacy of our teaching is dependent upon how students perceive us. Once we step into the classroom, we cannot avoid being "competency models." Next to parents we are the most accessible models. This existential fact should lead us to be introspective about the image we present to our students.

The impressionable individuals we face have every right to measure what we say by what we are. We have assumed the task of developing young people during the stormiest period of their lives. Are we aware of what it must feel like to be an adolescent today?

Marshall McLuhan suggests that the twentieth-century child is the hardest working in history because he must absorb more in order to master his environment. While we are busy plying our "content," the adolescent is groping to understand the real world, attempting to fabricate a satisfying image of himself. He is hungry for direction. Mass communication has made his world small; he is often deeply involved beyond his own knowing. His consciousness is bombarded by subliminal advertising, "hip" philosophy punctuated by the big beat (via 45 rpm records) and by magazines and paperbacks of varying quality on every conceivable subject placed and priced democratically so that anyone can read whatever he wishes.

To be one more "fact dispenser," one more contributor to the welter of unrelated information seems insanity. Yet, isn't this what is happening? Couldn't we have just one faculty member who could stand *with* the student and help him interpret, analyze, and discriminate what is beamed at, through, and around him? One person who adopts the "let's explore this together" instead of the "listen and you'll learn something" approach. Being with them doesn't mean being their buddy; it means tuning in to their world, find out where they live, and establishing a live base for communication.

If we are trying to "shape" adolescents, it's time to harness ourselves to the present. Arthur Combs supports this contention in his article, "Seeing is Behaving" (*Educational Leadership,* October 1958). Combs feels that we have little chance to change an individual if we believe that behavior is "the result of all the things that have happened to him in the past." In fact, we might just as well forget about school. Combs offers an alternative hypothesis: "If it is true that behavior is a function of perception, then the causes of behavior lie fundamentally in the present and not in the past." If we accept this assumption, we can take youngsters where they are and begin helping those whom Combs calls "prisoners of their own perceptions." To accomplish this, we must free ourselves of our media biases and become attuned to what's "out there" and how all of us are perceiving it. This is one way we can reverse what McLuhan calls the "rear-view mirror" approach to education.

Assisting students in escaping from the provincialism of their own culture is a major task of education. The high level of technology must be understood as the product of civilization. Today's teenager must become both mediate and the possessor of a long memory. How do we do this? Not by annual pilgrimages to the shrines of Chaucer, Milton, and Shakespeare, but through interdisciplinary exploration of environments and media. We must put together a team of English, social studies, art, and science teachers, and explore the history, structure, function, and social effects of such a medium as television. Such a team attack would go far beyond the unsure skirmishes that now take place in English classrooms. It might also insure that future generations might be the first in history to exploit media for human betterment.

What I am suggesting goes beyond the capabilities of the present classroom situation. We must give up another long-cherished security blanket—the slavish attachment to our discipline. McLuhan has long acknowledged the need for a complete reprogramming of our education system. He has noted that:

> all the talk about instructional aids in the classroom from electronic means is nonsense. You cannot introduce electronic forms into the classroom without rescheduling the whole process of instruction, and this is impossible under our unwieldly, fragmented conditions of classroom use. ("From Instruction to Discovery," *Media and Methods,* October 1966)

English teachers have long been haunted by the specter of the mass media. Yet, all attempts at media study prove unsatisfactory. This certainly is not due to any lack of sincerity or effort, but to the obvious confining influence of the linear structures they work from. It has been impossible to thoroughly study media such as TV, motion pictures, and magazines in the English class because there are economic, scientific, and political forces to be dealt with, and these lie outside the English teacher's expertise.

Once teachers reorganize into interdisciplinary teams the mass media will lose its amorphous white whale quality. Whole environments can be probed, and the shaping powers of technology will be laid bare. The environment outside school will be constantly scrutinized and sifted and will serve as referent when explorations into past or foreign environments are undertaken. Would it be difficult to assemble a team to compare the Elizabethan environment with our own? This type of project would require considerable planning and ingenuity, but it would be a far cry from the piddling Globe Theater Slide Tour that so many of us have taken in trying to give students a sense of Shakespeare's time.

Such cross-fertilization would inspire not only a thorough sense of Elizabethan living, but, I wager, it would lead teenagers to make discoveries about their own situations. Each succeeding venture—fifth-century Greece, nineteenth-century Russia, or even the World Community of the twenty-first century—would be enhanced by past environmental explorations. It would also be possible to probe urban ghettos, suburbia, Polynesia, and various African cultures. Each environment would be a mosaic in which its customs, technology, literature, religion, geography, architecture, music, art, etc. would be examined. Teachers could direct students in meaningful research that could be shared with the group. School libraries could be stocked with books devoted to areas to be studied. Films could be rented that provide insight into the area being studied.

The ecological approach that I am posing necessitates a radical change in school organization and procedure. First, the 30—desk classroom must go. Large group and seminar situations would be needed. When students are not involved in presentations or discussions, they could be working on research or skills that need attention. Personalized instruction would become a reality. Teachers who are not engaged in large group instruction could give tutorial attention to individuals. This is where many of the new tools of educational technology could be creatively used. Programed texts, 8 mm film loops, kinescopes, and other teaching machines could assist a teacher in "customizing" a good program for *every* student.

The motto of this movement might be "Slow Down and Learn" or "Slow Down and Enjoy Education." The pace of school days would naturally follow the more thorough and leisurely interdisciplinary studies. Gone would be the fragmented, bell-ridden, subject-matter centered curriculum. Such a stopgap solution as modular scheduling could be eliminated, and the nongraded school would flourish in a conducive setting. Most important, the Humanities would be the heart of school programs, not the apologetic, makeshift intruder now struggling against the linear, utilitarian, and scientific influences that predominate. The school that I envision would literally be an environment that contrasts with the fouled environments we all inhabit. Schools of this nature would fulfill the "reconstructive" role that John Dewey so ardently worked for a half century ago.

Popular Culture and Negro Education

Richard L. Beard

INTRODUCTION

The introduction of the examination of popular culture into the other academic chores now performed by students is a desirable goal, and coherent calls for scholarly examination of the mass medis as instruments of socialization have been sounded with some results. In recent years there have been reversional trends with regard to the judged worth of communications as an area fertile enough to bear an academic discipline all its own; still, on balance it appears there is now a growing awareness of the social and educational significance of popular culture, and this concern is reflected in the growth of departments of communication and American studies.

If, however, it has been recognized that popular culture as cultural phenomenon merits the attention or academic thought and research in specialized classes in specialized areas, it is yet to be realized that the study of popular culture can be utilized as an important instrument in general liberal education.

While the assumptions which motivate the remarks here are predicated on the notion that strong education in general assumes serious concern with popular culture, the ambition of this discussion is limited in scope. The central notion of this paper is that thorough analysis of popular culture on the part of Negro students is exceedingly valuable and desirable. Such desirability is a function of the relationship between the educational system and the demands of the socio-cultural system. Some brief account of these demands on the educational process is in order, to be followed by an analysis of how the study of popular culture can help to solve problems created by social and cultural imperatives. That many Negro students are not faced with the problems to be discussed here, that many will indeed reject the cultural imperatives of the current educational process, is obvious, and need not be further noted.

From Richard L. Beard, "Popular Culture and Negro Education," *Journal of Negro Education* 38 (Winter 1969): 86-90. Copyright © 1969 by Howard University. Reprinted by permission of the publisher.

HISTORICAL BACKGROUND

Any educational system is necessarily a cultural outgrowth from the dominant societal institutions, and of the dominant class interests responsible for the preservation and perpetuation of the institutions. The Negro participant in the system immediately encounters a set of institutionalized circumstances which have prevailed over time, and continue to feed on the system that spawned them. The educational system and its guiding forces have in actuality changed almost imperceptibly since Veblen wrote *The Higher Learning in America* where he applied the yardstick for American education:

> The primary test is usefulness for getting an income. The secondary test, practically applied where latitude is allowed in the way of "culture" studies, is the aptness of the instruction in question to fit the learners for spending income in a decorous manner.

Certainly Veblen's remarks are not out of place in the corporate society; if anything, his analysis, now almost a half century old, has lost its heretical tone, and is accepted as legitmate—indeed as quite appropriate by far too many. For now, it appears to have been firmly established, education is a "tool"—tool being a sufficiently industrial term. With rare exception, the stuff of education to be had today has little to do with the education of *human beings*. On the other hand, "education" today is extremely important as an economic tool, and in the narrow sense of the term, education is important "socially."

As the myth system would have it, a simple formula appears: all any student has to do is learn the predominant value system and methodology of the dominant class interests, incorporate same sufficiently into his own world view, and take his place within the social order. The acceptability of such an approach, the sense of realism which propounds it, both are vulnerable to attack on both ethical and intellectual grounds. What is assailable is not necessarily unreal, unfortunately, and the reasons advanced for education structure the nature of the eductional process. Moreover it is evident that the educational rationale advanced above does represent, if somewhat crudely, the guiding force of almost all American institutions of the higher learning. How the Negro student, with his own special problems, can help make such a system more meaningful, and some of the problems he has in the process, are the areas to be commented on in a discussion of the analysis of popular culture in the classroom.

SIGNIFICANT AREAS OF CONCERN

It appears that there are two generalizable problems common to very many Negro students, and especially those who attend Southern Negro colleges: (1) a lack of ability to relate meaningfully to the broad socio-cultural context, and (2) an infirmity of background in the print tradition. Clearly these problems, one substantive, the other procedural, exist anywhere and everywhere, and among anyone and everyone, but the concern here is with how these problems are asserted, and solved, within the assigned context.

The ability to relate to the national culture meaningfully assumes a thorough knowledge of the culture, if not a thorough contact. Almost all of the ideas and events studied in texts, heard in lectures, and found in suggested readings are descriptions of the activities and thoughts of Caucasians, and are written for the most part by Caucasians. Negro students who have over time-related events and ideas to a subculture, or different culture, are not accustomed to viewing the stuff of education through the accepted prism of the larger culture. The value systems and myth systems held in awe by the larger culture are often not meaningful in terms of subcultures. There is, then, the problem of being able to fit new facts and theories into an operational perspective.

Possibly the chief difference in the predominantly Negro classroom and the predominantly Caucasian classroom is a function of the communications traditions of each group. Whereas in the Negro class the professor may be completely satisfied with the class progress on the basis of oral interchange of ideas and skill in argument only to be disappointed in the outcome of a written exam, in the Caucasian class he can usually expect to worry about whether he has made any impact at all until he can read the results of a written exam, which indicates a dependence on successfully gathering the information from print and relating it in written form. Since education is yet geared almost entirely to absorbing information through books, the lack of a strong print tradition among Negro students poses difficult problems.

The problem is thus twofold, substantive in that the student must expand his frame of reference to be able to put in perspective the ideas and events which are dominant in the broad socio-cultural context, procedural in that the standard means of gathering the information which will allow the building of perspective is through the print tradition. Moreover, the problem is compounded when it is taken into consideration that both aspects must be solved at once, at least in the absence of another information gathering method.

There is another information gathering method, however, and it is through examination of popular culture. Popular culture here is taken to mean the product of the mass media, with perhaps a side definition to be that popular culture is all informational culture just under what we often term "high culture," and offered primarily for its entertainment value. To be sure, study of popular culture cannot take the place of reading; nothing can. What strong analysis of popular culture can do is to allow the student to continually consider and generate ideas while working to obtain skill in the print tradition. In this way, the development of the student's ability to abstract and express can be carried on without the delay so often caused by nothing more than a lack of print tradition.

THE NATURE OF POPULAR CULTURE

If there were no secondary gains to be had from the introduction of popular culture study into the classroom, the effort would be worthwhile, simply because of what popular culture "is" and what it "does" in American society.

Popular culture is the mirror of the socio-culture structure. As such it provides the culturally assigned answers to the existential questions of "who we are," and what we are "supposed to do," and "in what way" we should carry the tasks out. When George Gerbner, Dean of the Annenberg School of Communication, refers to the mass media as the "cultural arm of industry" he remarks the objective role played by communications institutions in supporting the beliefs and values necessary to the maintenance of the socio-cultural status quo. In such a role the popular cultural product is, among other things, a guide to proper behavior for members of the social system.

Experience has demonstrated that popular culture can be relied on to legitimize questionable decisions made by dominant interests in the social system. This legitimization process is complex, but predictable in at least one aspect: in order to explain and defend social and political decisions necessary to the perpetuation of the ongoing social system, popular culture will always be found relying on the myth and folklore which serve as the underlying assumptions of the socio-cultural system.

From such functions, it becomes clear that popular culture is a powerful educational force in society. Indeed, popular culture is the majority of information on which the public makes decisions. That popular culture as an educational medium is pervasive can be observed in many different ways. One example should suffice here. One has only to think of the five year olds he has known. How many of them, called upon, could define the concept of peace? How many of them even have any idea of what peace means? Probably none could give a satisfactory definition or answer. Indeed the closest might be an answer which reflected the notion that peace is the absence of war. But what if these same youngsters were asked what war means? It would not be extraordinary to find that at this tender age most youths could give a satisfactory, perhaps even a sophisticated answer. Brief reflection on the media, and its product of popular culture, easily explains the individual's storehouse of information which will respond to certain areas and not to others. The claim here would be that popular culture can be, should be, viewed as a broad, informal yet powerful educational institution, in capacity to mold minds fully on a par with formal educational organizations. It is in this context that a call can be voiced for the increased utilization of popular culture analysis in the classroom.

THE STUDY OF POPULAR CULTURE

Popular culture is *the common medium.* It is available to all, and given the structure of the mass media, makes the same information available to all. The student who analyzes popular culture can be made to understand that popular culture is the reflector of the nature of the social system which he must understand, deal with, and live in.

Popular culture indeed may not picture life as it "is," but it will picture life as it "should be," according to the dictates of the continued successful functioning of the social system. When the student examines popular culture products he can gain critical insight into what the dominant social and cultural interests feel his role should be. He learns who society thinks he is, and the position he therefore should assume, from the messages the society sends through its cultural voice. It may well be that the student of the media finds this role totally unacceptable; this in itself is a good sign in terms of academic procedure, for the student has at this point demonstrated analytical power. We will consider the substantive aspects of this problem later.

As a measuring instrument, careful analysis of popular culture will reveal the extent to which the intellectual concepts and assumptions dealt with by professors have actually moved into the common experience. Popular culture not only reports events, but in the very selection of those events there is a relationship between event and idea. Clearly the study of an event pictured by popular culture may demonstrate that, in the very process of the occurrence of the event, a highly regarded idea has been subverted. Even here, however, what is important is that subverted or not, there *is* a relationship between event and idea, and it *can be seen* through examination of popular culture. Such pursuit offers the student a way to observe the application of theory and myth in practice, and to make qualitative judgments about the worth of the abstract concepts. One can ask for little more in a learning situation.

The claim has been made that study of popular culture is a sort of surrogate for the rapid development of critical reading skills, and some defense is in order. First, in its commonality, popular culture is geared to a broad based audience. Certainly there would be no argument that the electronic media are geared at mass audiences, nor would there be much concern with the assertion that newspapers and large circulation magazines are structured and aimed by much the same process. The ideas advanced in these media are no less serious and important because they are given in simple presentation. Also, to the extent that the information quality of the popular cultural products suffers because of techniques which require mass appeal, the student will soon realize that important decisions are often reached on the basis of inadequate information, simply because the mass media has created such a broad dependence.

Even the "intellectual" magazines are geared to a sufficiently broad based audience that they lend themselves readily to a much more rapid analysis than do textbooks and scholarly journals, the sources of information now most common for students. Too, the "intellectual" magazines are precisely those media which present the student with discussions concerning current relationships of myths, ideas, and events.

Popular culture products, then, are common to everyone, and can serve as a relevant means of identifying and understanding the value, belief, and myth systems which are often so painfully difficult to separate from the normal text. As the student begins to study popular culture products, he is at the same time developing his skills in the print tradition, yet without having to hold back his pursuit of the meaning of ideas for lack of skill with print.

SOME FINAL REMARKS

It has been suggested that study of popular culture can work to solve problems of student identity with the total socio-cultural context and to build an operational perspective which can better assimilate ideas, events and the relationships between the two. Further, it has been argued that popular culture, as a mirror of socio-culture structure, provides the student with an alternative to printed matter in his search for knowledge about social and cultural organization and operation.

Whether or not the student agrees with the messages sent him by the society through popular culture is the subject of another paper. The claim here is that through study of popular culture the student can learn to perceive the messages sent to everyone from the dominant institutions in society. The student who wishes his educational posture to be such that he can readily perceive and cope with the imperatives of the culture, whether by rejection or acceptance, can find the analysis of popular culture of singular import.

Violence and the Mass Media: Challenge to Education

Charity M. Mance

Violence is a fact of American life, and it has been since the beginning of our national life. It was present in the early encounters of the settlers with the Indians; it erupted in incidents leading to and culminating in our separation from England; it marked the extension of the western frontier; and it now marks our present attempts to grapple with the pressing domestic and international issues confronting our society.

Now, as never before, the various manifestations and expressions of violence

From Charity M. Mance, "Violence and the Mass Media: Challenge to Education," *Educational Leadership* 26 (April 1969): 655-56. Copyright © 1969 by the Association for Supervision and Curriculum Development. Reprinted by permission of the Association for Supervision and Curriculum Development and Charity M. Mance.

are viewed with increasing alarm as they threaten the foundations of our social order. This widespread concern results from the greater awareness by our population as a whole of the extent and nature of violence as presented by the mass media. Unlike earlier times, when news traveled slowly and people learned about situations after they happened, many of these violent demonstrations now are presented while they are actually in progress and are viewed on television by millions of Americans.

These outbursts of violence are regarded by many as threats to personal and national security. Today not only are crimes perpetrated against individuals on the increase, but mass demonstrations have been directed against practically all phases of American life. Significant among these phases are politics and government, race, and education.

The widespread publicity, the space and time devoted by the mass media to violence, has become an issue in itself. This phenomenon has posed the question of whether or not this emphasis has had positive or negative results, whether it has presented an image which has served to create or stimulate further violence. Arthur Schlesinger, Jr., states that one reason for the climate of violence in the United States is:

> ... surely the zest with which the mass media, and especially television and films, dwell on violence. One must be clear about this. The mass media do not create violence. But they reinforce aggresive and destructive impulses, and they may well teach the morality as well as the method of violence.[1]

The function of news media in a free society is to keep the public informed. These media are fulfilling their responsibility only when the news is accurately and objectively presented.

The National Advisory Commission on Civil Disorders, in its report of March 1, 1968, states that it found a significant imbalance between what actually happened in our cities and what the newspapers, radio, and television coverage of the riots reported.[2] While the original impressions gotten from the media were corrected as a result of the Commission's follow-up study, millions of Americans who must rely on mass media also formed incorrect impressions and judgments about what happened.

A sampling of the reaction of a limited number of college students to the presentation of scenes of violence on television indicated that they feel that such news should be presented. However, many felt that the presentations tend to "sensationalize and glorify violence" in that many young persons identify emotionally with those engaging in violence and are stimulated to join in the act, thus causing violence to spread.

The reports on violence indicate that the majority of the participants are teenagers or young adults. The Walker Report[3] states that 66.2 percent of those arrested in the Chicago demonstrations ranged between 18 and 25 years of age and 32.6 percent of those arrested were students. This involvement primarily of teenagers and young adults presents a definite challenge to the schools.

As a major social institution, charged with the responsibility of guiding the youth in the development of the basic moral values which we say we cherish, the schools can put forth greater efforts to "practice what they preach." In the organization itself, in financial support, in administration and instruction, the schools can move toward the realization of that basic tenet of democracy which advocates respect for the integrity of human personality, the dignity and worth of the individual human being regardless of race, color, or creed.

By making this element of our democratic philosophy of life a reality in the schools, a major attack can be made on one of the underlying causes of increasing violence on the American scene. Quality education should be provided for all rather than for the affluent only. Respect for law, rather than engaging in devious and subtle practices to evade the laws regarding discrimination and segregation, could set a fine example for teaching the young respect for law and order.

Schools must provide more wholehearted, sincere, and realistic involvement of students in decision making on issues affecting them. Such involvement would enable them to gain valuable experience in problem identification, analysis, and the planning of intelligent courses of action.

Vitalized curriculum content which is relevant to today's issues and problems will enable the young to see some meaningful connection between school life and the significant issues they must confront from day to day. Firsthand experience in dealing with controversial issues vital to American life and relevant to the present needs of adolescents and young adults will prepare them to deal more effectively with some of the underlying causes of violence.

Let us hope that, along with the loud cry for force in suppressing violence, the schools will exercise more effective leadership in helping today's youth shape a better world for tomorrow.

NOTES

1. Arthur Schlesinger, Jr., *Violence: America in the Sixties (New York: The New American Library, Inc., 1968), pp. 50-51.*

2. *Report of the National Advisory Commission on Civil Disorders* (Washington, D.C.: Superintendent of Documents, U.S. Government Printing Office, March 1, 1968), pp. 201-2.

3. The Walker Report, *Rights in Conflict* (New York: E.P. Dutton & Co., 1969), p. 357.

Mass Media Curriculum: Fantasy or Reality?

Martin A. McCullough

Young people are major consumers of the mass media fare. Their appetites for commercial television, magazines, movies, and even newspapers appear to be without limits. The typical youngster spends an average of one-sixth of his waking hours watching television, and by the age of 16 has spent more time in front of a television set than he has in the classrooms of his schools.[1]

The movie industry sees young people as the major audience for their products today, either as a member of a family group or with their peers. Recent mergers in the publishing industry give all of the major publishers of monthly periodicals at least one magazine for the "younger set."

However, the bulk of time devoted to the mass media is spent on commercial television. In many ways television is typical of, and reflects the posture of, the other media. All are commercial enterprises and in the final analysis look to the profit sheet for determining success or failure. Their offerings, whether printed or filmed, are similar, and television manages to program much of what is available from the other media. Therefore, many of the following remarks which refer to commercial television are also applicable to other components of the mass media.

THE PLANNED MASS MEDIA CURRICULUM: LESS THAN REALITY

The mass media offerings can be conceptualized as a curriculum. Using commercial television as a model, there are generally accepted objectives, a body of research knowledge, carefully defined content, scope and sequence charts, program dissemination strategies based on age groupings, and thorough evaluation procedures.

The mass media curriculum, as planned, produced, edited, and offered to

From Martin A. McCullough, "Mass Media Curriculum: Fantasy or Reality?" *Educational Leadership* 26 (February 1969): 447-50. Copyright © 1969 by the Association for Supervision and Curriculum Development. Reprinted by permission of the Association for Supervision and Curriculum Development and Martin A. McCullough.

young consumers, is surprisingly simple and direct. On the basis of research and audience reaction, the mass media, and especially the television industry, have a major commitment to fulfilling the fantasy needs of young people. Schramm identified the purposes for watching television in the past decade, and the 1960s have seen the mass media orient their offerings on the basis of his and other research. Schramm states the need of young people for fantasy experiences as the primary reason for watching television, with the need for programs concerning real events a poor second.[2] These needs, along with some social usage, determine the current strategies behind the offerings of the mass media.

The overwhelming capability to produce fantasy experiences vicariously for all ages and types of children accounts for the majority of time they spend in front of a television set, in a movie theater, or between the covers of a paperback book or magazine. Within their own set of objectives, the curriculum developers of the mass media are successful. It is not possible to overlook the omnipresence of commercial television and the rest of the mass media. A basic fact is obvious that they have identified a low but generally acceptable level of young people's fantasy needs and taste.

THE CONSUMED MASS MEDIA CURRICULUM: LITTLE MORE THAN FANTASY

The basic commitment tends to influence materials about real events. The curriculum makers of the mass media realize correctly that youngsters carry over their criteria for fantasy consumption to other types of reading and viewing. The young reader or viewer wants reality presented in a fast-paced, exciting, and action-packed manner. Since youngsters get what they want from the mass media, reality-oriented material, even when committed to "telling it like it is," ends up "giving them what they want." The difference does not necessarily subordinate the truth but does allow the young consumer to sit back and be entertained again.

It is obvious that youngsters do change as a result of watching commercial television and utilizing the other mass media. The depth of these changes is largely unexplored and there is a need to seek answers to many basic questions. How have the mass media affected the values of young people? Do the young look more favorably on direct, even authoritarian action and control? Are they so exposed to violence and crime that they are more prone to accept this behavior? Or even to copy it?

In the absence of substantial research data, the position can be taken that the mass media do not influence greatly the basic values of the vast majority of young people. The introduction to books and television early in life on a fantasy-fulfillment basis and the continued expectation to be entertained in this way have, in effect, cut off the mass media from the real developmental process of growing up. There are major exceptions to this generalization, but it appears that value determination continues to center around the core of home, school, peer group, and church. The influence of the mass media revolves on the periphery and fills in gaps where there is no prior influencing or is selected when leverage is needed to pry loose from imposed restrictions.

Youngsters' reactions to the recent assassinations of three national leaders can serve as an example. Young people were shocked and sickened as were adults with the tragedies. It is interesting to note that the mass media which had brought so much violence and death as fantasy in no way prepared them for the shock of seeing death come to real people. This violence and the subsequent sadness of the families and the entire world did more to show youngsters the true nature of violence than the thousands of hours of fantasy consumption prior to these events.

The real curriculum of the mass media is determined by the individual. The mass media do not command a captive audience of young people. In the case of commercial television, research concludes that:

> It seems clear that in order to understand television's impact and effect on children we have first to get away from the unrealistic concept of what television "does to children" and substitute the concept of *what children do with television.*[3]

Most youngsters use the mass media for relaxation and recreation, but for others it becomes more than fantasy. Aside from matters of taste and style, the impact of the mass media and especially commercial television could be relegated to an unimportant position except that some young people do not use the mass media in ways anticipated by producers and editors. Consumption in these instances is a symptom of deeper problems that should be recognized by school personnel. In some instances too much dependence and too much time are committed to the mass media for vicarious experiences that are unrelated to life.

In other instances the dependence on visual "inputs," whether photographs, films, or video tapes, creates an unrealistic desire for new or different experiences at a faster pace than that at which they are provided in real life. A third pattern is typified by the popularity among lower socio-economic youngsters of situation comedies that take place in middle-class families. Here the planned curriculum of comedy is used as fantasy to compensate for deprived environments.

FANTASY AND REALITY: IMPLICATIONS AND STRATEGIES

The roots for developing strategies for coping with the influencing mass media usage are found in a realistic approach to the whole business. Basic to this providing fantasy experiences for young people and, to a much lesser degree, serve as a window to the world around them. Young people, as a whole, use the mass media as expected with no real adverse effects. Those who do not so use the mass media need the help and concern of school people because misuse of mass media fare is not a discrete phenomenon but is symptomatic of deeper problems. The curriculum of the schools should acknowledge the existence of is the acceptance of the mass media as a normal, healthy outlet for young people. They do place a wealth of information literally at the fingertips of young people. On the negative side, the mass media are basically anti-intellectual, though this is of their own choosing. They focus on crime, violence, and other baser human acts but usually couch these acts within the womb of fantasy fulfillment. If these facets can be accepted, then the job at hand is to influence the manner in which individuals relate to the mass media.

If the assumption is accepted that a certain amount of mass media usage is normal, then one strategy is to "contain" the quantity of consumption. This can be done by involving young people in learning or recreational activities that include satisfying interaction with others and opportunities for use of one's own personaltiy in task-oriented situations. This task will not be easy since many youngsters use television to compensate for their reluctance to become involved. These are the shy ones who seldom speak or make contributions to classroom discussions and who are the social and personality "dropouts" in our schools. Teachers and other professionals too often look without concern on this type of behavior and see this docility and compliance as a welcome balance for other more aggressive children. These young people are not receiving the satisfactions of being involved so they "escape" to the fantasy involvement of television and the other media.

It is not feasible to compete for the hours of the day that are spent watching television. But it is possible to enhance the process of being involved through sensitive and consistent structuring of school activities, so that involvement will be able to compete with the projective, vicarious experiences found through mass media consumption.

To achieve meaningful, satisfying involvement for the over-consumers of the mass media who occupy the inconspicuous middle sections of our classrooms, it will be necessary to make basic changes in many typical classroom procedures. Student involvement will result when teachers release their hold on instructional planning and classroom time and let students do some of the important things that go on in any learning situation. Student involvement can occur when the risk-level of the classroom is reduced so that students can share feelings and ideas without fear of embarrassment or condescension.

Obviously, the second strategy would deal with making the young user more sophisticated in his use of the mass media. Young people need the opportunity to experience the mass media as technical, business, social, and artistic entities. The first steps would involve the study of units devoted to developing a body of knowledge about the realities of corporate business and the use of technology in the communications and publishing sectors of the economy. A second step would be the study of the characteristics of the various media and how they are used within our society. A final step would be the development of the concepts of style and taste based on an appreciation of the artistic functions of directing, writing, acting, etc.

In conclusion, the mass media and especially commercial television have largely replaced the comic books of yesteryear. They fulfill a function by the mass media by encouraging greater understanding and appreciation of the mass media as a complex and essential enterprise. Perhaps then a start can be made toward changing the "locked-in" habits of the young consumers of the mass media.

NOTES

1. Wilbur Schramm, Jack Lyle, and Edwin B. Parker, *Television in the Lives of Our Children* (Stanford, Calif.: Stanford University Press, 1961) p. 30.
2. Ibid., p. 170.
3. Ibid., p. 169.

Image and Reality

S. I. Hayakawa

Up until November 26, 1968 (it was at that time I became a college president), I was an intellectual. The pressures of this job are so great that now I find I have no time to read books, and my intellectual life has come to a dead standstill. But even more related to this particular occasion is the fact that I have no time to write speeches. As recently as the middle of November 1968 I would not have confronted an audience like this without a carefully prepared outline, if not a complete manuscript. Today I come before you not knowing what I will say; I won't know until I've heard myself say it.

It's a very startling experience, this whole business of being caught in the middle of a tremendous wave of excitement and public concern about the presidency of an educational institution. A long series of events at Columbia University, the University of Wisconsin, Michigan State, the University of Michigan, and the University of California at Berkeley preceded the action at San Francisco State College, and because of the long year and a half or so during which this business was building up, there was a fantastic concentration of public interest upon our school from the moment I took office. Then something very strange and peculiar happened—in the first few minutes of my administration. All of you know about the incident, but you do not know my account of that famous incident of the sound truck. I went to the college before

From S. I. Hayakawa, "Image and Reality," *The Bulletin of the National Association of Secondary School Principals* 53 (May 1969): 35-48. Copyright © 1969 by the National Association of Secondary School Principals. Reprinted by permission of the NASSP.

eight o'clock that morning. I rarely got there by eight o'clock on previous mornings, but since becoming president I have to do that pretty often—that's one of the gruesome things about it. Anyway, I got there before eight o'clock that morning, and despite orders that there were to be no sound trucks or sound equipment on campus, here was this sound truck up on Nineteenth Avenue, blaring away. I went to notify the people in the truck that this was not authorized, but they wouldn't listen. I tried to borrow a microphone to notify the crowd that they were not supposed to be gathering at that point, but they snatched it away from me. Since they wouldn't let me use the microphone to make my announcement, I jumped on top of the sound truck—a reasonable thing to do, I think. When I tried to make my announcement, they turned up the sound track so loud so that no one could hear me. Well, I responded quite quickly; I just pulled the wires out of the equipment. It did no damage to the equipment, because they just screwed the wires back on again later on.

MEDIA MAKES AN IMAGE

The strange thing about all this is that this completely ordinary incident would have remained unspectacular if it were not for the four television cameramen who were around in order to cover the opening of school and who watched every bit of this, so the whole United States, if not other parts of the world, saw this thing going on. Now, what I want to tell you educators about this incident is very, very important. I have never touched on this incident so profoundly before. There was a moment in which an image was created, the image of this angry little guy in a tam-o'-shanter pulling the wires out to keep education going. This is an image to which many of you, something like 99 percent of the public, have responded with great warmth, and like most images it's only partly true and an awfully lot of it is false. That is, the whole business of my being very tough and a man of tremendous capacity for direct action, some kind of academic United States Marine, is not a very accurate picture of me; at least I hope not.

I've devoted my life to semantics, as some of you know, to theories of communication which we resolve human difficulties by. I've given years of lectures on how important it is to listen, to see the world through the framed reference of the other fellow, no matter how crazy he may seem at first. You don't bat him around; you don't pull out his sound equipment. You listen to him. Actually, I'm a pretty gentle sort of individual—for years I've been reading poetry extremely well at women's clubs. However, this was not the image that was projected on that morning; and the image which was projected captured everyone's imagination.

THE ADVANTAGES OF AN IMAGE

An image has both pitfalls and advantages. Having found myself in this awfully responsible position, I must confess that I've freely exploited the advantages of my image. Because of that curious little image that was established right there and then which, through accidents of circumstance, happened only to me and not to other college presidents who have done far more for education than I shall ever do in my lifetime—because of that little accident I, as a dramatic figure, had access to television cameras, to the press, and to the public that I would never have had otherwise.

There is a terrible unfairness about the mass media, the kind of unfairness that, for example, Negro leaders have complained of so much. As some of the very distinguished black leaders I have known said to me, "For 30 years I have been working for the advancement of my people, and in two weeks Stokely Carmichael becomes a nationally known hero for black people." And it is very, very true that when you get on the networks and become a kind of image, you have additional access to the networks. To him that has shall be given.

Having discovered this fact, I have been grateful to the media. One of the things that makes me very happy—in a rather nasty way—is to imagine my enemies in the strike situation turning on their television sets and finding *me* there. They don't like that, so they turn to another channel, and there I am again. And they turn to still another channel, and there I am again. It must drive them crazy. This thought gives me a great deal of pleasure.

REACTIONS TO THE IMAGE

The public response to this assertion that I made in behalf of education has been so tremendous that it overwhelms me. A memorandum came from the office of the state college administration the other day which said that it and the governor's office have received since last fall some 186,000 pieces of mail supporting the position that colleges must remain open and order must be maintained on campuses so that the educational process can continue. One hundred and eighty-six thousand pieces of mail, running 98 percent in favor of this position, only 2 percent against it. I've been receiving this kind of mail myself, bushel after bushel of mail that my secretary at home and my wife and their friends, and another bunch of secretaries at the office are still trying to open for me, and I've missed an awful lot—there isn't any possibility of my reading it all. But there, again, you have this peculiar excitement and enthusiasm, and in my case the mail has been running something like 99½ percent to ½ in favor of what I am doing. Now if that many people agree with you, you must be wrong somewhere.

But not only do I get so many letters from teachers at all levels from kindergarten to graduate school, I also get an enormous number of letters from students. Then there is the kind of letter from the man in the street, saying that he graduated from college in any year between 1915 to 1965 and that the college should be restored to what he used to know as college; namely, a place for thought, reflection, and study, where there wasn't a trace of uproar.

That is one kind of letter. But an even more touching kind of fan mail is that from people who never went to college, people who say they never got beyond the eighth grade, the tenth grade, the twelfth grade, or whatever: "I always wanted to go to college, but my father died, my mother died, I was poor; I always wanted to go to college. The young people who are able to go to college are so privileged, they're so happy, they're so lucky. And why are they doing it? Why are they destroying that which all our lives we hoped to get into." And sometimes a kind of letter comes to me in an almost illiterate scrawl, saying, "I've always wanted my children to go to college, wanted my grandchildren to go to college if I couldn't make it myself." And to the people who have never been to college the idea that there should be such a thing as a college to open up the gates of opportunity to people is a very important thing.

I didn't realize how important colleges were to people until I got this kind of mail and this kind of sentiment from all kinds of people. The taxi drivers who stop their taxis in the middle of the street to say hello, the Chinese truck drivers in Chinatown who stop loading their supplies in order to shake hands with me—these are not college educated people. Yet, somehow they see the college and university as a very important kind of place, whether they ever get to it or not. It is somehow important to their idea of civilization. Why is this? This thought kept bothering me. And I thought about it in many ways. Perhaps one reason for this almost universal interest in the maintenance of education revolves around the complex issue of what constitutes meaning and security in our world.

We live in troubled times; that is clear. Also, we live in a time in which there are no clear sources of authority, nor any clear solutions to our problems of social or individual salvation. In the Middle Ages, the Church was what we turned to for all our hopes of salvation, and a better life in the hereafter—if not here. Therefore, somehow or other all human aspirations and hopes were centered around the Church. At other times, notice, human aspirations revolved around the military; that is, a nation felt that if it had a strong enough army that could clean up on everybody in sight, it would be a great nation and therefore very happy. A strong empire and a strong navy, and, by gosh, our problems as a nation are solved!

THE SEARCH FOR HOPE

Today we are living in a time when neither business, nor the military, nor the church, nor any tradition upon which we once rested our hopes is enough. Somehow, I think, the vast majority of human beings in the United States—both college educated and not college educated—is saying that maybe our real hope for salvation lies in the universities. Maybe in great places like Columbia, Berkeley, UCLA, and Stanford—maybe at those places they are working out the answers to some of the problems that make us so puzzled and anxious. Maybe the diseases of the world can be abolished by the great medical research laboratories at the University of Pennsylvania or Harvard, or somewhere. Maybe our social problems can be studied, our psychological problems studied, at these great universities. And maybe if I can send my children there, they can find some answers to questions for which I don't have answers.

In a curious way, education has proved to be the hope of salvation for an awful lot of people. I guess this is natural enough. Many of us here are immigrants or children of immigrants. Our first steps in adjusting ourselves to this culture were through the public school system. We thought that if we were lucky enough to get through high school maybe we could go to college, and then to graduate school.

So, the feeling that people get out of the uproar at the campus is the unhappy one that this citadel, namely, the entire American system of higher education, is under a terrible threat from *within*—from ungrateful, nasty students who don't know how lucky they are, and from subversive and disloyal teachers who are trying to break down that which gives them their position, their career, and their opportunity for social usefulness. This is the way people see it, I think.

Over and over and over again, as I study the mail that comes in, I have the sense that people are afraid that, somehow, the country is going down the drain, and someone—with or without a tam-o'-shanter—has got to stop that process. It is very strange. Therefore, as a result of accidents of mass communication in my own life in the situation at San Francisco State College, I find myself in a position that symbolizes the protection of higher education to a lot of people. They feel that the rest of education is going to be irrevocably hurt if San Francisco State College goes down. I don't think this is so, but I do feel that, insofar as people feel this way, the weight of my responsibilities is vastly increased.

People continue to ask, in one way or another, why these things happen in our time. Why is it that apparently well-educated young people want to tear up the place? Why do they not resort, as previous generations have done, to the usual orderly process of registering complaints, getting into discussions and hearings about them, arguing back and forth with administrators and professors, and solving problems as they come up? Why do they go into these tactics of violent confrontation? What is the matter with them? The people keep asking these questions with a great deal of urgency.

IMMEDIACY MAY DISTORT

I don't suppose I have any better answers than anyone else, but let me submit one, one that is basically a Marshall McLuhan type of answer. Electronic communications, especially television, have made social events—including racial injustice and the war in Vietnam—so much more vivid, so much more immediate, so much more instantaneous. We see things minutes after they happen; sometimes we see them *as* they're happening—and, hence, we all feel a greater sense of involvement than any previous generation. What you read in the newspaper is always history—yesterday's action, not today's. But often on television, you can see what is actually happening, and most of you must have felt, as I have, this immediacy not only about some of the events in Vietnam, but certainly about the events in Watts in 1965, or in Newark. When there are great urban disturbances going on, we felt personally involved.

Just as television fantastically magnified this trivial business of my pulling wires out of a loud speaker, it tremendously magnifies everything for which it is the medium. Consider what we used to notice with such amusement—although it isn't really amusing when you think of the implications: During campus disturbances now, as at Berkeley in 1964, students are getting involved in demonstrations and they're doing great dramatic things, and then they run home and watch themselves on the six o'clock news. If they don't manage to get into the center of the camera one day, then they may try again the next—not so much for the freedom of speech or academic freedom or social justice or anything else, as for the chance to dramatically project themselves on camera. What happens when they are successful is that they get phone calls from their relatives as far away as New York or Chicago saying, "Hey, Danny, I saw you on television last night." Doesn't that tremendously increase a person's egotistical sense of how important he is to the future of mankind and to changing the course of history by what he can do in the picket line or campus disturbance at Berkeley or anywhere else? We have, therefore, these instant heroes.

This notion of instant history fantastically exaggerates the importance of even trivial events and makes getting into the thick of things so much more worthwhile than writing an essay or a letter to the editor—no one is going to take a picture of you doing that. But getting out there with the pickets with a placard, getting yourself hit by a policeman, hitting him back—these are more effective ways of making your message heard than any 500- or 5,000-word essay or memorandum you may write, analyzing the social evils that you want to call attention to.

What I've said very often to my students is, Why don't you write a letter to the *Chronicle* or the *Examiner*; why don't you write letters to the major magazines or the *New York Times* calling attention to this problem? So often they look at me scornfully; it's like having to write a theme in a composition class. It is much more exciting to act directly and get some immediate public attention.

I have maintained that our present generation of young people between the ages of 3 and 18 who have been babysat by television have lost, if they watched television three to four hours a day all that time, something like 22,000 hours that they might otherwise have spent in learning how to interact with other people. For all the values television has, one thing you can't learn from it is interaction. Interaction, even quarreling with your little sister, is an experience we all need. What happens to you if you've lost 22,000 hours of practice in interaction—interaction with your relatives, your grandma, your brothers and sisters, neighbors, and friends, and so on? What happens if you miss out on that? Perhaps you don't know how to interact. I get the feeling very, very often that some young people in their late teens today do not have an earlier generation's ability to relate to other people.

An extreme case is a person who cannot relate to anybody else through making conversation, exploring somebody else's interests, revealing his own, making friendships, getting into quarrels, and learning how to get out of them. If he's missed all this experience, if he doesn't know how to relate to others, relating to others becomes a dangerous, terrifying, threatening experience. If someone feels this way strongly enough, he may drop out. And I wonder to what extent our dropouts—take our far extreme dropouts, who leave altogether the organized society of their parents and teachers and form little hippie colonies—I wonder to what extent they are the victims of their own 22,000 hours or more of watching television. I don't know. But certainly the relationship of the drug experience to television is clearly easy to establish. Both the drug experience and television depend upon turning on and waiting for something beautiful to happen. Both are entirely passive experiences. Perhaps, I have speculated, young people as they grow to adulthood may be disillusioned with the commercials, but they still miss the fantasy life that television offered them as little children. So they turn on toward another kind of fantasy life available through psychedelic drugs—maybe.

EXPERIENCING THE DEMOCRATIC PROCESS

While I'm speculating, I want to take a far-out instance of the inability to relate to others. Let me submit what I call the Little League Theory of social protest. I don't know how many of you have noticed it, but one of the peculiarities of young kids is that they can't play baseball nowadays without adult supervision. If you don't make Little League, you don't play baseball at all. This has been the case for some years, in many places that I know. But when most of the people in this audience were children and played baseball, they didn't have any adult supervision. As a result, they learned to settle playground quarrels quickly so that they could go on with the game. Today, without an adult present, they can never settle their quarrels.

I say that the experience of democracy is necessary for democratic citizens. And democracy must exist in a sandlot baseball game when you are quarreling with your peers as to whether Dick was out or safe at second base, for if you have to stop the game for three quarters of an hour to decide this little question, then there is no more ball game. So you learn to decide quickly and go on with the game. Many young people seem not to have this ability. In a sense, there is a lack of acquaintance with the democratic process. And I keep wondering about the role of television in all this. Television doesn't show you what the democratic process looks like.

The democratic process in most instances is a very boring, tedious process, in which conflicting groups appear, testify, and argue relentlessly over little boards of supervisors and city council or congressional committees, and they recite statistics by the hour, and they give measurements of the area they want set aside as a state park, or they want a variance for Mr. Jones' home up on Galenus Road, and he wants a variance to let such and such a thing happen to the road around his house, and so on. It is all very tedious. Democracy has never been glamorous; it has never been particularly exciting. The details of democracy are a real bore. But all of you, having sat through thousands of teachers' meetings and thousands of city council hearings and so on, know that you have to go through this process. Now I maintain that a generation of kids who spend 22,000 hours of their life in front of the television set have missed something of the democratic experience, because—notice—television is covered by the considerations of show business. For ABC to snatch its audience away from NBC, and for NBC to snatch its audience away from CBS, each one has to be more exciting and dramatic than the other. So television is governed, in spite of itself, by the necessities of show business. But democracy in action seldom makes good show business, and you therefore don't show the tedious hearings in the city hall on a television set.

Anyway, many youthful activists say that they are disillusioned with the democratic process. As far as I'm concerned, it seems to me that they're not so much disillusioned with it as they are unacquainted with it. All this seems to be a tremendous disparagement of television, and I don't intend it to be. I think one of the greatest compliments that has been paid to television is that paid by the government of the Union of South Africa. It is so profoundly opposed to social change that it won't let television into the country at all. That nation is the one technologically advanced society in our world today that doesn't have television.

Does television accelerate the rate of social change to a fantastic degree? Television is a fantastic equalizer. It works more powerfully in the direction of equalization than does radio. This may be a temporary phenomenon, as the number of television channels increases. But, you know, you turn on a radio and you look around, especially along the upper registers of that band, and you find all sorts of strange programs that you, as English speaking people, don't ordinarily listen to. You find in some towns Japanese programs, Chinese FM stations, certainly a lot of soul music (which white people don't usually listen to), Mexican-American programs, Spanish language programs, and certain little evangelical sects which keep on going all night long.

Radio divides its audience into little splinters, because radio stations are relatively cheap to maintain. But a television station is so darned expensive that you have to appeal to the masses to keep going at all. This means then that any television program addressed to the white majority is also addressed to blacks, Mexicans, Orientals, and anybody else who happens to be within transmitting distance. Now think of the effect of this. Television has told all its audiences, including the poor, the illiterate, the disadvantaged, that they should try *this* cake mix, should use *this* detergent, should look at the new *Buick* and test-drive it, should have *this* kind of luxurious wall-to-wall carpeting, should have *this* kind of household appliance. Television says to everybody: You are American; you are entitled to eat, drink, and wear what other Americans are entitled to eat, drink, and wear; you are a member of the national community of Americans. And the poor man with his undernourished children and a nasty little southside apartment in Chicago watches that television and wonders why the hell he isn't being cut in on all these wonderful things that the culture offers. It's curious that if he's unemployed he has even more time to watch television, and therefore even more time to get his resentment and his anger boiling up about what the culture produces and is denying him.

The advertising profession prides itself on its ability to create demand. And, by gosh, it does create demand! After the great disturbances several summers ago in Detroit, it was observed by many reporters, and even by police present, that when the looting of stores began, it was curiously lacking in racist motivation. People would drive up in cars, and whites would help Negroes and Negroes would help whites take loot out of the stores and pack it into their cars. All this was done in the spirit of fine interracial brotherhood. It was reported that a holiday atmosphere prevailed, because suddenly everybody could grab all those things that had been advertised and that they had been wanting so badly.

Relatively prosperous people were horrified by that looting, but looting is idealized, in a curious way, by the advertising industry itself. There is a TV program in which a bunch of housewives go into a supermarket with baskets and see who can get the largest amount of expensive goods in the shortest period of time and dash up to the checkout counter. That's a glorification of looting; whoever loots fastest gets the prize, naturally. I've watched a kind of contest with some fascination on which a startled young woman—let's say a housewife—is told that she's getting a new dryer as a result of giving the right answer. Her face bursts into ecstacy as this is announced. In one program I saw, this same woman was given a dryer, and then she was given a color television set. Then it went on and on until she got a Chevrolet Impala, too, on top of all the other consumer goods. First the dryer, then the color television set, and then fantastic broadloom carpets, and ultimately a brand new automobile. The fascinating thing was to watch that woman's face. She went from ecstacy to ecstacy to ecstacy, and when they announced that Chevrolet she practically had an orgasm. Right there in public! The basic message that television beams into every household day after day, hour after hour, 15 or 20 hours a day, is that the ultimate in happiness is the collection of all these consumer goods. Good gosh! No wonder they call us a materialistic culture.

CONFLICTING MESSAGES

Against all this sort of thing, the educational system has got to beat out its own messages. The basic message of education is to be thoughtful, to be intelligent, to be rational. The basic message of commercials is to disregard thoughtfulness and reflection—the important thing is to get as many consumer goods as you can get hold of, and then you're above the next guy who hasn't got these things. These two kinds of messages are not in harmony with each other and in some very, very profound way, all of us in education are fighting other systems of communication, especially advertising, which promotes a set of values which we as educators could never wholly accept, no matter how much we ourselves may enjoy many of the products of our rich consumer economy.

Regardless of how much we enjoy them, we know they are not the end of life. The end of life is being a rich human being—rich, of course, in a sense that is totally independent of monetary values—rich in mind and heart, because of a wide range of knowledge, understanding, and human sympathies. The educational system must communicate this message, but the commercial networks offer powerful competition. So we do have a responsibility that the more powerful the networks become in beaming their messages, the tougher our responsibility becomes to send out certain counter-messages stressing other values than commercial and consumer.

I want to submit one other of my hypotheses. When people ask what's wrong with the colleges, what's wrong with the generation of young people that you've got in college today, I'm often tempted to break down the question as follows. You take the college disturbances, you look at the arrest records of students arrested, you take photographs and see who is marching in the picket lines, you see what classes are shut down because of the absence of the teacher or the students on a strike, and you find curious unevennesses. For example, the School of Business and the School of Engineering are totally uninvolved at San Francisco State College. Classes go on as if nothing were happening. That is also true of the School of Music, curiously enough, but not of the School of Art. I don't know why. The School of Home Economics, the School of Nursing, and most of the School of Education function as usual. Almost all the trouble comes from the humanities, and to some degree from the social sciences.

When you see the professors and demonstrating students, you see one after another: English majors, philosophy majors, art majors, speech majors, a few psychology and sociology majors, but a curious absence of people from other disciplines. So when someone asks, "What's wrong with the young student generation of today?" I am often tempted to say, "That's not the question; the right question is, 'What's wrong with the people in humanities and the social sciences?' Other people are all right." The absolute determination to go on with education comes from practically everywhere except the humanities and social sciences, though the social sciences have a smaller percentage of activists than the humanities.

One of the curious things about English and philosophy departments is the idea they sometimes impart to a student that he somehow belongs to an intellectual elite because he gets a Ph.D. in English or philosophy. I shall call this the Elitist Theory; that is, somehow the possessor of a Ph.D. in philosophy or English is a being superior to those awful people out there who have Ph.D.'s in education, or biology, or metallurgy, or some such low discipline—which are not really intellectual disciplines at all, you understand, from the point of view of the English department.

Now if you're really elitist, then somehow you have a profound conviction that you're superior to all these other people. However, the people in power in this world are politicians, business executives, military men; they exert all the power, they make the ultimate decisions, and we in the English department are left out. So this is a very unjust world; it's a world without any real sense of values—it doesn't value what smart guys we are, in English. In a better world, we who are real intellectuals—not phony intellectuals like Ph.D.'s in education and stuff, but real intellectuals like us—should really be governing the world. We should really have a place in high councils where decisions are made, but we don't. Therefore, there must be something wrong with this culture.

But I appeal to those of you who are my colleagues in the humanities. We in the humanities are not of a superior order, above those who have Ph.D.'s in physical education, mathematics, metallurgy, biochemistry, or agronomy. All these disciplines which are united in the educational system are important to human life; all of them are of equal worth. We must respect each other as fellow educators and fellow teachers above all, and we must unite to preserve the institutions that give us the academic freedom we enjoy. This is at the heart of our problem at San Francisco State College—it is not so much rampaging students as it is segments of the faculty who do not believe in higher institutions and do not believe in the institution of San Francisco State College itself. They seem willing either to overthrow it or to grab entire control of it to run it their own way. But I am going to fight for the preservation of San Francisco State College for all our students—all our physical education majors, our history majors, our music majors, as well as the humanities majors; I'm going to try to preserve San Francisco State College for all the people of California, no matter what it takes or whom I have to fight.

Film, Television, and Reality

Clifford Solway

One of the distinctions of our culture is its use of film as a guide to reality. We treat film as a mirror image of the physical world and simply assume its essential accuracy as a picture of the times.

The idea of film as a reproduction of external reality is the basis of television journalism. It is influential in other areas of film making as well, for instance among certain schools of cinematic realism which attempt to capture unstaged, "living" drama in the surrounding world or to recreate natural situations with ordinary people as actors. Under the impact of television, film makers have been

From Clifford Solway, "Film, Television, and Reality," *Teachers College Record* 68 (December 1966): 197-99. Copyright © by Teachers College, Columbia University. Reprinted by permission of the publisher and the author.

trying to break down the distinction between film and reality, to approach and to simulate (for that is the effect) so-called actuality, which is to say, the event itself, shown as it occurs.

Film as a reproduction of reality presupposes that the finished product retains the spatial and temporal character of the original. In fact, film construction involves editing which is a skillful rearrangement of the film footage to suit the needs and conventions of the medium. The Russian silent film director V. I. Pudovkin long ago called editing "the foundation of the film art";[1] it is also what in the end distinguishes a filmed version of an event from a "live" television broadcast of the same event.

EDITING FOR EFFECTS

The editorial bench with its rewinds, viewers, and splicers is so remote from the scene of filming, and the continuity of the final product is so convincing that audiences rarely appreciate the editor's contribution or the plasticity of his medium. His very isolation is significant. He constructs his film out of the assorted new footage delivered by the cameraman to the processing laboratories and from stock shots found in the film library. He does not try to match his synthesis of this material with an invisible outside world; the outside world doesn't interest him. The purpose of his craft is to make something that holds the viewer's attention. To this end he manipulates his shots freely for dramatic effect.

A good editor is an opportunist. If he can't get what he wants one way, he tries another, always working within the limits of the available film. His final arrangement of shots represents a painstaking attack on the viewer's eye and emotions, a mixture of instinct and cinematic cliché adhering to all-important rules of film continuity and emphasizing pace, visual excitement, movement within each shot, and the cumulative impact of the story.

The result is a unique form, Hollywood's motion picture, television news' film story. Part of its uniqueness lies in the ability of the editor to create something brand new, something that was not in the original and indeed never really happened in the outside world, out of the juxtaposition of unrelated shots. Standard editorial practices such as intercutting, cutting away to reactions and montage also generate meanings and emphases not implied in the original. These practices are legitimate. They are part of the film art and produce a highly compressed, selective reconstruction of reality.

Editing is basically the same for every kind of film ranging from educational to Hollywood escapist. Remarkably, the authenticity of the "factual" film is rarely seriously questioned. This intrinsic authority derives as much from a general failure to grasp the essentials of film making as from technological bias. The inherent surface realism of the picture on the screen contributes to it as well. Thanks to advanced cinematography, the picture is sharp and clear, the detail unambiguous. The entire frame is a glowing rendering of familiar surfaces. Everything about it is so real, the film "puts people there." The viewer's awareness of place, of physical situation, is acute.

PROJECTED IMMEDIACIES

It is at this point, where the picture is so astonishingly life-like, that the film and television media converge. The tendency of television news, in particular, is to use film in a way that apes "live" coverage. A "live" telecast is assumed to have greater flair and impact than film and in any case to be the best use of the medium. Television news therefore fosters a direct "you are there" relationship between the viewer and the filmed event, even when the film is days old. It stylizes its coverage to project the feeling of immediacy, a feeling which the reporter on the scene does all he can to heighten.

The consequent decay in reportorial technique is everything a McLuhanite might wish for. Simulated actuality relieves the reporter of the need to ask questions. The unfolding event is important in its own right and justifies the presence of cameras. If this isn't clear visually, the reporter removes every doubt with his terse, tense ringside manner. In the last resort he becomes a participant himself and makes news, often as a victim, right in front of the viewer's eyes.

As he covers a continuing news story such as a long war, the television reporter is under pressure to maintain a steady supply of fresh pictures. He feels a strong temptation to alter his perspective periodically, if only to prevent a boring repetition of shots. This tendency appears to generate conflicts in interpretation not only with nonpictorial journalists, but with the government as well. These conflicts are likely to continue. Television news coverage may even tend to dampen the appeal to patriotism in wartime.

THE FILMED AND THE SEEN

The evident distinction between actuality—the event itself—and an edited film version of it is usually ignored by both newsmen and viewers. The lapse is not surprising. But film makers of an earlier period were very much aware of the contradictions inherent in their medium. They wrote and talked incessantly about "the cinema and reality." It was never a noticeable part of their aesthetics to attempt to duplicate the directly felt dimensions of life. Exponents of the film art, even of the documentary, made much out of the distinction between nature seen and nature filmed. Raymond Spottiswoode was representative when he wrote, in *The Grammar of Film,* "the differences between ... [them] ... constitute the chief value of the cinema and the source of most of its enjoyment."[2]

Outstanding documentary directors of the past, men like Robert Flaherty and Pare Lorentz, tended to deal with the physical world through an expressive visual imagery which evoked, for them, underlying truths. They were concerned with the visible and invisible effects of time on rooted lives. Time fascinated them. As it passed, man's surroundings changed, his way of life was transformed. The camera was able to catch the nuances in the landscape, to isolate stark, powerful images that spoke of human determination and defeat. Necessarily, these film makers learned to express the passage of time cinematically, using both optical and symbolic effects.

SUPPRESSING TIME

The use of film to simulate actuality involves, on the other hand, the suppression of time. An overpowering awareness of the present characterizes it. Everything happens *now,* in a continuing present, right before our eyes. Film for television generally reflects the stress on what is urgent and immediate. Even the numerous dramatic series, which are filmed in Hollywood by and for the networks, contain few pronounced jumps in time, so that a genuine development of character, for instance, is rarely achieved in them. Their characters are ready-made.

The tendency to suppress time may, of course, be traced to the television viewer's notorious impatience and short attention span. Or it may have interesting psychological implications. In any case it reflects the influence of electronic media which aim at the immediate engagement of the whole sensory apparatus of the viewer. Nevertheless, film editing implies certain gradual or rhythmical effects evolved through the composition of separate shots, effects which work in time, not instantly.

A film, in short, is not a "happening." It is a didactic arrangement of camera shots, charged with meanings and implications nowhere in the original, organized for cumulative impact. When it purports to be untampered actuality, it is actually misleading and illusory. Dropping his mental reservations about "watching a film," the viewer may tend to assume he knows what a participant alone knows, or he may generalize from what is on the screen to what is not. Film used in this way tends to be uncontrollable in its suggestiveness; it exploits the absolute conviction of the viewer that he is there, witnessing the real thing, at ringside.

Films do not capture "events in their full context, embedded in rich complexity, burdened with secondary and tertiary side effects,"[3] to borrow from Gerald Holton's definition of experiential reality. For the mind to be prodded into thinking about causes and contents, the viewer still requires an intelligent presence, someone who knows how to use the film medium without being used by it.

NOTES

1. V. I. Pudovkin, *On Film Technique* (London: Vision Press, 1950).
2. Raymond Spottiswoode, *The Grammar of Film* (Los Angeles and Berkeley: University of California Press, 1959).
3. Gerald Holton, "Conveying Science by Visual Presentation," in G. Kepes, ed., *Education of Vision* (New York: George Braziller, 1965).

Suggested Discussion Questions and Activities

1. **DISCUSSION** McLaughlin's attacks on the present school environment and his proposal for an "ecological approach" suggest that a revolution must occur in education.

   a. Do you agree or disagree with his disapproval of the present school environment?
   b. Should the schools adopt a motto of "Slow down and learn" or "Slow down and enjoy education"?
   c. Is an "interdisciplinary exploration of environments and media" needed to facilitate a learner's acquisition of mediacy? Why or why not? What other options, if any, are there?

2. **ACTIVITY** McLaughlin asks whether we are aware of "what it must feel like to be an adolescent today." Investigate the typical life of an adolescent 50 years ago, 25 years ago, and today. Organize your findings in such a way as to illustrate the similarities and differences; compare your findings with others.

3. **DISCUSSION** Beard discusses the problem resulting from a weak print tradition in Negro students. While this problem may exist, is it limited to blacks? If not, who else can you identify with this problem and why? Do you agree with Beard's suggestions? Are there other options available for helping "print-weak" students?

4. **ACTIVITY** Mance believes that by "practicing what they preach" schools could promote respect for the individual. From your reading and personal experience, list ways schools presently deny "the integrity of human personality" and make suggestions as to how these situations could be altered.

5. **ACTIVITY** McCullough believes that some young people who "are not receiving the satisfactions of being involved . . . 'escape' to the fantasy involvement of television and the other media."

a. Prepare a poll to find out what popular media your students, or a group of young people you work with, are using. Ask them to keep a diary for about two weeks, indicating the medium, the content, and the time spent (a prepared form would help them and you).
b. During the same period, try to identify those students who are involved, somewhat involved, and seldom involved in the classroom or other activities under your supervision.
c. Compare your findings.

6. **DISCUSSION** McCullough, Hayakawa, and Solway all deal with "reality" and/or the lack of it in the modern media. Expanding on their illustrations, identify other contrasts between reality as you know it and the "reality" of the many media. Are there any dangers if many people continue to see the media as essentially accurate "pictures of our times"?

7. **DISCUSSION** Brainstorm and discuss possible long-range advantages and disadvantages of popular media study in the secondary school.

SECTION TWO

An English Teacher's Challenge

The following scene is a dramatization. The names and comments are real although the situation is contrived. The scene is a roundtable discussion of contemporary issues in the teaching of English.

MODERATOR: What would you identify as a major challenge facing the English teacher today? For example, Father Ong, you have indicated that voice is "coming into its own," but you have also talked about the complex forces which both favor and work against it. What can be done?

ONG: We can arm ourselves and our students only by vigilant awareness of what is going on about us. In particular, teachers and students of language and literature must cultivate sensitivity to the more profound significance of the media of popular culture—which is not the same thing as either uncritical acceptance of popular culture or entrenched hostility to all its manifestations.

CULKIN: A sensitivity to the characteristics of each medium can lead to a greater insight into all media and the relationships among media . . . The general challenge can be stated in two ways:

1. To improve the student through the media.
2. To improve the media through the student.

McLAUGHLIN: I'm suggesting we wiretap the AM world. This means closing textbooks, educational journals and turning on the radio and TV set, hitting the local movie house about once every two weeks, listening to young singing groups making the rounds, and browsing through magazines . . . High culture addicts will accuse you of selling out at this point. Don't listen to these posterity-peddlers; their contempt for the present has helped make it what it is.

SCHMITTROTH: Our first step is to acknowledge and then begin to learn about the student's culture. Our role for the next ten years is that of learner . . . The teacher's role is to learn along with his students . . . . Times they have changed, brother. We must.

FRANSECKY: If we are to help students renew and reconceive themselves as new world citizens, then we would be wise to examine the modern media that are turning them on, and on, and on . . . We must be aware that we are confronting a student who is terribly present tense, whose world is immediately reflected on radio, television, and disc, and only occasionally in print.

Wired for Sound: Teaching, Communications, and Technological Culture

Walter J. Ong

From the time of ancient Greece, communication processes have always been at the center of western education. Early academic study focused on grammar, which gave birth to rhetoric. Rhetoric formed a matrix for dialectic and logic, and all these conjointly help shape physics and medicine, and ultimately modern science. Through the Middle Ages, the Renaissance, and into the nineteenth century, education began with grammar, rhetoric, and dialectic or logic, the *artes sermocinales* or communication arts.

From Walter J. Ong, "Wired for Sound: Teaching, Communications, and Technological Culture," *College English* 21 (February 1960): 245-51. Copyright © by the National Council of Teachers of English. Reprinted by permission of the publisher and Walter J. Ong.

Teachers are still especially interested in communication, not merely because they are incidentally involved with the process but because their work itself is communication *par excellence.* At the point where teaching is going on, the knowledge which men have accumulated and communicated to one another out of the past thousands or hundreds of thousands of years is being communicated again to inexperienced youth, to give this youth that experience reaching far back beyond one's own years which sociologists call culture. But as teachers channel this knowledge to succeeding ages, they do so by talking it over, rethinking it, and recommunicating it among themselves. In the person of the teacher, who is the depository and communicator of knowledge, mankind constantly reviews what it knows, revaluates its knowledge, revises it, detects its deficiencies, and sets up the framework for new discoveries.

The teacher's work involves him in a constant interior dialogue with the past, the present, and the future. Since the only source of knowledge is the experience we have had up to the present time, or in other words past experience, he has to communicate with the past to raid it for what it has to tell him. With his students, he puts out feelers into the future to orient his knowledge effectively. And he has to bring his knowledge of past and future into focus within the present system of communication, the one in which he has actually to do his teaching.

Hence it is not strange that teachers are sensitive more than other men to changes in communication processes. And teachers in the field of language and literature are most sensitive of all. In these fields a great deal of restlessness is observable today. The furor about why Johnny can or cannot read, the agitation concerning foreign language programs, the tendency of structural linguistics to replace older grammar, and the general overhauling of language-teaching and literature-teaching processes which has been taking place for the past 30 years or more are symptoms that something is stirring. What is it?

Probably a great many things are stirring; but it is certain that many of them can be summed up by saying that we are leaving the Gutenberg era behind us. As we move further into a technological civilization, we meet with abundant signs that the relationship between the teacher and the printed word and hence those between the teacher and a large area of communication, which includes practically all of what we generally mean by "literature" are no longer what they used to be. These relationships were set up in the Renaissance when a typographical civilization appeared, climaxing the intense development of a manuscript culture which had marked the preceding Middle Ages. The present swing is to oral forms in communication, with radio, television (oral in its commitments as compared to typography), public address and intercom systems, or voice recordings (to replace or supplement shorthand, longhand, typing, or print). As a result of this swing, older relationships are undergoing a profound, if not often perceptible, realignment.

Early teaching was aural and oral in cast. Socrates taught by means of person-to-person dialogue. Although Plato in great part extinguished this dialogue when he and his followers captured, stiffened, and mounted it on the written page, he nevertheless thought of himself as preserving dialogue itself by preserving its form or "idea." And although Aristotle seems to have moved further away from the dialogue form than Plato, a careful and astute reading of his works by Werner Jaeger, Joseph Owens, and others has shown how strongly the dialogic approach persists in them. Cicero's whole framework of culture was oral in a way in which the text-oriented Renaissance Ciceronianism could never be. To bring Greek culture to Rome, Cicero did not simply read books but went to Athens to listen to the oral exposition of philosophy there and thus to learn what to transmit viva voce to his compatriots. It is well known that Cicero first spoke what he had to communicate, delivering his orations first and writing them afterwards. St Augustine remains similarly oriented. He was disillusioned less by Manichean writings than he was at the oral presentation of Manichean teaching by Faustus, who, after exciting the highest hopes, explained so little and so unconvincingly. When Augustine heard the fateful words, *Tolle et lege*—we know from what he has to say elsewhere about reading habits in his day—he took up the Scriptures and read to himself *aloud.*

By contrast with the ancient world, the Middle Ages produced a more purely manuscript culture. But their teaching methods retained massive oral-aural commitments. Socrates' dialogue, to be sure, was reduced to the university master's monologue, eventually styled a "lecture" or "reading," since it was typically a commentary on a written work and itself regarded as something committed or to be committed to writing. Yet the practice of testing intellectual prowess by oral methods alone, such as disputations, was retained. Written assignments or written examinations after grammar school remained unknown and apparently unthought of. A thesis was not something one wrote but something one asserted and defended orally as one's inaugural act upon induction into the teaching profession. Medieval culture is thus a transitional culture, oral-aural at root but scriptural in bent.

The printed page completed the pedagogical shift away from the oral. It silenced the medieval disputation and, as Marshall McLuhan so well put it in the volume *Mass Culture* "created the solitary student," and the school textbook as well. From the beginnings of printing the greatest source of revenue for book publishers has been the classroom and its purlieus. Early publishers liked to ally themselves with humanist educators. The massive plaque on Erasmus's tomb in the Münster at Basel is erected by three grateful publishers, whom he helped make affluent: Amerbachius, Frobenius, and Episcopius. At a time when not more than a few pages of any book could be kept standing in type at any one time, the Wechel firm of Paris and Frankfort-on-the-Main published at least 172 editions of one or another work, almost all for classroom or academic use, by Peter Ramus and his literary lieutenant Omer Talon (Talaeus). Erasmus, Ramus, and Talon are only three among thousands of textbook authors whose works are published and read more than those of almost any "literary" writer.

The connection between printing and teaching was from the beginning as subtle and profound as it was financially successful. The notion of "storing" unassembled letters (and consequently dismantled words and books) in "fonts" of prefabricated type, which lies at the heart of the typographical developments of the fifteenth century, exhibits a close psychological connection with the doctrine of the *loci communes* ("commonplaces" or simply "places") taught in rhetoric and dialectic or logic classes in fifteenth-century schoolrooms. One "drew arguments" from the places as one drew type from a font. As the printed book took over, and with it faster and faster silent reading habits, the commitment to eloquence and oral expression lingering as a heritage from the Renaissance devotion to classical antiquity became, more and more, lip service. The "elocution contests" of a generation or two ago were the dying gasps of the old tradition. It seemed that the printed book had won the day.

It still seems so in the sense that it is unlikely that printing (or its recent manifold variants such as mimeographing or planographing) will ever be done away with in teaching or elsewhere generally. It is incontestably convenient to have the spoken word frozen in space, and frozen in exactly the same space for everyone among one's auditors. The teacher is not likely to forego the luxury of being able to say, "Everyone now turn to page 83, line 4 from the top, and look at the third word from the left." This luxury is too hard-won. For such a directive was entirely impossible before the invention of printing, when, if the students had manuscript books, every book would have every word in a different place from every other book. Except in certain academic horror stories, no one really seems convinced that the modern world is going to regress into a pretypographical or a preliterate culture. What is happening is more complicated than this. If students are losing their hold on reading and on grammar, this is in great part because, in their relationship to the other items involved in communication, reading and grammar are not what they used to be. They are still there, and will be, but the constellation in which they exist is shifting its formation.

One of the principal causes of the shift in status of reading and grammar is the increased importance of oral-aural communication in our technological society. It is paradoxical that a society given so much to the use of diagrams and to the maneuvering of objects in space (from giant aircraft to atoms) should at the same time develop means of communication which specialize not in sight but in sound. Yet the signs of a shift are everywhere. Grammar, which was originally the study of written language (gramma in Greek means a letter of the alphabet) and which, as normative grammar, has rules based less upon what speaking people do when they talk than upon what literate people do when they write, is yielding to linguistics, which, while it includes grammar, is rooted in the study of oral performance. The trend toward discussion groups has been under way for a long time. It manifests itself not only in the classroom under such guises as "Deweyism," but also in business, where meetings of all sorts have multiplied beyond calculation in the course of the recent managerial revolution. The same elaborate business organizations which solve many of their problems by computing machines have found that back of the Univac there must be large-scale and deliberate confrontation of person with person. Interest in group dynamics serves as a counterbalance to electronic computers. Often the most efficient way to attack a problem has been found to be the "brainstorming" session, where members of a group stimulated by the rest of the group as an audience, suggest orally whatever solution to a practical problem may stray through their heads, no matter how zany the solution may at first blush appear.

Libraries themselves have undergone significant reorientations. The oldstyle Renaissance public or semipublic library, with its books chained to keep the users for carrying them away, yielded some years ago to the lending library. Both these institutions were spectacularly quiet. The new library makes allowance for noise, and utilizes noise. It includes seminar rooms and all-purpose rooms for larger meetings. Acoustic insulation, of course, has made these possible. But, by whatever means the effect has been achieved, libraries have recently become places where people can get together to talk. Our attitude toward books, our concept of what they are, is sure to be affected by such a change, especially as more libraries are being run on an open-stack plan. Librarians, including librarians of early lending libraries, until recently appear to have existed chiefly to keep books in the library, from which they would issue them with ill-concealed reluctance, placated only by thought of the savage reprisals which would result if the books were not returned by the detested borrower almost immediately. Today's librarians all want books to go out and feel frustrated if they do not. The result is that more and more books are now read in a world alive with sound, to musical backgrounds provided by radios and hi-fi sets.

The oral-aural emphases of today run counter to certain typical phenomena of the Gutenberg era as diverse as the invention of printing and the exploration and observation of the surface of the globe. These activities reached their peak together, and both focused attention in space and thus vaunted sight. The microscope and telescope, developed as epiphenomena of printing and exploration, did the same. But a new age is upon us, and its shift from sight-emphasis to increased sound-emphasis spans this entire area from the diffusion of the word to the exploration of one's surroundings. In the realm of words, dictaphones replace shorthand writing, and audio charge systems replace written library records. Exploration no longer depends on moving the human body through space. It is conducted by radar and radio-telescopes (more informative in many ways than visual-type telescopes), and by sputniks, which are launched into space as little speaking voices. In these devices, sight, of course, plays a role, but no longer so exclusive a role as before. Press reports on the first nearly successful moon rocket noted that at its apogee it could not be seen even with the most powerful lens telescope on earth, but that it could be heard.

In their whole trend, modern developments in communications, while they have not slighted the visual, have given more play to the oral-aural, which a purely typographical culture had reduced to a record minimum in human life. The sequence of development running from silent print through audio-visual telegraph to the completely aural radio is an obvious instance of increasing aural dominance. Even television belongs partially in this visual-to-aural series, being only equivocally a regression to visualism. For the visual element in television is severely limited. The amount of detail feasible on a television screen is far less than that visible on a movie screen and not remotely comparable to that tolerable and easily discernible in photographs. Details on television have to be filled in aurally, by explicit vocal explanation or by suggestion through music and sound effects. Silent television is hardly an engaging prospect.

Heightening the oral-aural element in a culture does much more than merely deemphasize vision. It subtly heightens the personalist element in a culture. For the plenary development of sound, the human voice, is a manifestation of the person. Even more than it is a manifestation of an understanding of objects, speech is a calling of one person to another, of an interior to an interior. Sight presents always surfaces, presents even depth as a lamination of surfaces, whereas sound presents always interiors, for sound is impossible without some resonance. The post-Baconian preoccupation with sight and "observation" produced the world of the Enlightenment, a world of objects and things without convincing personal presences, giving us the strangely silent universe which Newtonian physics and Deism both supposed. Printing was the harbinger of this Newtonian world, for printing is spectacularly allied with surface or "object" treatment of reality. Picasso's collages use bits of printed posters or newspapers to establish a sense of flat surface because print is sensed as indissolubly allied with surface. Scraps of printing in the collages serve precisely the function of returning the eye from the perspective depths in other parts of the assemblage to the plane surface of the painting—it is unconvincing to imagine print on anything other than something relatively flat and smooth.

Strangely enough, although it is in part a visualist development, television has moved away from this effect of print. It has been a personalizing, not an objectifying, medium. The discussion panel, with its interchange of personalities, is properly a television phenomenon. Such personal interchange was difficult to manage on radio, for there individual persons could only with difficulty be kept distinct. Hence the use of voice was not brought to its fullest fruition. By the same token television is a more feasible means of education than radio. This is not because it can use visual aid devices (figures written on a blackboard on television cannot be seen by any viewer unless the camera is turned on them—they lack the permanent availability of figures on a classroom blackboard). It is because television better implements personal rapport between instructor and student.

But television is not the only manifestation of the growing interest in the human person which accompanies the resurgence of voice in our culture. Another manifestation is the self-conscious personalism of our times. The twentieth century, from one point of view the most mechanized of all the ages of mankind, is from another point of view the most personalized. No other age has generated a whole philosophy of personalism such as one finds in the works of Martin Buber, Gabriel Marcel, and others. At a much less reflective, more superficial, and nevertheless significant level, no civilization before our technological civilization has given such attention to problems of personnel and personality in matters even of industrial performance. The "I" and the "thou" have never been the objects of more explicit treatment than now. In the future, alongside the digital and analogue computers and other mathematicizing developments, such as western culture has specialized in more and more over the past few hundred years, the human person will receive more and more attention, not in every quarter but in significant milieus and ways.

One may object that earlier civilizations were, and other contemporary civilizations are, more personal in certain aspects of their structure than ours. Modern Arab culture, syled by Marcel Jousse "verbomotor" (verbomoteur), is still almost exclusively personal in orientation (as a preliterate culture must be). acting in terms of personal loyalties and without much "objective" insight into issues. Such cultures can be both anarchical and, as Albert Camus well knows, absorbingly interesting from a human and literary point of view. This is because of their personalist orientation. But from another point of view, and an utterly basic one, such cultures leave much to be desired in this same personality orientation. Their respect for the elementary personal right to life can be quite minimal.

The influence which the present cultural shift toward the oral-aural is having on language and literature study and teaching is probably most important where it is least crass and striking. To think of adapting courses to present trends by exploiting as gadgets the spectacularly evident new media—radio, television, tape recordings, intercom—is to a certain extent to miss the point. These new media are now just new gadgets to be employed for what we are already doing with other less efficient gadgets. They are part of a shift which is inexorably affecting our very notion of what communication itself is. The question is not how to adapt television or tape recording to present courses in educational institutions or present courses to television and tape, for the present shift is sapping the very notion of a "course" itself. A "course" (Latin, *cursus*) means a running through. The concept of a "course" in a subject, derivative from the process of teaching by "running through" a text, is a relict of manuscript and typographical culture. Moving in a more oral-aural setting, Socrates never gave a "course" in anything, and indeed had no notion of what such a thing as a "course" might be.

This is not to say that "courses" in language and literature or in anything else are on their way out. Evolution does not proceed by jettisoning earlier developments completely in working toward new ones. It tends rather to preserve earlier developments, even though these may have to be given new guises. Courses in language and literature are evidently going to be with us for a long time, perhaps for good. Nevertheless, their psychological significance is undergoing subtle and complex, but inexorable, change.

One way to express the nature of this change is to say that the old focus of literary studies on rhetoric is being replaced by a focus on dialogue. In ancient times, and through the Middle Ages, the cause of literature was the cause of rhetoric—which is to say the cause of the art of oratory. Poetry and all "ornate" expression was commonly referred to an eloquence which was associated basically with the oration or public speech before a group of persons. In contrast, the dialectic which split off from rhetoric and modulated into logic, first in Aristotle but more definitely through the Middle Ages, has pulled away from literature and helped generate modern science. The Renaissance sought to return from dialectic to literature by reemphasis of eloquence and rhetoric, but the Renaissance effort foundered in the combined currents of an always ebullient scholasticism and of the modern scientism so closely related to scholasticism. Rhetoric and the areas of communication which it represented failed to develop any mature theoretical structure viable in the post-Newtonian world where neat theories seemed to account for everything else.

For some time now the Newtonian universe has been broken down, and the result has been a recrudescence of interest in language and literature. But the interest no longer centers on rhetoric, the art of persuasion, which in our day is much more the province of the advertising man and marketing specialist than of the *litterateur*. The more effective ally of literature has turned out to be the sense of dialogue which marks important philosophical developments of our age (and which is notably missing or *ersatz* in advertising). Literature is no longer standing so much alone as it did when "mere" rhetoric was arrayed against dialectic. It is painstakingly picked over by psychologists, physicians, sociologists, anthropologists, theolgians, and others. Certain typically modern philosophies of the "existentialist" sort have been described as literary philosophies, conscious of and using literary form, as exploited by Camus, Marcel, Sartre, and others. We have become explicitly aware in our time of the intimate linkage between the process of communication and human thought itself. Many of the illusions of the Enlightenment concerning private thought and psychological privacy generally have been dissipated since the discovery of evolution, of depth psychology, and of the processes involved in the history of human thinking. We are intimately aware, as Gaston Fessard and others have put it, that science itself is only arrested dialogue. Voice is not an accretion, but a necessary adjunct or even a necessary dimension of human thinking. (It should be added that the "dialogue" meant here is neither medieval dialectic nor Hegelian dialectic, although it is related somewhat to both. Dialogue refers here to actual vocal exchange between person and person.)

It is through awareness of the paramount role of voice in human activity that students of English or of any other language today must seek to understand the reactivation of the oral-aural element in human culture. Voice is coming into its own as never before. But the ways in which it is doing so, and the elements in our culture which favor voice as well as those which militate against it, are complex in the extreme. We can arm ourselves and our students only by vigilant awareness of what is going on about us. In particular, teachers and students of language and literature must cultivate sensitivity to the more profound significance of the media of popular culture—which is not the same thing as either uncritical acceptance of popular culture or entrenched hostility to all its manifestations. Any kind of genuine sensitivity to literature of any age or culture has become thoroughly impossible unless a person has grown seriously, not phrenetically—reflective about contemporary communications media. Men today—and, above all, high school, college, and university students—live englobed in a universe of sound emanating from radio and hi-fi sets which surpasses anything any earlier human culture has known, both in the total decibel output at any given moment and in incessancy. Reflection on the condition of the new media and the changes they are effecting in human life will probably produce no pat formulae either to describe the totality of the present situation or to prescribe highly simplified lines of action. But it should enable us to live.

An Extension of Film and Television Study

John M. Culkin

Today's students are immersed in a sea of communications. One does not have to be a card-carrying McLuhanite to acknowledge the pervasive presence of media and messages of all kinds. If we are interested in students, we should want to teach them how to swim in these new and uncharted waters.

One of the great contributions of the film study and screen education movements has been to focus attention on the need for respecting and dealing with media normally experienced *outside* the school environment. The logical extension of this thrust should be to develop awareness for all the media which reach and influence the student. Popular music, for example, is probably the most accurate barometer of the sense and sensibility of students. And then there is the barrage of sights, sounds, and feelings which come at them from screens and pages of all sizes, from stages, radios, record machines, and just from a stroll downtown. It is almost impossible even to add up the hours of involvement with these media. It's a total environment rather than a series of acts.

From John M. Culkin, "An Extension of Film and Television Study," *Audiovisual Instruction* 13 (January 1968): 11-13. Copyright © 1968, Department of Audiovisual Instruction, NEA. Reprinted by permission of the publisher.

This environment belongs to this century. Many have reacted to it, few have reflected about it, and fewer still have done anything about it. If the unexamined life was not worth living in Socratic Athens, it may be lethal in "The Global Village." Within the brief span of 50 years we have moved from a speech- and print-dominated culture into a total information and polymedia culture. Intelligent living within such a culture demands an understanding of all these media.

The rather hortatory and somewhat minatory tone of the foregoing paragraphs reflects a personal concern with the growing competence gap between the commercial and noncommercial communcations in the student's world, between those who are interested in making money and those who are interested in making people. Cigarette commercials, for instance, cost about $30,000 per *minute* to produce. The average instructional television program gets produced for considerably less than $1,000 per *half hour.* The cigarette pushers also tend to study their audiences harder and to get fired faster if communication doesn't take place. The commercials are produced with considerably more care than the programs they sponsor. Marya Mannes suggests that this insistent appeal to commercial interests has produced the overtone for almost every tone struck in our society—"But will it sell?" Her book by that same title is the stuff of which teachers' meetings should be made.

But however positive or negative the motivation may be, the need for some systematic attention to the media is still with us and will be increasingly pressing itself upon our attention. Susan Sontag offers a nice formulation of the goals. "What is important now is to recover our senses. We must learn to *see* more, to *hear* more, to *feel* more."

This seeing, hearing, and feeling should be applied to the whole battery of media in common usage for the education, manipulation, entertainment, and elevation of audiences. It would include television, painting, music, sculpture, newspapers, magazines, advertising of all kinds, radio, comics, computers, plays, films, photography, opera, telephones, ballet, phonographs, tape recorders, speech, print, and related and combined forms of these media. The neutral word "media" has the advantage of being inclusive and of avoiding the tedious discussions about whether or not certain media qualify as art forms. They all qualify as facts within the student's experience and that would seem to be sufficient reason to examine them.

"Mediacy" is a new word which may be useful in describing the skill needed to interpret all the media of communication. It is to all media what literacy is to print. Like all neologisms it has a quality of the precious and the unfamiliar about it. Like all new words it will survive only if it proves useful. The word is considerably less important than the skill it is meant to describe. The rationale for mediacy has been cogently stated by Edmund Carpenter:

English is a mass medium. All languages are mass media. The new mass media—film, radio, TV—are new languages, their grammars as yet unknown. Each codifies reality differently; each conceals a unique metaphysics. Linguists tell us that it's possible to say anything in any

language if you use enough words or images, but there's rarely time; the
natural course is for a culture to exploit its media biases.

This insight takes us beyond any merely "fallout shelter" approach to the media
and introduces us to very basic questions about cognition, perception, and
values. The media are not mere envelopes which carry all messages indifferently;
they shape both the message and the perceiver.

A sensitivity to the characteristics of each medium can lead to a greater
insight into all media and to the relationships among media. Students who come
to life through experience with one medium tend to come alive across-the-board.
The concept of mediacy is far from an attack on or minimizing of the spoken
and printed word. It is, however, an acknowledgement of the fact that the
introduction of new media in a culture must of necessity change the role of the
older media. The printed word is not served best by those who ignore what is
currently happening and silently hope that the new media will silently fade
away. To deal with these realities in no way implies any automatic or blanket
approbation of them. Marshall McLuhan stated the case in the introduction to
Exploration in Communication:

> *Exploration in Communications:*
> The aim of this anthology is to develop an awareness about print and the
> newer technologies of communication so that we can orchestrate them,
> minimize their mutual frustrations and clashes, and get the best out of
> each in the educational process. The present conflict leads to elimination
> of the motive to learn and to diminution of interest in previous
> achievement: it leads to loss of the sense of relevance. Without an
> understanding of media grammars, we cannot hope to achieve a
> contemporary awareness of the world in which we live.

And those who may be unmoved by the theoretical urgency of understanding
media can almost assuredly find motivation by looking around their schools or
homes at the current breed of high school students. Bob Dylan sings: "The times
they are a-changin'," and "Because something is happening but you don't know
what it is, do you Mister Jones?" Most of us "tweenagers," caught between the
generations, can empathize with Mister Jones. No culture has ever had to
experience so many new things in so short a time. The fact that we haven't
developed ways of dealing with this speeded-up rate of change shouldn't be
either a surprise or a source of regret. There were no precedents for the whole
thing. Now is not a bad time to begin. The media are not a bad place to begin.

The fact of the media is challenge enough. The information levels are, for the
first time in history, higher outside the classroom than in it. The student lives in
both these worlds. What is unified in his experience should also be unified in his
understanding. The general challenge can be stated in two ways: (1) to improve
the student through the media, (2) to improve the media through the student.

The first stresses the positive contribution of the rich and varied experiences
available to the student through all the media. The second underscores the fact
that the media, especially the commercially exploited ones, respond to the

demands of their audience; improve the audience and you improve the medium.

An idea like media study which can touch upon such basic issues of theory and public policy can also generate a number of eminently practical questions concerning implementation. Here again the experience gained in the nascent film study and screen education programs can provide guidelines for media study, which is actually an extension and coordination of these programs and of existing programs in literature, the arts, and the humanities. Education is like a snake. If you touch it at any one part of its anatomy, you get a response from the whole organism. Any new idea will, therefore, inevitably raise questions about such items as scheduling, grades, styles of teaching, examinations, budget, teaching materials—the whole catastrophe.

The following headings sum up a few of the practical issues now faced in film and television study and which will also be involved in a more extended program of media study. We are still in the first five minutes of the movement and these statements should be read as one man's probes into a field where we will all be well served to hear from all the precincts.

TEACHERS

The idea will be as good as the teachers. One problem is that the students frequently have had greater experience of the media world than the teachers. It's their turf, their territory. This suggests that the style of teaching most appropriate to this new situation will be an inductive or heuristic one which builds on an analysis of the experiences which the students already have. Teachers can be assisted in a variety of ways through short- and long-term workshops or institutes. On the practical level it is urgent that summer institutes include media study as a legitimate focus for those preparing to work in educational media, English, and programs for the disadvantaged.

TEACHING MATERIALS

While the concept of "teacher-proof" materials is repugnant, the realization that both teachers and students can be assisted enormously by well-produced teaching aids is valid enough. The new media raise new problems of legal and residual rights and, since the schools to date haven't provided a concerted enough voice for these materials, the issues still have not been faced. The schools will need full films and TV programs, excerpts, discussion materials, films about the media, sound and video tapes, new books and magazines. At present *Media and Methods* comes closest to the type of magazine most useful to the teacher who has to walk into the classroom on the morrow. Most important of all will be that these materials are prepared not by those who would exploit this new market, but by those who are both competent in the media and who care for the student. A unique man like Tony Schwartz, the sound artist, who is involved at the highest level of his profession and is simultaneously a teacher of both high school and college students, is a hopeful prototype of the practicing artists who could become involved with the schools.

CURRICULUM

Here more than anywhere else there will be no single answer. Inventive teachers are already working on media programs within English or the more flexible units in arts and humanities. Some schools have courses or units titled "communications" or "communication arts." Many film study and screen education programs also analyze photography and commercials from all media. The schools are tending to break down many of the artificial walls between items in the curriculum, and media study should profit from this trend.

ELEMENTARY SCHOOLS

Most of the current programs in media study are in the high schools, but there is a growing and hopeful interest on the part of elementary school teachers. This makes great sense. The time to help the kids with their media experience is when they are going through the experience. From a more positive point of view, the media can also be used to train and tune up the senses of three-, four-, and five-year-old students so that they are aware of the full powers of their own humanity.

LEARNING BY DOING

Dewey and Montessori never sounded more contemporary than today. Apart from any vocational or professional interest, students should get involved in trying to communicate through the media. Some beautiful, but all too infrequent, examples exist of what they can do when given the chance to express themselves through film, tape, photography, paint, and the other media. Some claim that such active work in the creative end of the media may be the only valid route for training intelligent consumers of the media. One thing is certain—there are no unmotivated students when it comes to making a movie.

AUDIOVISUAL DIMENSION

Media study can offer the media specialist a new and enlarged role within the school. Since the media are his area of competence, he can take a more responsible role in the instructional program. Both as a teacher of the media and as a consultant to the faculty, he can become a more integral part of the instructional team. His judgment can also influence the school program through the choice of films, records, and slides which have value not only for their ancillary purpose in the curriculum, but which have merit in and of themselves as complete experiences and as works of art.

The theoretical and practical issues, however, should not obscure the fact that at the heart of the school is the student. Independent of our theories or desires about him is the fact of his immersion in the new media. Harley Parker has defined art as "anything which illuminates the environment." As a bonus most teachers will find that in working with students in media study they are also illuminating their own environment. The teacher then joins the student *in* learning rather than enjoins him *to* learning.

A Recipe for Triggering Relevance

Frank McLaughlin

INGREDIENTS

1. A willingness to take the spotlight off the teacher and put it on the student.
2. More tolerance for ambiguity, noise, and adolescents with long hair.
3. A commitment to the present instead of the future.
4. Scholarship in such areas as folk-rock music, current films, newspapers, and magazines and less concern for the usual academic niceties of the past.
5. A realization that everything teaches but not everything is worth learning.
6. Giving up the teacher as authority image, and its necessary tool—the lecture method.
7. Looking upon your classroom as a learning laboratory, not as place where information is transmitted.
8. A sincere attempt to try democracy in the classroom; law and order should take a seat behind learning when priorities are considered.

If students don't appropriate knowledge, there is no learning. If skills are not acquired, if important concepts and values have not been internalized, then whatever has taken place is either wasted or has produced negative learning. Sooner or later we all have to face up to this. We must honestly question whether two way communication really exists in our classrooms.

Can we communicate, make the necessary connections? More specifically, can

From Frank McLaughlin, "A Recipe for Triggering Relevance," *Media and Methods* 5 (January 1969): 23-26. Copyright © 1969 by Media and Methods Institute, Inc. Reprinted by permission of the publisher and Frank McLaughlin.

a middle-aged, weary English teacher make contact with teenagers in schools where such innovations as team teaching, modular scheduling, and nongradedness aren't even considered? Despite the obvious disadvantages of being structurally straitjacketed in 30 desk classrooms five periods a day, I maintain that meaningful communication and learning can take place.

Learning (unless it is peripheral) won't take place until students are "engaged" with tasks they feel meaningful. How do you engage their attention? How do you draw them in, involve them? Certainly not by continuing to be "cultural curators," parading artifacts from the past and expecting teenagers to be moved by *Beowulf,* "Il Penseroso," or *Tale of Two Cities.* Isn't it a mite ludicrous for an English teacher to try to pump up interest in *Silas Marner* when his teenagers are bombarded by the fast-paced humor of *Laugh-In* or the multiscreen swinging action of *The Thomas Crown Affair,* which they might have half seen (the top half) at a drive-in last Friday night? Furthermore, shouldn't we question the amount of time we spend teaching the novel and short story? Isn't it likely that our students will choose their vicarious experiences in the future more from motion pictures and television than from the genres we've trained them in?

The point is we know too much about the past and too little about the present. We have also adopted a security blanket mentality about our subject matter. Our training as English teachers gives us a language and a sanctified corpus of works to teach; unfortunately, it often becomes just one more impediment between kids and the world they must make sense of. Our subject matter training should not serve as a set of perceptions to be passed on to our students but as a series of conceptual and affective referents to be brought into play in fresh contexts.

To develop this idea from another angle, we could approximate formal rarefied subject matter (meant somehow to fill kids up with the *right* information) as *FM,* and the loud, insistent, often banal racket that characterizes the actual world as *AM.* No matter how much we improve the quality of *FM* transmission (which is unfortunately what most graduate courses and institutes are about), it is still essentially a foreign and frequently irrelevant language.

Most English teachers shy away from the *AM* world. It's vulgar, it's populated by a lot of long-haired school and society dropouts, and besides there are no study guides available. We forget that Marlowe, Byron, and Blake were once *AM* outcasts who have only become academically safe since they died and were interred in textbooks. They certainly were not that unlike such contemporary troubadors as Paul Simon, Jim Webb, and Frank Zappa. The latter three can help us make connection between the "now" generation and academic lessons we deem important.

I'm suggesting we wiretap the *AM* world. This means closing textbooks, educational journals and turning on the radio and *TV* set, hitting the local movie house about once every two weeks, listening to the young singing groups making the rounds, and browsing through magazines like *Mad, Rave, Car and Driver, Playboy, Eye, Motor Trend, Seventeen,* and a half dozen movie and *TV* publications. When you take the time to discover the media-mod environment, you are learning the turf. Being able to draw from it will give you "common ground" to share with your students. High culture addicts will accuse you of selling out at this point. Don't listen to these posterity-peddlers; their contempt for the present has helped make it what it is.

The subversion I'm suggesting is not easy in most of the schools we teach in today. Many of us need to adopt radical techniques in our present situations to bridge us into the "schools for kids, let's-work-together, learn-by-doing" education John Dewey dreamed of nearly a century ago. What follows are some ways an English teacher can start the movement in his own class. If you're in a particularly repressive school, shut the door and post a lookout before you try the following:

THE MEDIUM IS MUSIC

The New Youth of the Rock Generation has done something in American popular song that has begged to be done for generations. It has taken the creation of the lyrics and the music out of the hands of the hacks and given it over to the poets.

RALPH GLEASON

These words appear on the back of the Simon and Garfunkel album, *Parsley, Sage, Rosemary and Thyme.* Gleason's praise will seem lavish until you listen a half dozen times to songs like "The Dangling Conversation," "7 'Clock News Silent Night," and "Scarborough Fair Canticle." Several of the songs on this album could be used as vehicles for getting into such themes as Alienation, War, Personal Identity, etc. To the teacher who feels that Simon and Garfunkel are an isolated and unfair example, some listening is in order. The Free Design, The Beatles (who have matured considerably since "I Want to Hold Your Hand"), and The Doors are worth listening to. Soloists like Bob Dylan, Joan Baez, James Brown, and Phil Ochs also provide much fodder. The last folk singer has a great album that an enterprising social studies teacher might also find fascinating. It has the superb title, *All the News that's Fit to Sing.* The individual bands touch upon a dozen topical events. Two final popular music examples will help demonstrate how relevance can be triggered with a "hunk of environment." If an English teacher wanted to create a unit, "The Authentic Life," he might use two recent 45's "The Proper Ornaments" (by the Free Design) and "Mr. Businessman" (by Ray Stevens) to introduce the theme. Both records vigorously attack the rampant materialism in America, our penchant for pursuing the short range goals and middle class values. The first of these records has beautiful harmony, and kids will have to listen closely to the points being made; the latter is a bit too blatant for my taste, but it contains several fine phrases and raises issues that teenagers are concerned about and want to talk about. By conveying what the "inauthentic" life is, both records would nicely set the stage for a meaningful journey through Thoreau's *Walden.*

Simon and Garfunkel's "I am a Rock" could be contrasted with John Donne's "No Man is an Island" segment in his seventeenth meditation. Bob Lind's "The Elusive Butterfly" could also be played and analyzed in conjunction with Donne's metaphysical conceits or with the use of figurative language generally. The possibilities are endless; all that is necessary is that we tune in and listen.

THE MAGAZINE BIT

Another gambit begins by collecting every conceivable magazine you can lay your hands on. I have carefully selected more than 150 over a two-year period. They range from *Flying* to *Psychology Today,* from *Chettah* to (ugh . . .) *College English,* from *Forbes* to *Movie Teen Illustrated.* When my ouija board tells me the time is ripe, I lug my magazines into school and ask each student to bring in between two and five magazines apiece. We spread them all over the room. By this time there are usually more than 300 around, and the room is a colorful mess. If you are visited by an unfriendly spirit at this point, tell him you are creating a powerful learning environment or (know your medium) that you and your students are collecting magazines for a church rummage sale. Better yet, keep your door locked.

If you have done your work well, magic will soon happen. Kids will find a particular magazine that captures their fancy. You help to insure this by some perceptive card stacking. Make sure the magazines you brought cover a wide range of experiences and individual issues contain features or articles that will arouse all but the most dormant curiosity. I usually devote a day to wallowing in the magazines. No directions. No homework. You will quickly discover that nonreaders quickly become readers when the right carrot is placed before them.

After students have discovered a magazine or two, they choose one to study. They determine how it's put together, where the magazine gets its advertising, the ratio of editorial to advertising content, who the readership is, what methods the magazine employs to get feedback, how the magazine compares to its competitors, etc. What you are really after here is the in-depth study of a medium. You probe for the structure, function, and variety of magazines. A good concluding activity would be to make magazines.

THE NEWSPAPER GAMBIT

I'm hooked on cartoons. McLuhan would call them a cool medium (low in definition, demanding involvement). We might use them as mini-lessons. Instead of giving kids Warriner Handbook type theme topics like . . . My first date . . . My favorite astronaut . . . An embarrassing moment . . . or some other such weighty topic, cut out cartoons from your local paper (and/or from magazines like *Playboy, The New Yorker, Saturday Review, Esquire,* etc.) and prepare them for use on the overhead projector.

You might project eight or ten good cartoons and have your students use them as points of departures for themes. Better yet, let them bring some of their own in for the same purpose. You can also use cartoons as a triggering device to get you into a new topic or unit, or they can serve to bridge you from one unit to another, or to establish a new point of view on some topic you're exploring.

The newspaper itself is a great teaching machine. It is a mosaic of voices that digests, reports, persuades, interprets, discusses, and lists information. Look at the first page. Notice how the reader can scan the page before he chooses what he wants to read; notice how he can read bits and pieces before finishing a single article or column, if he so desires. We can take the different sections of newspapers and analyze them. Contrast the editorial voice with the cold, impersonal voice of legal notice. Contrast the reporting with the advertising copy, etc. We might question why many people consider *The Christian Science Monitor* such a good paper. We might bring it and the *New York Times* in class and compare them with local newspapers. Walker Gibson's "speaking voice approach" offers a good strategy for working in this fashion.

It's also about time that we stopped using those "safe" academic writing models that abound in textbooks and began utilizing some of the fine writing that can be found in daily newspapers and magazines. How about bringing James Reston, Russell Baker, Arthur Daley, Jim Bishop, and Art Buchwald in the classroom. The short stories in *Esquire* and *Playboy* are often superb; *Playboy's* interviews are among the best any magazine offers; *Sports Illustrated* often contains writing worthy of emulation. To do this means getting your nose out of Addison and Steele, Francis Bacon, and other worthies of the past. Don't turn kids off with Montaigne when you can turn them on with Nat Hentoff or William Buckley.

Finally, while you are exhausting yourselves with media probes and encounters with race relations, the authentic life, the individual vs. society, make room for humor. Humor is the best but least used tool in the educator's arsenal. I've had the misfortune of sitting through classes where English teachers dealt with humor or comedy (usually in genre form), and there were few laughs or good times. Don't make humor one more boring unit.

Use Mike Nichols and Elaine May recordings. Bill Cosby, Flip Wilson, the Negro comic who lost rhythm because he attended a white school, and Burns and Schreiber have very funny albums that contain good social commentary and satire. Sprinkle it throughout your year's work, and use it at the end of long units when both you and your students need a change of pace. Humor teaches. Cool Medium Much Involvement. Use it. Kids are hungry for learning. Appetites, however, not only go unsatisfied, they are not even recognized. English teachers who know *only* how to trot out works from the past to arm kids for some value future ought to switch to selling insurance. . . . There they might make better connections between past and future that will benefit clients. Kids live in the present tense. Teachers who can't relate to the present inhibit growth.

HALF TIME SPEECH

*Unflinchingly assume responsibility for classroom
communication. If teenagers don't learn, it's our fault. If
they don't appropriate the knowledge we expose them to it's
because we haven't demonstrated its efficacy.*

If your heart doesn't beat a little faster when "Kaliedescope," or "Classical
Gas" is being played, if you don't know who Procol Harum, Glen Campbell, The
Association, or The Mothers of Invention are, if you haven't tuned into a Jean
Shepherd monologue or read McLuhan or seen *The Graduate* or *Yellow
Submarine* or *Of Black America,* it might be time to set aside your textbooks
and lessons plans, skip the courses in *FM* transmission, and discover the *AM*
world at your fingertips.

Tool, Weapon, Fine Instrument

John Schmittroth

"Times, they are a-changin'."
English classes ain't
Oh, it's the sure road to extinction
Unless—
Here's a way back, brothers.

At this moment in history, the composition class should be the pulse of the
university. Alive young people have something to say. English teachers can show
them how to say it—efficiently, emphatically. But nothing is happening. Because
we are not listening. We don't know our students.

Today's student is not the crewcut ex-*GI* of the fifties; the funster of the
forties "digging" the big-band sound; the flasked roadster-driver of the thirties.
He is a phenomenon looking for his own thing. An historical analogue is the
clerk of medieval times, on whose thin shoulders rested the mind of mankind;
one who would gladly learn and gladly teach and riot at Paris and riot at
Oxenford.

Today's college freshman is turned on, tuned in; he is the offspring of multimedia; his is an electronic culture whole and intact. He has spent 15,000 hours with television and watched only 10,800 hours of school; he has seen 500 full-length films. He is plugged in to a new electronic literature which shows man in multi-image—from the bland, powdered pimp of Madison Avenue to the lonely long-distance runner; *Hud* and *Cool Hand Luke*; *The Graduate* and *Bonnie and Clyde; 2001, A Man and a Woman, Lord of the Flies*.

Because of the immediacy of electronic media, because they have taught him so many things so quickly, today's student feels he can sniff out hypocrisy. He has seen the war in living—and dying—color; it is his symbol of our sickness. He has seen his freedoms everywhere strangled—students clubbed in Chicago; Eldridge Cleaver made to flee the country; a young deserter pulled from a church by the *FBI*; himself and his friends forced into the army against their will. This scene to him is the Establishment. Big Brother who denies him a voice on campus, denies him a vote in local, state, and national elections, but allows him to pay tuition and taxes.

What can he say, do, be? He can get angry, picket, sit in, confront. But best of all he can plug in to his sound.

Subtle, complex, affecting, and effective, his music tells it like it is. Some of it is bad and loud; some of it is good and loud; and some of it comes very, very close to very good art, to first-rate poetry—John Lennon, Donovan, Soul, Simon and Garfunkel (who sing Robinson's "Richard Cory"), Acid Rock, Joni Mitchell (who writes exquisite "poems"), The Underground, Leonard Cohen (a poet who chants "new folk"), Rod McKuen, Judy Collins (who sings Yeats's "Song of Wandering Aengus" under a new title of "Golden Apples of the Sun"—the album title, too), Bob Dylan (who took his name from Dylan Thomas and whose protest "poems" are perhaps the best of all), Joan Baez (with a whole album of "literary" things said and sung, *Baptism*), and Jacques Brel, who flays the mad world in a song called "Next". . . .

Where do we go from here?

Our first step is to acknowledge and then begin to learn the student's culture. Our role for the next ten years is as learner. What follows is a way to begin.

The composition class should be a workshop in which the whole class or groups within the class work within semester-long "molds" or "models" of Now culture.

The teacher's role is to learn along with his students and, while learning, to teach the students the craft of writing.

All writing done in the class must be functional—every writing assignment should pertain to the semester-long study. And, most important, writing should be aimed at some kind of "publication"—a Xeroxed "magazine"; school newspaper, local or national papers or magazines; radio, television, or films; live drama.

Whenever possible, the students should do original research. The classroom should be fluid, with groups moving in and out as necessary. There should be tape recorders and movie cameras available for creativity and for documentation.

(If no funds are available for these, drop the tired $7.00 reader and charge a "materials" fee of $7.00.) Artists and controversial figures should be brought into the classroom, or the "classroom" should be taken to them. In several of the projects, two or three members designated by the class should be flown, with movie camera and sound equipment, to film an interview that the class has spent the semester preparing; all effort should be made to "publish" the completed project on campus or local television.

Writing assignments, in addition to the term project, may include a daily log of group work; weekly or biweekly progress reports; critiques of the work of others; letters to the editor of the campus paper or of local or national papers; book reports and book criticisms of primary or secondary material used in research; reports of meetings; transcribings of taped interviews; préces; unassigned creative work; articles and features for a projected publication.

The following are 33 "molds" or "models" for semester-long study in an English workshop, by a class or by small groups within the class:

1. On Defining the Establishment
2. Black Consciousness
3. Censorship (local, state, national)
4. Pop Music: A Classification (Start with Ellen Sander, "Pop in Perspective: A Profile," *Saturday Review*, October 28, 1968.)
5. A Readers' Guide to "Now" Culture
6. The Film as English (starting from scratch and making a film)
7. The Rhetoric of Campus Politics (or local, state, or national politics if an election year)
8. An Ideal Curriculum for a Freshman Composition Course (student-eye view)
9. Eldridge Cleaver
10. *TV* Advertising
11. The Beatles (*See* "Letters to the Record Editor," *Saturday Review*, March 29, 1969, for an interesting "source" of the song "Julia.")
12. Simon and Garfunkel (*See New York Times* Magazine, October 13, 1968.)
13. Writing a Book of "Now" Songs (actually doing it)
14. On Defining Student Power
15. Writing and performing a play, scenario, *TV* documentary
16. Black Music in America
17. Community Dialects
18. Astrology
19. Leonard Cohen: The Poems and Songs
20. Donovan: The Poems and Songs
21. On Defining Soul
22. Folk: New and Old
23. Black Theater
24. Rod McKuen: Poems and Songs
25. Jacques Brel (Who at the Moment Is Alive and Well and Living in Paris Preparing *Man of La Mancha)*
26. *The Graduate:* Novel and Film
27. S.D.S.
28. Leroi Jones: The Plays (comment and performing scenes)
29. Pop Music: Black and White

30. The Role of Sex (tape recorded interviews with psychologist, sociologist, priest, lovers, married couples, etc.)
31. Underground Music
32. Underground Newspapers
33. Underground Film

Finally, if Tom Paine were alive and well in an English class today, he would probably be asked for a theme on model airplanes or a book report on *Little Dorrit*. As in no time in the past, we have an eager audience to whom we can show that English is a tool, a weapon, a fine instrument. Times, they have changed, brother. We must.

Modern Media and Teaching: A Raid on the Inarticulate

Roger B. Fransecky

> At 16 our convictions are hills from which we look; at 40
> they are caves in which we hide.
> F. SCOTT FITZGERALD

Success, Prestige, Power, and Advancement, those compelling symbols of human accomplishment so long sought by an energetic society, are dying. Today's youth, the inheritors of a new highly visual culture, are turning away from the values which guided so many of us. In doing so, says Margaret Mead, they are like fresh settlers in a new land. These are our students, these babes in unisex toyland, who turn to media for some measure of experience, some continuity of expression, some special responsiveness not found in textbooks or classrooms, even in excellent schools. If we are to help students renew and reconceive themselves into new world citizens, then we would be wise to examine the modern media that are turning them on, and on, and on.

As professional teachers, we must be able to react to this new culture and its unique in-school manifestations with responsive attitudes and skills, some not taught in English methods classes. We must be aware that we are confronting a student who is terribly present tense, whose world is immediately reflected on radio, television, cinema, and disc, and only occasionally in print. Awareness of this cultural gap is crucial to the English teacher who is discussing, Gawd forbid,

Roger B. Fransecky is Director, Educational Media, at the University of Cincinnati. This article was written expressly for this book.

Silas Marner with members of a senior class who have been bombarded with Benjamin and the Beatles who lured them down Abbey Road with a tune far more inciting than any that we can play.

In a recent interview in that now-almost-respectable magazine, *Playboy*, Marshall McLuhan responded to an inquiry about the present state of our educational system and the reason the young aren't finding a sense of personal identity within that system with these words:

> Because education, which should be helping youth to understand and adapt to their revolutionary new environments, is instead being used merely as an instrument of cultural aggression, imposing upon retribalized youth the obsolescent visual values of the dying literate age, our entire educational system is reactionary, oriented to past values and past technologies and will likely continue so until the old generation relinquishes power. The generation gap is actually a chasm, separating not two age groups but two vastly different cultures. I can understand the ferment in our schools, because our educational system is totally rear-view mirror. It's a dying and outdated system founded on literary values and fragmented and classified data totally unsuited to the needs of the first television generation . . . The challenge of the new era is simply the total creative process of growing up—and mere teaching and repetition of facts are as irrelevant to this process as a dowser to a nuclear power plant.[1]

Some teachers might react negatively to McLuhan's rhetoric, but we cannot deny the reality of the "generation gap," or McLuhan's suggestion that it is, in reality, a "chasm." Nor can we hide from his accurate suggestion that much of our educational system is "rear-view mirror." Our challenge as teachers is still to provide the rear-view mirror, which allows the experiences of past cultures to become relevant to *now* but also to respond to the present and future—through a mixed media "package" of print, disc, and cinema.

IS CULTURE OUR BUSINESS?

McLuhan's newest "probe" into the age of electric information, *Culture Is Our Business*,[2] suggests that the 1970s are a "new tribal time." The tasks of selecting and processing information today are immense, if not overwhelming. McLuhan suggests that ads and televison commercials are the cave art of the twentieth century. Like cave paints, ads are not to be simply studied, but rather they exist to exert an ESP-like influence on us at a distance. They are, in McLuhan's terms, "varieties of collective power, masks of energy invented by a new tribal man."[3] Today all teachers of these new "tribal men" must help to be less passive as receivers, more discriminating as consumers, and more sensitive as communicators.

The reluctance on the part of English teachers to "teach" the media has been reflected in several reports of national English meetings in recent years. Although now over five years old, the reports of the Anglo-American Seminar on The Teaching of English which met at Dartmouth College in 1966[4] are still significant today. While English teachers were not overtly hostile toward the inclusion of mass media in their classrooms, which many regarded as the most powerful competitors of literature today, the international participants reflected the concerns of many English teachers about the quality of program content, the exploitation of violence, sadism, and sex. Teachers also have been sensitive to the differences between earlier folk cultures and the synthetic, commercialized "package" culture today, one that is often cynically manufactured *for* the people, often cashing in on their worst tastes.[5]

THE TEACHER AS STUDENT

The implications for teacher education of the new media are immense. Often teachers resent what they regard as the intrusion of technology in their classroom, for the film, the videotape, the slide-set, may be magnificent means which have obscured the important question of ends, of goals, of specific learning objectives. Teachers rightly ask if mediated materials are responsible, and not merely "stimulating." Many teachers feel that many mediated learning materials (and their developers) reflect the intellectual void which Yeat's described: "The best lack all conviction, while the worst are full of passionate intensity."

The middle sixties marked the beginning of what might be termed "The Educational Technology Decade." Experiments in computer-assisted instruction, for example, have demonstrated that technology has far outdistanced the available "software" programs. Emmanuel Mesthene, director of Harvard's Program on Technology and Society, warns, however, "What's good for educational technologists is not necessarily good for education."[6] Mesthene and other technologists are cautioning educators to monitor the use of technology in education to make certain hat humane human development is the major goal of instructional technology. The battle ranging in English education between the behaviorists and the anti-behaviorists is reflected by the audio-visual-instructional technology movement in education.

Audo-visual education has recently been described as a "study in despair" by a visiting British scholar, Ford Fellow Peter Harkness, at the close of a one-year study of audio-visual practices in American education. The very phrase itself—audio-visual instruction—suggests a technique rather than an environment. But the complex educational process involves expectations, assumptions, private and social actions. If education is to become "ecstasy" as George Leonard suggests, education must become a physical and phychological environment, embodying individual self-realization and actualization. If we are to provide alternatives to revolution for students who find their educational experience reactionary and oriented to past values and technologies, we must understand how we can adapt the media—the electronic gospel—to the needs and priorities of the new environmental man.

Before educators can design educational programs that smack both of mediacy and immediacy, they would do well to consider the hunting metaphor used by the French existentialist, Jean-Paul Sartre, to describe the characters in a Faulkner novel. Sartre wrote that Faulkner's characters behaved within the artistic structure of the novel as if they were all trapped within a moving vehicle hurling forward at breakneck speed, but each character was strapped in a seat turned backward to view the journey through a rear window. The front and side windows were blacked out, the only view of the journey was through the rear window . . . hurling forward through a present they could not study, a future they could not see, viewing only the past through the rear window: characters trapped in a timeless present. How often do our students feel that they are trapped within a timeless present? What then are the alternatives?

EXIT THE GURUS

One of the major teaching alternatives is the use of films in English teaching. The sixties saw many teachers using film because somehow it "worked." Many classrooms became models of James Moffitt's "universe of discourse" where *writing out, speaking out, acting out,* and *seeing out* became discursive activities appropriate for that special "room with a view." There were many claims for the use of film in English: films "turned 'em on," "films delivered," "films were relevant," "films were a silent language," etc. Teachers today are suspect of many of these claims. A new firmness in the rhetoric of teachers, a new demand for the honesty so important to the kids of what Charles Reich calls "Consciousness III"[7] has supplanted the jive talk by those Bob Geller insightfully terms "faded gurus proclaiming the panaceas for the ills of ed. biz."[8]

Even film conferences are moving from the darkened hotel ballrooms still dank with last evening's Shriner's party, to school cafeterias at the end of long school days. Students and teachers are making films together. Administrators are receiving angry disdain for all those questions about cost and relevance; teachers are becoming more tough-minded, more certain, and more aware of the potential of media. Even in conservative, budget-conscious communities, teachers are getting "into" media. The gurus are leaving us, and teachers are moving into English classrooms. Neill, Kozol, Kohl, Friedenberg, Reich have been the real teachers of most of our "new" English teachers. Now there is talk of "reality therapy," "human potential," "self-actualization," among teachers who are convinced that they will not stand impotent, frightened, and disheveled in front of their students.

MEDIA AND DISCOURSE:
A MODEL FOR ANALYSIS

Today mass media, from public television's *Great American Dream Machine,* to CBS's *Sixty Minutes* offer legitimate models worthy of close analysis in English classrooms. The traditional categories of discourse: drama, narrative, exposition, and argumentation have become redefined by media professionals. Now all levels of discourse, what I term "languaging," are appropriate for study.

James Moffett in *Teaching the Universe of Discourse* provides a useful framework for analyzing any discourse—in a textbook, in a drama, on a film, in a television public affairs broadcast. Moffett suggests a model that moves from *interior dialogue* (Piaget's "egocentric speech"), through "socialized speech," through the models of language *recording* ("the drama of what is happening"), to *reporting* ("the narrative of what happened"), to *generalizing* ("the exposition of what happens") to *theorizing* ("the argumentation of what may happen.")[9]

Moffett's spectrum of discourse, although abstract and linear, does suggest a model which might be used to analyze any print or nonprint language experience. The major streams of perception, memory, chronology, and other logics are found on every level. There is also room in the model for an examination of both information-processing and fictionalizing. The Moffett model is but one type of discourse useful in assisting pupils with the task of analyzing the tangible and intangible qualities of any media experience. Many media teachers share the concern that media study needs to be grounded in the direct discursive experience of the learner. Media means messages; media is "discourse"—it is soliloquy dialogue, and monologue—and students analyzing "languaging" in the media should utilize the potential of media to model language, to help them participate in the experience of creating discourse. In so doing, a pupil of language is using media to high purpose and to its fullest potential.

A television program, a fine film, a simulation game, or a recording of a sonnet, belongs in a classroom. A teacher using media to help a student extend his understanding of his language, and the way language helps frame and order human experience, becomes a more humane, more mindful, and more responsible teacher. We must dare to be this kind of teacher, one who can help the pupil diminish the tensions and the disparities between the powerful societal forces that "educate" in the large sense, particularly mass media, and the schools wherein we attempt to bring order to ourselves and so, eventually, to the larger society.

NOTES

1. Marshall McLuhan, *Playboy* 16, no. 3 (March 1969): 61.
2. Marshall McLuhan, *Culture Is Our Business* (New York: McGraw Hill Book Co., 1970).
3. Marshall McLuhan, *Culture Is Our Business* p. 1.
4. Herbert J. Miller, *The Uses of English* (New York: Holt, Rinehart and Winston, 1967).
5. Ibid, p. 138.
6. Emmanuel G. Mesthene, "Computers and Purposes of Education," in Wayne H. Holtzman, ed., *Computer-Assisted Instruction, Testing and Guidance.* (New York: Harper & Row, Publishers, 1970).
7. Charles Reich, *The Greening of America* (New York: Random House, 1970).
8. Robert Geller, "Exit the Gurus," *Media and Methods* 7, no. 6 (February 1971): 52.
9. James Moffett, *Teaching the Universe of Discourse* (Boston: Houghton Mifflin Co., 1968), p. 47.

Suggested Discussion Questions and Activities

1. **DISCUSSION** Ong, writing in 1960, challenged students and teachers to arm themselves with a "vigilant awareness" of their environment. Do you think students and/or teachers accepted this challenge? What evidence can you cite to prove or disprove Ong's observations of a swing to oral forms of communication? Why is his title, "Wired for Sound," an increasingly appropriate one for the 1970s?

2. **ACTIVITY** Culkin belives media study will only be "as good as the teachers" and points to the need for more teacher education in media.

   a. Identify the philosophy, values, skills, and behaviors you believe a teacher must have to work in media education.
   b. Identify your personal strengths and weaknesses for each of the items you have noted in part (a).
   c. Review your answers to a and b when you finish reading this book.

3. **ACTIVITY** Throughout this book references are made to several media sources. Begin a list of these references. One entry should be *Media and Methods* magazine, edited by Frank McLaughlin ("On Mediacy" and "A Recipe for Triggering Relevance") and referred to in the Culkin article, which was reprinted from *Audiovisual Instruction,* another entry for your list. Also, investigate opportunities for media education through national, state, and local conferences in addition to university and local school pre- and in-service programs. For instance, a major meeting of value to all educators and students is the annual media conference sponsored by John M. Culkin and his staff at the Center for Understanding Media, Inc. in New York City.

4. **ACTIVITY** Both *Media and Methods* and *Audiovisual Instruction,* as well as many other educational journals, provide not only sources of ideas but also sources of materials for media study. Write to each of the

advertisers who regularly appear in these journals and ask for their descriptive literature; also ask to be added to their mailing list.

5. **DISCUSSION** McLaughlin provides an AM/FM analysis of the contemporary English classroom. Do your present plans and/or activities lean more toward AM or FM? Consider his recipe; do you agree with any or all of the ingredients? Would you include any others?

6. **DISCUSSION** Schmittroth refers specifically to "molds" or "models" for the university composition class. Would his suggestions be just as appropriate for the secondary school English program? If not, what modifications would you suggest? Why?

7. **ACTIVITY** Fransecky suggests the use of "the Moffett model" for analysis of a media experience.

   a. Familiarize yourself with the Moffett model.
   b. Develop a classroom lesson(s) by applying any or all of the model to one or more of the popular media.

8. **ACTIVITY** Using some form of convenient media (film, slides, comics, cartoons, magazines clippings, etc.), create graphically the English teacher's challenge as conveyed by the authors in this section.

SECTION THREE

Understanding McLuhan

A classroom discussion of the television program *Laugh-In* once prompted a student of mine to ask for an explanation of the line, "Marshall McLuhan, what are you doin?" Knowing that the effective teacher taps the resources of his learners, I asked for someone else to offer the explanation.

"It's an 'in-joke'—you know the show is full of them!"

"No! Marshall McLuhan is on *Gunsmoke,* opposite *"Laugh-In."*

"No, dummy, that's Marshall Dillon!!!"

"Oh, yes."

"I think he's a former army hero or something like that; didn't he have something to do with World War II?"

"Yea, we just studied about Tito and they called him marshall because he headed the army of Yugoslavia. This guy's probably like him . . . I mean *as* him . . . You know what I mean!"

Yes, I knew what he meant, and I also realized that Marshall McLuhan was not a household word for that group. At the time it didn't concern me, but recently, with college students of English, a similar situation came up. While I was surprised at how few in the class could identify McLuhan, I was further perplexed by the few who had read McLuhan. Further "research" disclosed a general familiarity with the name, but little cognizance of the messages.

PRE-TEST

Marshall McLuhan is

a. a World War II Yugoslavian hero

65

b. a New York City television newsman
c. an up and coming fiction writer
d. all of the above
e. none of the above

Answer
If you selected a, b, c, or d, you probably should read this section; if you selected e, you may not have to read this section, but it does offer three views of the McLuhan influence.

The Gadfly and the Dinosaur

Ted Palmer

> *The discovery of the alphabet will create forgetfulness in the learners' souls, because they will not use their memories; they will trust to the external written characters and not remember of themselves . . . You give your disciples not truth, but only the semblance of truth . . . they will appear to be omniscient and will generally know nothing*
>
> SOCRATES: *The Phaedrus*

The animal is large, but sleek; it moves ponderously, but rhythmically. In its linear journey, it crushes, eats, bends, regurgitates, digests, and defecates the lush imaginations of the secondary school students who foliate its world. It is an educational system in its prime. But into its exclusive world darts a gadfly who, with irritating persistence, pokes and probes its tender parts forcing it to pause to regain its mental balance. During such a pause, the dinosaur notices that the vegetation of his environment has been becoming less palatable, in fact, almost indigestible—it is smaller and not of the type to which he is accustomed. As a species, the dinosaur must adjust or die.

The gadfly, mutating frequently, slips easily from change to change. Yesterday's technique is treated with respect, but not with servitude. He perceives change quickly, describes it succinctly, and reacts relevantly. In 427 B.C., he was Socrates; today he is Marshall McLuhan. To English teachers, who perhaps may be the most conservative limb of a mastodonian educational system, he is an irritating threat because "their own ego seems to have been typographically conditioned so that the electric age with its return to inclusive experience threatens their idea of self."[1]

English teachers, even apart from their personal preferences, are expected to be the bastions of the print culture which McLuhan calls the Gutenberg galaxy. It is a culture which was born 3,000 years ago with the phonetic alphabet and which reached maturity 1,500 years later with Gutenberg's invention of the printing press. It has been with us so long that it has seldom been questioned. Yet there is little, apart from longevity, which makes it deserving of reverence.

The phonetic alphabet itself consists of "semantically meaningless letters used to correspond to semantically meaningless sounds" (Understanding Media, p. 83). Print, a ditto device, made this arbitrary set of jottings so repeatable that a dramatic change occurred in the ratio between our different senses. Whereas sound and touch were even more important than sight in the preliterate world, the Gutenberg press' ability to make the visual medium repeatable and portable, made sight predominant. This was not merely a change in emphasis, but had an inverse effect on the ratio between the senses, because "any sense when stepped up to high intensity can act as an anaesthetic for the other senses."[2] Thus we create a world in which sound, in particular, loses much of its significance and we treat the man who writes as necessarily wiser than the man who speaks.

Such an arbitrary evaluation is unjustified. The two greatest teachers, Socrates and Christ, did not commit their teachings to writing. Pope explains the deficiency and harm of print in pointing out that print feeds the fogs of dullness because "Wit, the quick interplay among the senses is . . . steadily anaesthetized" (Gutenberg Galaxy, p. 259). Does print actually contribute to a really wise population or does it, as Socrates suggested in The Phaedrus, merely supply a veneer of knowledge behind which ignoramuses may hide?

As English teachers, we frequently equate our articulateness with wisdom and often judge students on the basis of their verbal facility. It is not possible that the most inarticulate student in the class might be the most sensitive, imaginative, and artistic (in a nonverbal way)? McLuhan avers this possibility in suggesting that preliterate tribal societies "may be greatly superior to western cultures in the range and delicacy of their perceptions and expressions" (Understanding Media, p. 84).

Print, in communicating its lineal bias,[3] prejudices us against the mosaic and the intuitive. Thus, we equate deductive reasoning with perception and ignore the value of intuitive reason. Our I. Q. tests, if they succeed in nothing else, do in fact test the linear verbal capability of the students. They test, in reality, the student's ability to cope with a print culture. Along with I. Q. tests, the Gutenberg galaxy gives us exams as we know them today: "The portable, uniform book creates the uniform exam" (Gutenberg Galaxy, p. 211). Such exams, according to McLuhan, are one of the major evils of our educational system. As he pointed out in a television appearance on Telescope (CBC) in July 1967, we have made "Shakespeare unreadable for life by the expedient of exams."

The Gutenberg galaxy has made a great impact on our attitude to poetry and our ability to experience it. With the invention of print came the divorce between poetry and music (Gutenberg Galaxy, p. 200). Poetry, which is primarily an audial experience, has become, since print, a visual one. Only the use of recordings and quality readings by teachers in the classrooms (with students' texts closed) can poetry become the "musical experience" it was meant to be. Our appreciation of the "content" of poetry is also inhibited by our lineal bias. We discuss the "levels" in a poem such as *The Ancient Mariner*. For preprint societies, however, poetry was mythical experience in which all levels were simultaneous. Until we can lead our students back to this type of unified experience of a poem, they will continue to approach poems as grammarians rather than as artists.

For the Gutenberg galaxy is the grammarian's galaxy. There was no bad grammar until print, since only when words were printed in transportable form was it possible to compare versions and to make value judgments. For centuries now, we had reverenced the writing of the "best" people as grammatically "correct." Only in the last decade have we begun to realize that grammar involves social, not moral questions and that the question of "correctness" is merely relevant. Thus, only after many centuries are we English teachers able to agree with McLuhan that we have unduly reverenced "a culture based upon the printed word" and have tolerated "snobberies which ought to be cast aside" *(Gutenberg Galaxy*, p. 2).

Casting aside we must do, for our Gutenberg galaxy is currently interfaced with an imploding electronic galaxy. Once again, we are "living mythically and integrally, as it were, but we continue to think in the old fragmented space and time patterns of the pre-electric age" *(Understanding Media*, p. 4). Radio, television, telephone, and motion pictures all employ the spoken word either centrally or exclusively. Thus, we are returning to an oral mode of existence, which dramatically involves all of the senses, rather than merely the visual. In such a world, even the visual becomes a mosaic as may be seen in the popular Beatles' movies and the Monkees' television program. The modern media are "no longer tied to rational sequential modes of thought," *(Time* review of *The Medium Is the Massage)*, and our students no longer think according to linear, Newtonian logic.

The English teacher, caught on the razor edge interface between the Gutenberg explosion and the electronic implosion must, if he is going to teach effectively, be willing (as McLuhan was himself) to study their students' popular culture to set up a more meaningful dialogue.[4] He must realize that a sensitive intuition based on a mosaic of experience may be more valid than ponderous proof based on carefully delineated evidence. Only when he sets aside his print-oriented prejudices will he be able to objectively sense the "world" which his students bring to the classroom. He might even be willing to admit that McLuhan is correct in asserting that "Slang offers us an immediate index to changing perception."[5]

There is no need to stop studying written literature and to terminate our writing programs merely because we are now in an electronic age. The English teacher must realize, however, that much modern literature (especially James Joyce and other artists of the stream of consciousness) has adopted many of the characteristics of the electronic media. Similarily, he must realize that clarity and organization in a written composition are not so important as the total impact made by the student's creation. The twentieth-century teacher must not, as immature children do, discard all the possessions of his parents. He might find, however, that essays can be spoken (oral presentation in class or submitted on tape) and that students' efforts in short story and drama should be acceptable on celluloid (e.g., 8 mm film) as well as on paper. The classroom, like the world of the 1960s, should be a mosaic of printed and electronic experiences. Otherwise, the teacher is conducting a nineteenth-century classroom in the midst of a pulsating twentieth-century world.

The a go-go rhythm of change in our century is both its attraction and its problem, for every change in technology creates its own environment, and we are so immersed in our environment that it is invisible to us. Yet the technological changes of our age are so rapid that, to gain time, to adjust, the human "central nervous system rallies a system of general numbness to the challenge of the specialized irritation" *(Understanding Media,* p. 44). It is during this period of numbness that man is most likely to be victimized by that of which he is unaware. Thus, for McLuhan, education should be "Civil defense against media fall-out" *(Gutenberg Galaxy,* p. 246).

Therefore, "If there is any villain in McLuhan's world, it is education, since in his eyes the traditional 'rear-view mirror' approach is incapable of *touching* today's kids" *(Media* review of *The Medium is the Massage).* In other words, rather than treating the new media as new and unique, too many English teachers treat them as merely slightly altered styles of the novels, short stories, and essays they have traditionally taught. We fail to realize that media themselves are active processes and that to understand them we must learn their grammar as thoroughly as we learned that of the old. We should be establishing curricula now according to that which will enhance our students' perception of the media that will enclose them when they graduate. Movie and television appreciation should be a part of all English courses of study. As McLuhan argues, "media themselves are both aids to learning and proper objects of study."[6]

English teachers, as the main proponents of the "arts" in any school system must understand the role of the arts as antienvironments. McLuhan "argues with Pound that the artist is the antenna of his race."[7] The artist reacts integrally to experience, seeing the present in its perspective between past and future. The poems, short stories, and novels we teach, therefore, can act as DEW lines warning us of the ultimate impact of our technologies. The English teacher himself must be an artist, one who is capable of seeing more than his single point in linear time; one who not only makes his students pregnant with information, but is also willing to stay around for the day of delivery.

A real problem today is the fact that students are anything but information virgins the day they enter school. They come brimming with information (Culkin, p. 72), much of it vicarious "adult" experiences, because of the pervasive influence of the teacher-in-the-home: television. For two or three years he has been taught by "Captain Kangaroo," "As the World Turns," "Batman," and maybe even "Peyton Place." And this teacher has involved him in a way that few classroom teachers will ever succeed in doing. Television, with its low definition, its mesh of black and white dots, forces the viewer to participate actively in filling the empty areas. The viewer becomes the screen in a tactile experience. Yet, after experiencing this medium with its visual, audial, and tactile implosion, he enters the one-dimensional visual world of the classroom. He is frustrated when he tries to read books in "depth" the way he has "read" TV in depth and thus "encounters the world in a spirit antithetic to literacy" (*Understanding Media,* p. 334).

The English teacher must make literature a depth experience. He can achieve this by treating television as an ally rather than as an enemy. Since TV is a "reaction" medium which draws attention to processes rather than products, it might be particularly effective to teach poetry via this medium. Students might thus be able to respond integrally to the mosaic pattern of images in the poem. McLuhan outlines experiments which tend to prove that "students performed better with TV channelled information than they did with lecture and print" (*Understanding Media,* p. 311). He also asserts that the TV teacher is "reverenced" more by the students than is the classroom teacher. Such experiments, however, are not altogether convincing in view of the lack of success in teaching English to university students via TV.[8] This lack of success, however, may be due to the character of the teacher chosen for the TV lecture—all personalities are not suited to this medium.[9]

Regardless of who is the content of a program, it is the medium itself which is the message. Far too many English teachers spend their time searching wheelbarrows for obscenity while the wheelbarrows themselves continue to skip past their guardposts. The content of a book, a movie, and a TV program may be identical, and that content may soon be forgotten, but the impact of the medium itself on methods of thinking and experiencing is inerasable. McLuhan makes his deepest cut into the traditional English teacher when he propounds that "Our conventional response to all media, that it is how they are used that counts, is the stance of a technological idiot" (*Gutenberg Galaxy,* p. 18). Television wraps itself around us, caresses and massages our senses until our perceptual habits are changed. Our only defense against becoming servomechanisms of this seductress is the English teacher who will study media as messages in themselves.

Your classroom as an environment may be more important than what you say in it. The English classroom should implode upon the student in a way that demands involvement. Bulletin boards should be lively changing mosaics of experiences in our subject. Seat arrangement in the classroom should be flexible—a circular or parliamentary formation each carries its own message to the student before you give oral instructions. Visual aids (e.g., overhead projector slides) and audial aids (tape recorder, record player) should be employed frequently, and pictures and other relevant articles should be passed around the class to give a tactile experience. Only if the whole sensorium of the student is participating will the student be truly involved.

Since the medium is the message, our present content fixation is unjustified. Our emphasis should not be "on content or detail but on the postulates, ground rules, frames of reference, and premises of each discipline" (Culkin, p. 72). Examinations in English should not be based on memorized outlines of plot, character, theme, and setting, but should be "sight" work which tests the student's ability to apply the premises and skills of our subject. The present content anxiety which manifests itself in the "gotta finish the course" syndrome is an anachronistic misinterpretation of the function of English.

But all the content of McLuhan that could be applied to English teaching is in itself of minute importance compared to the medium McLuhan himself uses. Although reviewers have criticized his "soporific syntax and mastodonian metaphors" (*Time* review, *The Medium is the Massage*), it is his style that makes him memorable and valuable. McLuhan doesn't pronounce like an oracle; he probes. He sets before the reader (especially in the *Gutenberg Galaxy*) a mosaic of ideas with the implied instruction: "Try them on." He is the poser of the searching conundrum and openly admits that he doesn't always agree or disagree with his own ideas, that he deliberately exaggerates, and that he might quickly contradict himself. His approach is antirational, but elicits a mental involvement seldom received from a reader.

If English teachers, in their classrooms, were to apply the "probe" approach, they might find that students were really reacting for the first time. One might initiate a literature lesson with a paradoxical statement that causes the student to probe himself and the work under consideration. The teacher must be ready to switch his own point of view to provoke reaction to a comment which is being swallowed without being chewed. Many of McLuhan's probe techniques can be used in our classrooms to intensify or elicit student involvement.

But even more important than the medium that McLuhan uses is the medium that McLuhan is. Call it "McLuhancool" or what you will, the man is a successful teacher. Students who have studied under his guidance remark that they took no notes, can remember little course content, but sense a tremendous educational impact. For McLuhan, like TV, is a cool medium who elicits a participation on the part of the student.

McLuhan asserts concerning all media that "If the medium is of high definition, participation is low. If the medium is of low intensity, then participation is high" (*Understanding Media*, p. 319). Thus the lecture is a hot medium while the seminar is cool. Certain teachers, because they are cool, are more effective in seminars than in lectures. Such awareness of personal differences should be of immense help to those planning a team teaching program. The teacher, who can initiate a probe and then withdraw from the center to allow his students to take the idea from there, will probably find that he has left his students with a more inclusive, integral experience than one who at all times holds the center hammering his points across with pneumatic drill impact. Even here, there are no precise linear rules. The hot and cool are matters of degree in a given teacher, in a given class, or in a given school. But there will be a revolution in our attitudes once we accept the fact that there are matters of degree in a high school—that teachers and teaching situations are not homogeneous units that can be casually interchanged in a lock-step linear curriculum. We must acknowledge, as anti-rational as it may appear, that television, classroom, teacher techniques, and teacher character are usually more important than curricula content.

McLuhan has been "called the King of Popthink, Canada's intellectual comet, oracle of the electronic age, an apologist, a nut, a con man, a genius, a comedian, the most important thinker since Newton, Darwin, Freud, and Einstein, and a communications expert who can communicate" (CBC Times, July 7, 1967). All these appellations are probably justified to some degree and constitute parts of any mosaic that would attempt to define "teacher" insofar as what that term must mean as we live on the interface between two great technologies. Our role as English teachers is an uncomfortable, but an admirable one. Like Socrates before us and like McLuhan around us, we must be gadflies stinging our society, particularly the educational system, into an awareness of the invisible events that shape its existence. Our educational system is probably one of the largest (in terms of Gross National Product devoted to education), one of the best organized and best equipped. Like the dinosaur, we continue to grow and appear invulnerable. Today, dinosaurs are fossils; the gadfly is as lively as ever.

NOTES

1. Marshall McLuhan, *Understanding Media: The Extensions of Man* (Toronto: McGraw-Hill Book Co., 1962). p. 289. All subsequent quotations come from this edition.
2. Marshall McLuhan, *Gutenberg Galaxy* (Toronto: University of Toronto Press, 1960). p. 24. All subsequent quotations come from this edition.
3. There is no perspective or third dimension in art until the phonetic alphabet and print.
4. Comment made by McLuhan on the CBC *Telescope* program on July 12, 1967.
5. Ibid.
6. John M. Culkin,, "A Schoolman's Guide to Marshall McLuhan," *Saturday Review,* 18 April 1967, p. 72.
7. Harry J. Boyle, "Marshall McLuhan," *Weekend Magazine,* 1967, p. 8.
8. Freshmen classes at the University of Windsor were found to be unruly when left by themselves with the TV and many dynamic classroom teachers were unsuccessful in the television lectures.
9. A review of a McLuhan TV appearance asserted concerning McLuhan that "the live, in person master, however, did not fit well the cool montage: he was 'hot,' too highly defined, too complete, literal."

Cooling Down the Classroom: Some Educational Implications of the McLuhan Thesis

Robert T. Sidwell

When Nietzsche's Zarathustra announced the death of God, the people continued to laugh and dance. Concluding that his inauguration of the period *post mortem Dei* was somewhat premature, the prophet retired once more to his mountain. Nietzsche (and his alter ego, Zarathustra) was, as he somewhere wryly conceded, born posthumously. Our modern seer, Marshall McLuhan, on the other hand, announced the death of the mechanical technology and was awarded the Albert Schweitzer professorship of a $100,000 chair in the humanities at Fordham University. "The times," as Bob Dylan sings "they are a-changin'."

Soren Kierkegaard describes a scene wherein a clown is called upon to announce a fire in a theater. He was greeted with laughter and applause (the melancholy Dane suggested that such would probably be the popular reaction to the end of the world). Laughter and applause have, by and large, been the reaction to Professor McLuhan's revolutionary thesis (in addition to outright bewilderment), possibly because he too tends to play the clown at times. In our admiration, amusement (or bewilderment), however, let us not lose sight of the fact that the McLuhan thesis *is* a revolutionary document, particularly for the educational profession.

Unlike Marx and Engels, McLuhan does not call for a revolution; he in fact describes one that is to a large degree a *fait accompli*. McLuhan's description is of a technological revolution, the replacement of the mechanical age by the electronic age. This is the content of the revolution, and, as such, is scarcely very exciting news to anyone over the age of twenty. The McLuhan thesis, however, does not rest on this obvious transformation from mechanical media to electronic media. The new medium of electric technology, suggests McLuhan, treated formally, is itself (like any medium) a "message" quite divorced from the sum of its contents. As a matter of fact, a preoccupation with the content of any medium or process is, from McLuhan's perspective, to ignore the message of that

From Robert T. Sidwell, "Cooling Down the Classroom: Some Educational Implications of the McLuhan Thesis," *The Educational Forum* 32 (March 1968): 351-58. Reprinted by permission of Kappa Delta Pi, An Honor Society in Education, owners of the copyright.

medium *qua* medium. As he has so catchingly phrased it, "the medium is the message."

McLuhan's contention that not content but the medium itself is the message is predicated upon his belief that "any technology creates a totally new human environment."[1] It, in fact, introduces a change of scale, or pace, or pattern into human affairs.[2] The real "message" of any medium, then, is to be found in those changes in perceptual patterns of sensual ratios that it, *qua* medium, engenders. That such changes *are* made, says McLuhan, is due to the fact that technological media represent an extension (or amputation) of some human faculty—psychic or physical.[3] Thus, the wheel is an extension of the foot, the book an extension of the eye, clothing an extension of the skin, etc. Furthermore, " . . . such extension demands new ratios or new equilibriums among the other organs and extensions of the body."[4] One cannot avoid these adjustments or accomodations. Media alter the environment and evoke in us, willynilly, " . . . unique ratios of sense perceptions. The extension of any one sense alters the way we think or act—the way we perceive the world. When these ratios change, men change."[5]

Although we cannot avoid these changes, we can, since McLuhan, be intelligently aware of them and of their implications.

"There is absolutely no inevitability as long as there is a willingness to contemplate what is happening."[6] As Father John Culkin notes, "Such influence [of media] are deterministic only if ignored."[7]

McLuhan's contention of an intimate relationship between technological process and modes of societal perceptions and sensual ratios has been shared by a number of other thinkers, usually in less explosive terms and with a more peripheral emphasis. Husserl, for example, noted that:

> The scientific abstraction from concreteness, the quantification of qualities which yield exactness as well as universal validity, involve a specific concrete experience of the *Lebenswelt*— a specific mode of seeing the world.[8]

To put this into McLuhan's terminology, the "specific concrete experience" is provided by the technological media of that world, and the "specific mode of seeing the world" is the "message" of the media.

Herbert Marcuse has provided a similar analysis of the "message" of the science of Galileo, when he observed it " . . . is the science of methodical, systematic anticipation and projection . . . that which experiences, comprehends, and shapes the world in terms of calculable, predictable relationships among exactly identifiable units."[9]

In reducing matter to quantifiable qualities, Marcuse suggests, science (Galilean) provided a new mode of seeing the world. This new perceptual framework tended to relate men to one another "in accordance with quantifiable qualities. . . ."[10]

McLuhan himself has devoted a considerable number of words to a description of the "message" of the media of the past age—the highly literate and mechanized age. The revolutionary impact of the McLuhan approach lies in his assertion that that is a *past* age. To glimpse some of the significant implications of the McLuhan thesis for education, it is necessary to look briefly at *The Gutenberg Galaxy,* which was " . . . intended to trace the ways in which the *forms* of experience and of mental outlook and expression have been modified, first by the phonetic alphabet and then by printing."[11]

Pre-alphabet man was predominately an auditory creature—the ear was the dominant sensory organ. He lived in "acoustic" space—undifferentiated, intuitive, total. His medium of communication was speech, and its "message" was a specific patterning of perception and sensual ratios. In this (auditory) patterning, action and reaction were simultaneous and demanded a total involvement. McLuhan's term for this modality of life is "mythic," by which he means a " . . . mode of simultaneous awareness of a complex group of causes and effect."[12] The mythic dimension that characterized pre-alphabetical life has been maintained in literate cultures (as the Chinese) which uses a nonphonetic (ideographic) script that " . . . enables them to retain a rich store of inclusive perception in depth of experience . . . For the ideogram is an inclusive *gestalt,* not an analytic dissociation of senses and function like phonetic writing [as such, it] . . . invests each ideogram with a total intuition of being and reason that allows only a small role to visual sequence as a mark of mental effort and organization."[13]

That pre-alphabetical man's perceptual patterns *were* radically different has been eloquently demonstrated by S. Giedion's studies of spatial conception in prehistoric art. He concludes that:

> The distinguishing mark of the space perception of primeval art is the complete independence and freedom of its vision . . . In our sense there is no above and no below, no clear distinction of separateness from an intermingling, and also, certainly, no rules of proportional size. . . . All is within the continual present, the perpetual interflow of today, yesterday, and tomorrow.[14]

Dorothy Lee has concluded that "The given as undifferentiated content is implicit in the nominal categories of the Wintu. . . . To the Wintu, the given is not a series of particulars . . . the given is unpartitioned mass. . . ."[15] Again, with regard to Malinowski's well-studied Trobrianders:

> Events and objects are self-contained points in another respect; there is a series of beings, but no becoming. There is no temporal connection between objects. . . . There is no arrangement of activities or events into means and ends, no casual or teleologic relationship. What we consider a casual relationship in a sequence of connected events is to the Trobriander an ingredient of a patterned whole.[16]

This totality of tribalistic involvement without differentiation of pre-alphabetical man (as reflected in his art and language) is the basis of the *Gemeinschaft* (community) so well delineated by Toennies—an organic rather than a mechanical formation.[17]

Then came the phonetic alphabet—its message, as McLuhan has so well shown, was devastating to the all-at-once-ness organicity of pre-alphabetical man's world:

> The alphabet is a construct of fragmented bits and parts which have no semantic meaning in themselves, and which must be strung together in a line, beadlike, and in prescribed order. Its use fostered and encouraged the habit of perceiving all environment in visual and spatial terms—particularly in terms of a space and of a time that are uniform, c,o,n,t,i,n,u,o,u,s and c-o-n-n-e-c-t-e-d.[18]

Man became linear, his activities fragmented, his thoughts sequential and departmentalized. From an undifferentiated all-at-one-ness, the phonetic alphabet encouraged a perceptual awareness of a sequential one-at-a-time-ness. Man became individualized (detribalized)—an individual and unrelated atom at large in sharply differentiated visual space:

> Phonetic culture endows men with the means of repressing their feelings and emotions when engaged in action. To act without reacting, without involvement, is the peculiar advantage of western literate man.[19]

The integral wholeness of pre-alphabetical man's world underwent a radical departmentalization—his sensual, emotional, imaginative facets were delineated and disassociated from the "whole," while he himself was individualized, detribalized, and specialized.

Such a world view is the *sine qua non* of applied knowledge and technology. Printing, McLuhan notes, is merely an extension and intensification of the visual orientation. David Riesman noted that "Print may be said to mark the epoch of the middle class—the time-attentive, the future oriented, the mobile . . . If oral communication keeps people together, print is the isolating medium par excellence."[20] Many a wife may have shared this feeling while staring at the back of her husband's morning paper at the breakfast table.

The supreme quality of print, McLuhan feels, is the simple fact of its repeatability—it is "a ditto device."

This fragmenting process of mechanized handicraft produced the "division of labor." Noting the detribalizing effects of this fragmented and linear perceptual pattern, Marx " . . . interpreted the division of labor as the social expression of self-alienation."[21] It would be interesting to hear what that dedicated rebel would have made of a recent newspaper item headed "Ten Specialists Required to Reset Phone Button."[22]

Another item in this same edition serves to demonstrate what may well be the epitome of visually dominated sensorium. Dr. Edward E. Burns of Texas A&M is therein credited with the statement that "People eat with their eyes." *See what I mean?*

The education of typographic man has been a faithful reflection of the "message" of his media—it too has been linear, fragmented, nonparticipatory, and sequential. Even the fragmented learning space (classroom) reflects this bias:

Print meant the possibility of uniform texts, grammars and lexicon visually present to as many as asked for them. The classroom, as we know it, was entirely the by-product of print.[23]

The typographic extension of man brought in, among other things, universal literacy and education—homogenized and uniform. So much is past history. Enter the age of electric technology and *its* unique message.

If all media are extensions of some human faculty, then electric circuitry is the penultimate extensiom of man—an extension of his central nervous system. As such, its message is totality, not fragmentation; a cluster configuration rather than the sequential, linear configuration of print. Electric circuitry is *speed,* the acceleration of information. "At the high speeds of electric communication, purely visual means of apprehending the world are no longer possible; they are just too slow to be relevant or effective."[24] The electric world demands an involvement of the total sensorium for its apprehension. Meaning is altered by acceleration, and the totality of electric simultaneity demands a totality of perception which sounds the death-knell for fragmented, serial, one-at-a-time-ness. It is a world of all-at-once-ness. The electric extension of the central nervous system constitutes, as Father Culkin has aptly put it, " . . . a single instantaneous and coexistant field of experience."[25] As such, the media demand an involvement and participation in depth of the whole being, a mythic dimension. Segmented, individualistic typographic man is being "retribalized" by his media; the atomistic *Gesellschaft* of visual space is being "massaged" by the media into an organic, universal *Gemeinschaft.* A glance at some of the strange (to a typographic perception) goings-on among the students at our higher institutions of learning reveals, if nothing else, the mythic demands of the electric age student for involvement, participation, organic role. The attraction of such participatory activities as the Peace Corps, Civil Rights, etc., are precisely their mythic qualities—an organic *role* rather than a linear *position.*

The church has its *aggiornamento* (up-dating) movement—an attempt to establish new (organic) relationships between the fragmented two cities of Augustine—a realization of the demand for the restoration of a mythic dimension in religion. The transcendent God of the fragmented typographic world has surely died; The electric world demands immanentism, not transcendent aloofness. "If anything characterizes the modern temper," writes theologian Gabriel Vahanian, "it is a radical immanentism."[26]

Easter Sunday, 1967. A group of some 10,000 young people gather in New York's Central Park for a "Be-In." "We wanted it to be an active celebration of being alive, of having that experience in the park," says Mr. James Fouratt, one of the organizers. "People in New York don't look at each other, don't see each other, don't talk to each other."[27]

Mexico City officials report that the Sunday afternoon band concerts became amazingly popular since jazz numbers were added to the traditional fare. The unprecedented crowds were "humming, clapping and shouting."[28] They were involved and participating because jazz is, in McLuhanese, a "cool" medium (one that is of low definition and demands participation or completion by the audience). The electronic age is cool, as illustrated by the TV screen which presents the audience with some three million "dots" of which only a few dozen are selected by the participant to form his visual image. As a product of these cool media of participation, the electronic age learner is a new breed of cat; he is involved and oriented to involve himself in depth, to live mythically. When this new learner is put into a linear, fragmented school environment (the creation of the typographic media) of low participation and high definition (as is print—a "hot" medium)—enter one big educational problem:

> The youth of today live mythically and in depth. But they encounter instruction in situations organized by means of classified information—subjects are unrelated, they are visually conceived in terms of a blueprint . . . The student finds no means of involvement for himself and cannot discover how the educational scheme relates to his mythic world of electronically processed data and experience that his clear and direct responses report.[29]

The implications of the McLuhan thesis are enormous for the educational profession (and threatening for linear educators). The student of the electric world is a participant in discovery and not the passive recipient of neatly prepackaged linear learning. The linear, analytic, and irrelevantly fragmented bits of information make increasingly less sense to the products of the electronic media. "Young people are looking for a formula for putting on the universe—*participation mystique*. They do not look for detached patterns—for ways of relating themselves to the world, *a là* nineteenth century."[30]

Actually, McLuhan suggests, the TV child in a social and educational world that is visually oriented is an "underprivileged cripple."[31]

Apparently one reason why Johnny can't read is that he tries to apply the set of perceptual patterns of his cool electronic media (involvement in depth of *all* senses) to a hot (print) medium which demands an isolated and extended *visual* sensuality rather than a unified sensorium. This seems much like attempting precise target shooting with a shotgun.

How then are we to cool off the classroom in order to get in phase with our media?

Education, it would appear, in order to reflect the message of the electronic media, must begin to dismantle its linear organization pattern on all fronts. It would have to become more "formal" and synthesizing, and less analytic and instructional:

> In our time John Dewey worked to restore education to its primitive, preprint phase. He wanted to get the student out of the passive role of consumer of prepackaged learning. In fact, Dewey in reacting against passive print culture was surfboarding along on the new electronic age.[32]

If, in fact, our school audiences have been massaged by their media to take a participatory role in the learning process, all is not as dark and linear in the educational world as it might seem. As Father Culkin has observed, the current educational innovations display an interesting similarity—a break with the linear, print-oriented pattern: team teaching, audio-lingual language training, multimedia learning situations, seminars (cool and participatory as opposed to hot, passive lectures), individualized learning (learning responsibility shifting from teacher to student).[33] The mythic (not mystic) East would certainly appear to be a topic of increased interest to educators attempting to totalize learning; the teacher who introduces Haiku poetry and the Zen koan to the elementary grades might be surprised at what the electric age learner can do with these forms of mythic experience.

Clearly, the message is involvement, not "scholarly" detachment; synthesis of knowledge and experience, not fragmented analysis; wholeness and convergence, not sequential linearity. From a position of a curricular luxury, the arts " . . . now become a dynamic way of tuning up the sensorium and of providing fresh ways of looking at familiar things."[34] "The arts," of course, include nonwestern as well as western sources. The "empty" spaces in classical Chinese painting, for example, should prove quite comfortable to the young products of the participatory electronic media (although their teacher may feel a linear annoyance at the "incompleteness" of the undifferentiated aesthetic continuum). In terms of educational theory, the multidisciplinary and cross-cultural emphases of such theorists as Theodore Brameld are very much in phase with the totality of electronics.

It is regrettably true that in the sharply linear groves of Academe, the pre-electrical perceptual pattern that resulted in fragmentation of knowledge, has been virtually reified in academic departmentalization. This (arbitrary) pattern of segmentation has acquired all of the sacrosanct qualities of an immutable natural law, a "ghostly objectivity" to borrow the apt phrase of Georg Lukács. That the reality is "ghostly" and merely the hypostatized human delineation is painfully obvious to the students of the electric age, who constantly complain that the course x bears absolutely no relationship to the activities in courses y and z (and none seem to bear much relationship to their increasingly mythic *Lebenswelt*).

If the McLuhan thesis is indeed the message (commercial?) on the screen ("handwriting on the wall" seems too downright typographical to apply to McLuhan), the educational implications are clear enough. The electronic age pupil requires an educational environment that does not ask him to consume a carefully weighed bundle of predigested and prepackaged knowledge, that allows him a maximum participation in discovery, that will relate and synthesize rather than linearly f/r/a/g/m/e/n/t knowledge. Not "rite words in rote order," but the unified all-at-once totality of instant automation.

"Paradoxically," McLuhan claims, "automation makes liberal education mandatory."[35] Should education persist in moving into the future looking steadfastly to the rear, continue the present fragmented unrelatedness of its curricular offerings, it will insure a future citizenry wholly alienated from the cybernetic world in which they will be living. "Control over change would seem to consist in moving not with it but ahead of it. Anticipation gives the power to deflect and control force."[36] Such anticipation may be seen in, for example, the new three-year college (tentatively named "Bensalem") which was to open its doors at Fordham University in July 1967. Perhaps this experimental college will be the archetype of future experiments in providing student participation in matters of curriculum.[37]

If education must be the "civil defense against media fallout," it must become aware of the message of the media—the depth and interrelation of the new world of electronic organization.

Perhaps the best understanding of the message of the electronic media for education is presented in the advertisements for the Berlitz Language Schools—"total immersion."

NOTES

1. Marshall McLuhan, *Understanding Media; The Extensions of Man* New York: McGraw-Hill Book Co., 1966), p. vi. Cited hereafter as McLuhan, *Understanding).*

2. Ibid., p. 8.

3. McLuhan and Quentin Fiore, *The Medium is the Massage* (New York: Bantam Books, 1967) p. 26. (Cited hereafter as McLuhan and Fiore, *Massage).*

4. Ibid., p. 45

5. Ibid., p. 41

6. Ibid., p. 25.

7. John M. Culkin, S.J., "A Schoolman's Guide to Marshall McLuhan," *Saturday Review,* 18 March 1967, p. 51.

8. Herbert Marcuse, *One-Dimensional Man* (Boston: Beacon Press, 1966), p. 164.

9. Ibid.

10. Ibid., p. 157

11. Marshall McLuhan, *The Gutenberg Galaxy* (Toronto: University of Toronto Press, 1962), P. 1. (Cited hereafter as McLuhan, *Gutenberg).*

12. McLuhan and Fiore, *Massage,* p. 114.

13. McLuhan, *Understanding,* p. 84-85.

14. S. Giedion, "Space Conception in Prehistoric Art," in Edmund Carpenter and Marshall McLuhan, eds., *Explorations in Communication* (Boston: Beacon Press, 1960), pp. 85-86. (Cited hereafter as Carpenter and McLuhan, *Explorations).*

15. Dorothy Lee, "Linguistic Reflections of Wintu Thought" in Carpenter and McLuhan, *Explorations,* pp. 12-13.

16. Lee, "Lineal and Nonlineal Codifications of Reality," in ibid., p. 141

17. Ferdinand Toennies, *Gemeinschaft and Gesellschaft,* quoted in Talcott Parsons, Edward Shils, Kaspar D. Naegle, Jesse R. Pitts (eds.), *Theories of Society* (New York: Free Press, 1961), 2 vols., I, p. 192.

18. McLuhan and Fiore, *Massage,* p. 44.

19. McLuhan, *Understanding,* p. 86.

20. David Riesman, "The Oral and Written Tradition," in Carpenter and McLuhan, *Explorations,* pp. 113-14.

21. Robert C. Tucker, *Philosophy and Myth in Karl Marx* (New York: Cambridge University Press, 1961), p. 185.

22. *The New York Times,* 29 March 1967.

23. Marshall McLuhan, "The Effect of the Printed Book on Language," in Carpenter and McLuhan, *Explorations,* p. 129.

24. McLuhan and Fiore, *Massage,* p. 63.

25. Culkin, op. cit., p. 70.

26. Gabriel Vahanian, *The Death of God* (New York: George Braziller, 1961), p. 188.

27. The New York Times, 27 March 1967.

28. Ibid.

29. McLuhan and Fiore, *Massage*, p. 100.
30. Ibid., p. 114
31. McLuhan, *Understanding* p. 332.
32. McLuhan, *Gutenberg*, p. 144.
33. Culkin, op. cit., p 72.
34. Ibid.
35. McLuhan, *Understanding*, p. 357.
36. Ibid., p. 199.
37. *The New York Times*, 6 April 1967.

A Schoolman's Guide to Marshall McLuhan

John M. Culkin

Education, a seven year old assures me, is "how kids learn stuff." Few definitions are as satisfying. It includes all that is essential—a who, a what, and a process. It excludes all the people, places, and things which are only sometimes involved in learning. The economy and accuracy of the definition, however, are more useful in locating the problem than in solving it. We know little enough about *kids*, less about *learning*, and considerably more than we would like to know about *stuff*.

In addition, the whole process of formal schooling is now wrapped inside an environment of speeded-up technological change which is constantly influencing kids and learning and stuff. The jet-speed of this technological revolution, especially in the area of communications, has left us with more reactions to it than reflections about it. Meanwhile back at the school, the student, whose psyche is being programed for tempo, information, and relevance by his electronic environment, is still being processed in classrooms operating on the postulates of another day. The cold war existing between these two worlds is upsetting for both the student and the schools. One thing is certain: It is hardly a time for educators to plan with nostalgia, timidity, or old formulas. Enter Marshall McLuhan.

He enters from the North, from the University of Toronto where he teaches English and is director of the Center for Culture and Technology. He enters with the reputation as "the oracle of the electric age" and as "the most provocative and controversial writer of this generation." More importantly for the schools,

From John M. Culkin, "A Schoolman's Guide to Marshall McLuhan," *Saturday Review*, 18 March 1967, pp. 51-53. Copyright © 1969 by Saturday Review, Inc. Reprinted by permission of the publisher and the author.

he enters as a man with fresh eyes, with new ways of looking at old problems. He is a man who get his ideas first and judges them later. Most of these ideas are summed up in this book, *Understanding Media*. His critics tried him for not delivering these insights in their most lucid and practical form. It isn't always cricket, however, to ask the same man to crush the grapes and serve the wine. Not all of McLu is nu or tru, but then again neither is *all* of anybody else. This article is an attempt to select and order those elements of McLuhanism which are most relevant to the schools and to provide the schoolman with some new ways of thinking about the schools.

McLuhan's promise is modest enough: "All I have to offer is an enterprise of investigation into a world that's quite unusual and quite unlike any previous world and for which no models of perception will serve." This unexplored world happens to be the present. McLuhan feels that very few men look at the present with a present eye, that they tend to miss the present by translating it into the past, seeing it through a rear-view mirror. The unnoticed fact of our present is the electronic environment created by the new communications media. It is as pervasive as the air we breathe (and some would add that it is just as polluted), yet its full import eludes the judgments of commonsense or content-oriented perception. The environments set up by different media are not just containers for people; they are processes which shape people. Such influence is deterministic only if ignored. There is no inevitability as long as there is a willingness to contemplate what is happening.

Theorists can keep reality at arm's length for long periods of time. Teachers and administrators can't. They are closeted with reality all day long. In many instances they are co-prisoners with electronic-age students in the old pencil box cell. And it is the best teachers and the best students who are in the most trouble because they are challenging the system constantly. It is the system which has to come under scrutiny. Teachers and students can say, in the words of the Late Late Show, "Baby, this thing is bigger than both of us." It won't be ameliorated by a few dashes of good will or a little more hard work. It is a question of understanding these new kids and these new media and of getting the schools to deal with the new electronic environment. It's not easy. And the defenders of the old may prove to be the ones least able to defend and preserve the values of the old.

For some people, analysis of these newer technologies automatically implies approbation of them. Their world is so full of *shoulds* that it is hard to squeeze in an *is*. McLuhan suggests a more positive line of exploration:

At the moment, it is important that we understand cause and process. The aim is to develop an awareness about print and the newer technologies of communication so that we can orchestrate them, minimize their mutual frustrations and clashes, and get the best out of each in the educational process. The present conflict leads to elimination of the motive to learn and to diminution of interest in all previous achievement: It leads to loss of the sense of relevance. Without an understanding of media grammars, we cannot hope to achieve a contemporary awareness of the world in which we live.

We have been told that it is the property of true genius to disturb all settled ideas. McLuhan is disturbing in both his medium and his message. His ideas challenge the normal way in which people perceive reality. They can create a very deep and personal threat since they touch on everything in a person's experience. They are just as threatening to the establishment whose way of life is predicated on the postulates he is questioning. The establishment has no history of organizing parades to greet its disturbers.

His medium is perhaps more disturbing than his message. From his earliest work he has described his enterprise as "explorations in communication." The word he uses most frequently today is "probe." His books demand a high degree of involvement from the reader. They are poetic and intuitive rather than logical and analytic. Structurally, his unit is the sentence. Most of them are topic sentences—which are left undeveloped. The style is oral and breathless and frequently obscure. It's a different kind of medium.

"The medium is the message," announced McLuhan a dozen years ago in a cryptic and uncompromising aphorism whose meaning is still being explored. The title of his latest book, and illustrated popular paperback treatment of his theories, playfully proclaims that *The Medium Is the Massage*—a title calculated to drive typesetters and critics to hashish and beyond. The original dictum can be looked at in four ways, the third of which includes a massage of importance.

The first meaning would be better communicated orally—The *medium* is the message." The *medium* is the thing to study. The *medium* is the thing you're missing. Everybody's hooked on content; pay attention to form, structure, framework, *medium*. The play's the thing. The medium's the thing. McLuhan makes the truth stand on its head to attract attention. Why the medium is worthy of attention derives from its other three meanings.

Meaning number two stresses the relation of the medium to the content. The form of communication not only alters the content, but each form also has preferences for certain kinds of messages. Content always exists in some form and is, therefore, to some degree governed by the dynamics of that form. If you don't know the medium, you don't know the message. The insight is neatly summed up by Dr. Edmund Carpenter:

> English is a mass medium. All languages are mass media. The new mass media—film, radio, TV—are new languages, their grammars as yet unknown. Each codifies reality differently; each conceals a unique metaphysics. Linguists tell us it's possible to say anything in any language if you use enough words or images, but there's rarely time; the natural course is for a culture to exploit its media biases. . . .

It is always content-in-form which is mediated. In this sense, the medium is co-message. The third meaning for the M-M formula emphasizes the relation of the medium to the individual psyche. The medium alters the perceptual habits of its users. Independent of the content, the medium itself gets through. Preliterate, literate, and postliterate cultures see the world through different-colored glasses.

In the process of delivering content the medium also works over the sensorium of the consumer. To get this subtle insight across, McLuhan punned on message and came up with massage. The switch is intended to draw attention to the fact that a medium is not something neutral—it does something to people. It takes hold of them, it jostles them, it bumps them around, it massages them. It opens and closes windows in their sensorium. Proof? Look out the window at the TV generation. They are rediscovering texture, movement, color, and sound as they retribalize the race. TV is a real grabber; it really massages those lazy, unused senses.

The fourth meaning underscores the relation of the medium to society. Whitehead said, "The major advances in civilization are processes that all but wreck the societies in which they occur." The media massage the society as well as the individual. The results pass unnoticed for long periods of time because people tend to view the new as just a little bit more of the old. Whitehead again: "The greatest invention of the nineteenth century was the invention of the method of invention. A new method entered into life. In order to understand our epoch, we can neglect all details of change, such as railways, telegraphs, radios, spinning machines, synthetic dyes. We must concentrate on the method in itself: That is the real novelty which has broken up the foundations of the old civilization." Understanding the medium or process involved is the key to control.

The media shape both content and consumer and do so practically undetected. We recall the story of the Russian worker whose wheelbarrow was searched every day as he left the factory grounds. He was, of course, stealing wheelbarrows. When your medium is your message and they're only investigating content, you can get away with a lot of things—like wheelbarrows, for instance. It's not the picture but the frame. Not the contents but the box. The blank page is not neutral; nor is the classroom.

McLuhan's writings abound with aphorisms, insights, for-instances, and irrelevancies which float loosely around recurring themes. They provide the raw materials of a do-it-yourself kit for tidier types who prefer to do their exploring with clearer charts. What follows is one man's McLuhan served up in barbarously brief form. Five postulates, spanning nearly 4,000 years, will serve as the fingers in this endeavor to grasp McLuhan:

1. 1967 B.C.—*All the senses get into the act.* A conveniently symmetrical year for a thesis which is partially cyclic. It gets us back to man before the Phoenician alphabet. We know from our contemporary ancestors in the jungles of New Guinea and the wastes of the Arctic that preliterate man lives in an all-at-once sense world. The reality which bombards him from all directions is picked up with the omnidirectional antennae of sight, hearing, touch, smell, and taste. Films such as *The Hunters* and *Nanook of the North* depict primitive men tracking game with an across-the-board sensitivity which mystifies Western, literate man. We mystify them too. And it is this cross-mystification which makes intercultural abrasions so worthwhile.

Most people presume that their way of perceiving the world is *the* way of perceiving the world. If they hang around with people like themselves, their mode of perception may never be challenged. It is at the poles (literally and figuratively) that the violent contrasts illumine our own unarticulated perceptual prejudices. Toward the North Pole, for example, live Eskimos. A typical Eskimo family consists of a father, a mother, two children, and an anthropologist. When the anthropologist goes into the igloo to study Eskimos, he learns a lot about himself. Eskimos see pictures and maps equally well from all angles. They can draw equally well on top of a table or underneath it. They have phenomenal memories. They travel without visual bearings in their white-on-white world and can sketch cartographically accurate maps of shifting shorelines. They have 40 or 50 words for what we call "snow." They live in a world without linearity, a world of acoustic space. They are Eskimos. Their natural way of perceiving the world is different from our natural way of perceiving the world.

Each culture develops its own balance of the senses in response to the demands of its environment. The most generalized formulation of the theory would maintain that the individual's modes of cognition and perception are influenced by the culture he is in, the language he speaks, and the media to which he is exposed. Each culture, as it were, provides its constituents with a custom-made set of goggles. The differences in perception are a question of degree. Some cultures are close enough to each other in perceptual patterns so that the differences pass unnoticed. Other cultural groups, such as the Eskimo and the American teenager, are far enough away from us to provide esthetic distance.

2. *Art imitates life.* In *The Silent Language* Edward T. Hall offers the thesis that all art and technology is an extension of some physical or psychic element of man. Today man has developed extensions for practically everything he used to do with his body: stone axe for hand, wheel for foot, glasses for eyes, radio for voice and ears. Money is a way of storing energy. This externalizing of individual, specialized functions is now, by definition, at its most advanced stage. Through the electronic media of telegraph, telephone, radio, and television, man has now equipped his world with a nervous system similar to the one within his own body. President Kennedy is shot and the world instantaneously reels from the impact of the bullets. Space and time dissolve under electronic conditions. Current concern for the United Nations, the Common Market, ecumenism, reflects this organic thrust toward the new convergence and unity which is "blowing in the wind." Now in the electric age, our extended faculties and senses constitute a single instantaneous and coexistent field of experience. It's all-at-once. It's shared-by-all. McLuhan calls the world "a global village."

3. *Life imitates art.* We shape our tools and thereafter they shape us. These extensions of our senses begin to interact with our senses. These media become a massage. The new change in the environment creates a new balance among the senses. No sense operates in isolation. The full sensorium seeks fulfillment in almost every sense experience. And since there is a limited quantum of energy available for any sensory experience, the sense-ratio will differ for different media.

The nature of the sensory effect will be determined by the medium used.

McLuhan divides the media according to the quality or definition of their physical signal. The content is not relevant in this kind of analysis. The same picture from the same camera can appear as a glossy photograph or as a newspaper wirephoto. The photograph is well-defined, of excellent pictorial quality, hi-fi within its own medium. McLuhan calls this kind of medium "hot." The newspaper photo is grainy, made up of little dots, low definition. McLuhan calls this kind of medium "cool." Film is hot; television is cool. Radio is hot; telephone is cool. The cool medium or person invites participation and involvement. It leaves room for the response of the consumer. A lecture is hot; all the work is done. A seminar is cool; it gets everyone into the game. Whether all the connections are causal may be debated, but it's interesting that the kids of the cool TV generation want to be so involved and so much a part of what's happening.

4. *We shaped the alphabet and it shaped us.* In keeping with the McLuhan postulate that "the medium is the message," a literate culture should be more than mildly eager to know what books do to people. Everyone is familiar enough with all the enrichment to living mediated through fine books to allow us to pass on to the subtler effects which might be attributed to the print medium, independent of the content involved. Whether one uses the medium to say that *God is dead* or that *God is love* (――― ―― ――――), the structure of the medium itself remains unchanged. Nine little black marks with no intrinsic meaning of their own are strung along a line with spaces left after the third and fifth marks. It is this stripping away of meaning which allows us to X-ray the form itself.

As an example, while lecturing to a large audience in a modern hotel in Chicago, a distinguished professor is bitten in the leg by a cobra. The whole experience takes three seconds. He is affected through the touch of the reptile, the gasp of the crowd, the swimming sights before his eyes. His memory, imagination, and emotions come into emergency action. A lot of things happen in three seconds. Two weeks later he is fully recovered and wants to write up the experience in a letter to a colleague. To communicate this experience through print means that it must first be broken down into parts and then mediated, eyedropper fashion, one thing at a time, in an abstract, linear, fragmented, sequential way. That is the essential structure of print. And once a culture uses such a medium for a few centuries, it begins to perceive the world in a one-thing-at-a-time, abstract, linear, fragmented, sequential way. And it shapes its organizations and schools according to the same premises. The form of print has become the form of thought. The medium has become the message.

For centuries now, according to McLuhan, the straight line has been the hidden metaphor of literate man. It was unconsciously but inexorably used as the measure of things. It went unnoticed, unquestioned. It was presumed as natural and universal. It is neither. Like everything else it is good for the things it is good for. To say that it is not everything is not to say that it is nothing. The electronic media have broken the monopoly of print; they have altered our sensory profiles by heightening our awareness of aural, tactile, and kinetic values.

5. 1967 A.D.—*All the senses want to get into the act.* Print repressed most sense-life in favor of the visual. The end of print's monopoly also marks the end of a visual monopoly. As the early warning system of art and popular culture indicates, all the senses want to get into the act. Some of the excesses in the current excursions into aural, oral, tactile, and kinetic experience may in fact be directly responsive to the sensory deprivation of the print culture. Nature abhors a vacuum. No one glories in the sight of kids totally out of control in reaction to the Beatles. Some say, "What are the Beatles doing to these kids?" Others say, "What have we done to these kids?" All the data isn't in on what it means to be a balanced human being.

Kids are what the game is all about. Given an honest game with enough equipment to go around, it is the mental, emotional, and volitional capacity of the student which most determines the outcome. The whole complicated system of formal education is in business to get through to kids, to motivate kids, to help kids learn stuff. Schools are not in business to label kids, to grade them for the job market or to babysit. They are there to communicate with them.

Communication is a funny business. There isn't as much of it going on as most people think. Many feel that it consists in saying things in the presence of others. Not so. It consists not in saying things but in having things heard. Beautiful English speeches delivered to monolingual Arabs are not beautiful speeches. You have to speak the language of the audience—of the *whom* in the "who-says-what-to-whom" communications diagram. Sometimes the language is lexical (Chinese, Japanese, Portuguese), sometimes it is regional or personal (125th Street-ese, Holden Caulfield-ese, anybody-ese). It has little to do with words and much to do with understanding the audience. The word for good communication is "Whom-ese"—the language of the audience, of the "whom."

All good communicators use Whom-ese. The best writers, film makers, advertising men, lovers, preachers, and teachers all have the knack for thinking about the hopes, fears, and capacity of the other person and of being able to translate their communication into terms which are *relevant* for that person. Whitehead called "inert ideas" the bane of education. Relevance, however, is one of those subjective words. It doesn't pertain to the object in itself but to the object as perceived by someone. The school may decide that history is *important for* the student, but the role of the teacher is to make history *relevant to* the student.

If *what* has to be tailored to the *whom,* the teacher has to be constantly engaged in audience research. It's not a question of keeping up with the latest slang or of selling out to the current mores of the kids. Neither of these tactics helps either learning or kids. But it is a question of knowing what values are strong in their world, of understanding the obstacles to communication, of sensing their style of life. Communication doesn't have to end there, but it can start nowhere else. If they are tuned in to FM and you are broadcasting on AM, there's no communication. Communication forces you to pay a lot of attention to other people.

McLuhan has been paying a great deal of attention to modern kids. Of necessity they live in the present since they have no theories to diffract or reflect what is happening. They are also the first generation to be born into a world in which there was always television. McLuhan finds them a great deal different from their counterparts at the turn of the century when the electric age was just getting up steam.

A lot of things have happened since 1900 and most of them plug into walls. Today's six year old has already learned a lot of stuff by the time he shows up for the first day of school. Soon after his umbilical cord was cut he was planted in front of a TV set "to keep him quiet." He liked it enough there to stay for some 3,000 to 4,000 hours before he started the first grade. By the time he graduates from high school he has clocked 15,000 hours of TV time and 10,800 hours of school time. He lives in a world which bombards him from all sides with information from radios, films, telephones, magazines, recordings, and people. He learns more things from the windows of cars, trains, and even planes. Through travel and communications he has experienced the war in Vietnam, the wide world of sports, the civil rights movement, the death of a President, thousands of commercials, a walk in space, a thousand innocuous shows, and, one may hope, plenty of Captain Kangaroo.

This is all merely descriptive, an effort to lay out what *is*, not what should be. Today's student can hardly be described by any of the old educational analogies comparing him to an empty bucket or a blank page. He comes to the information machine called school and he is already brimming over with information. As he grows his standards for relevance are determined more by what he receives outside the school than what he receives inside. A recent Canadian film tells the story of a bright, articulate middle class teenager who leaves school because there's "no reason to stay." He daydreams about Vietnam while his teacher drones on about the four reasons for the spread of Christianity and the five points such information is worth on the exam. Only the need for a diploma was holding him in school; learning wasn't, and he left. He decided the union ticket wasn't worth the gaff. He left. Some call him a dropout. Some call him a pushout.

The kids have one foot on the dock and one foot on the ferryboat. Living in two centuries makes for that kind of tension. The gap between the classroom and the outside world and the gap between the generations is wider than it has ever been. Those tedious people who quote Socrates on the conduct of the young are trying vainly to reassure themselves that this is just the perennial problem of communication between generations. 'Tain't so. "Today's child is growing up absurd, because he lives in two worlds, and neither of them inclines him to grow up." Says McLuhan in *The Medium is the Massage:* "Growing up—that is our new work, and it is *total.* Mere instruction will not suffice."

Learning is something that people do for themselves. People, places, and things can facilitate or impede learning; they can't make it happen without some cooperation from the learner. The learner these days comes to school with a vast reservoir of vicarious experiences and loosely related facts; he wants to use all his senses in his learning as an active agent in the process of discovery; he knows that all the answers aren't in. The new learner is the result of the new media, says McLuhan. And a new learner calls for a new kind of learning.

Leo Irrera said, "If God had anticipated the eventual structure of the school system, surely he would have shaped man differently." Kids are being tailored to fit the Procrustean forms of schedules, classrooms, memorizing, testing, etc., which are frequently relics from an obsolete approach to learning. It is the total environment which contains the philosophy of education, not the title page in the school catalogue. And it is the total environment which is invincible because it is invisible to most people. They tend to move things around within the old boxes or to build new and cleaner boxes. They should be asking whether or not there should be a box in the first place.

The new learner, who is the product of the all-at-once electronic environment, often feels out of it in a linear, one-thing-at-a-time school environment. The total environment is now the great teacher; the student has competence models against which to measure the effectiveness of his teachers. Nuclear students in linear schools make for some tense times in education. Students with well-developed interests in science, the arts and humanities, or current events need assistance to suit their pace, not that of the state syllabus. The straight line theory of development and the uniformity of performance which it so frequently encourages just don't fit many needs of the new learner. Interestingly, the one thing which most of the current educational innovations share is their break with linear or print-oriented patterns: team teaching, nongraded schools, audio-lingual language training, multimedia learning situations, seminars, student research at all levels of education, in,vidualized learning, and the whole shift of responsibility for learning from the teacher to the student. Needless to say, these are not as widespread as they should be, nor were they brought about through any conscious attention to the premises put forward by McLuhan. Like the print-oriented and linear mentality they now modify, these premises were plagiarized from the atmosphere. McLuhan's value is in the power he gives us to predict and control these changes.

There is too much stuff to learn today. McLuhan calls it an age of "information overload." And the information levels outside the classroom are now higher than those in the classroom. Schools used to have a virtual monopoly on information; now they are part-time competitors in the electronic informational surround. And all human knowledge is expanding at computer speed.

Every choice involves a rejection. If we can't do everything, what priorities will govern our educational policies? "The medium is the message" may not be bad for openers. We can no longer teach kids all about a subject; we can teach them what a subject is all about. We have to introduce them to the form, structure, gestalt, grammar, and process of the knowledge involved. What does a math man do when a math man does do math? This approach to the formal element of a discipline can provide a channel of communication between specialists. Its focus is not on content or detail but on the postulates, ground rules, frames of reference, and premises of each discipline. It stresses the modes of cognition and perception proper to each field. Most failures in communication are based on disagreement about items which are only corollaries of a larger thesis. It happens between disciplines, individuals, media, and cultures.

The arts play a new role in education because they are explorations in perception. Formerly conceived as a curricular luxury item, they now become a dynamic way of tuning up the sensorium and of providing fresh ways of looking at familiar things. When exploration and discovery become the themes, the old lines between art and science begin to fade. We have to guide students to becoming their own data processors to operate through pattern recognition. The media themselves serve as both aids to learning and as proper objects of study in this search for an all-media literacy. Current interest in film criticism will expand to include all art and communication forms.

And since the knowledge explosion has blown out the walls between subjects, there will be a continued move toward interdisciplinary swapping and understanding. Many of the categorical walls between things are artifacts left over from the packaging days of print. The specialist's life will be even lonelier as we move further from the Gutenberg era. The trends are all toward wholeness and convergence.

These things aren't true just because Marshall McLuhan says they are. They work. They explain problems in education that nobody else is laying a glove on. When presented clearly and with all the necessary examples and footnotes added, they have proven to be a liberating force for hundreds of teachers who were living through the tension of this cultural fission without realizing that the causes for the tension lay outside themselves. McLuhan's relevance for education demands the work of teams of simultaneous translators and researchers who can both shape and substantiate the insights which are scattered through his work. McLuhan didn't invent electricity or put kids in front of TV sets; he is merely trying to describe what's happening out there so that it can be dealt with intelligently. When someone warns you of an oncoming truck, it's frightfully impolite to accuse him of driving the thing. McLuhan can help kids to learn stuff better.

Suggested Discussion Questions and Activities

1. **DISCUSSION** What points in the McLuhan thesis can you cite that have specific implications for the secondary English program? Assuming you once did, do you still have questions about any of McLuhan's statements? If so, what are they?

2. **ACTIVITY** List the major McLuhan ideas explained in the articles of this section. As you read the remaining sections, note areas of agreement or disagreement with the McLuhanisms you have listed.

3. **ACTIVITY** If you have not already done so, read, *at least, Understanding Media* and *The Medium is the Massage.* Also, you might find *McLuhan: Hot and Cool* and *McLuhan: Pro and Con* interesting.

An Expanding View of Literature

Solomon Simonson

"We dare not spurn the legacy of literature bequeathed to us by television and films simply because we are print-bound. Let us not look a gift horse in the mouth ... A living literature awaits our attentive ears and disciplined sights."

Edmund J. Farrell

" ... if we are to present ourselves to students as persons who inhabit the world they know, we need to broaden our definition of literature to include television productions, films, records, and tapes as well as books. A picture *can* be worth a thousand words, and a play heard can be worth a dozen read silently."

Samuel D. Wehr

" ... much great literature exists only in print. Let's teach that to those who can read it. The great literature that exists in the lively art forms of film, records, living theater, recordings, and TV videotapes and video scopes, can be experienced through those media."

John Stuart Katz

"Both literature and film are liberating arts; they are part of the humanities. They make the viewer or reader aware of outward realities and of his own inward life. Both, as Northrop Frye says of literature, develop and educate the imagination."

Jack R. Cameron and Emma E. Plattor

"If the study of literature, for example, is to produce a 'literate' man and thereby fulfill its principal function of educating the imagination, it is important that literary experiences stimulate the student's imagination as strongly and as frequently as possible. For a variety of reasons, much of the literature that is taught from textbooks fails to achieve such stimulation."

Helen W. English

"I wanted the subject matter to be relevant, personal, and affective. I wanted students to be able to experience poetry as it happens—through an emotional experience rather than an analytical experience."

Charles Suhor

"The comic is American mirth, democratic mirth, the mirth of a nation so bent on equality and self-improvement that it must use its popular arts as media for education and as an outlet for the creative energies of its people."

Louis Penfield

"One highly effective experiment dealt with evaluating photography . . . Students discovered that photographs not only express a way of seeing but also explore every form of human emotion."

Is Literature Dying?

Solomon Simonson

The sceptre of literature has held sway over the western dominions of both entertainment and edification since the days of Homer. It is only in the twentieth century that the cultural sovereignty of literature has been challenged. Four times, during the past 50 years, new inventions in media of communication have made onslaught on literature. But the art of reading has withstood the ravages of one medium after another to wrest power.

From Solomon Simonson, "Is Literature Dying?" *The Educational Forum* 30 (May 1966): 423-26. Reprinted by permission of Kappa Delta Pi, An Honor Society in Education, owners of the copyright.

The movie industry was the first challenger as it visualized fiction in a spectacular sweep. Then, the colorful news-periodical capsuled nonfiction in such fashion that news events became a vicarious thrill of experience. Later, the radio broadcasters made capital of episodic programs and turned the soap-opera into a genuine part of the national folklore. The most recent challenger, the television empire, flooded the American home with rapids of amusement and instruction. But literature was not found in the proverbial barrel. Literature did not fall.

This description of the state of literature in our times is deceptive. If we look to an old Gestalt corollary, that the total impact of stimuli is greater than the sum of its parts, we shall be able to perceive that the collective forces of the mass media are driving literature in centrifugal direction, far off the center of the cultural forces of the nation.

If we add the national habits of one movie a week, six hours a day of television, an absorption on every other evening with a periodical, and the spontaneous responses of ears and feet to radio music and noise recordings whenever the spirit moves us, we have very little time left and almost no emotional resources in reserve for any response to literature.

When the potential readers in our society are found to be satiated emotionally, jaded in their interests, and saturated with continuous dosages of cultural drugs from all the media, the creative writers find that they have to compete with other media on a level unlike the poets, essayists, and novelists of other ages. The writing that is successful today has to have more than quality and more than those elements of *kitsch* that were sufficient in another period. The aspirant to successful writing has to pass a publisher's severe test, one that is not a measure of merit but of marketability. And what is marketable today is a psychologically oriented hodgepodge of slick stuff with the cold glare of gold and the icy finger of action. Check the *Goldfinger* box office receipts for confirmation or draw up a list of bestsellers and classify the common attributes.

Our national culture, nevertheless, has had its philosophic moments in essay-writing, its golden ages of poetry, its silver eras of oratory, its depth of narrative symbolism, and its dramatic glories. But, since the second world war, the best creative efforts have been somewhat sick. It was hardly an accident that John Steinbeck was selected for a Nobel Prize in the sixties for the contributions he made to the literary scene in the thirties.

In the February 1965 issue of the Author's Guild Bulletin, J. Donald Adams makes this scathing comment on the current literary situation:

> We stand in need of a critical journal of uncompromising honesty, clear-eyed in its assessment, unswayed by ephemeral literary fashions, savage in its attack on the phony, the pretentious, the muddled, and the degenerate.

Yet no critical journal can do more for a renaissance of literature than a courageous publisher or a truly uncompromised author. This is an age of mediocrity not because talent is unavailable and uninspired. Our plight is due in part to the fact that the national audience is well nigh impregnable. Although our teachers of literature are doing remarkably well in fostering reading responsibilities and book purchases for millions of students, the commitment to literature belongs to a literary elite, indeed a tiny segment of the population. As professional readers of literature in our time, the English teachers in our schools and colleges continue to delve into their Byrons and Shaws, their Emersons and Hawthornes. The graduates of our schools, however, do not carry over into habit any serious involvement with their teachers' enthusiasms. For these reasons, and many others, including the Publishers' Curtain and the economic need for mass readership, the genuinely creative writers cannot find or meet their audiences.

The scholars, many of them engrossed in distinctive research, will soon be somewhat enriched as a result of the establishment of a National Humanities Foundation. It can hardly be expected that the newly budgeted millions for the N.H.F. will do much more than provide allowances for some members of the American Council of Learned Societies to pursue individual esoteric interests. Literature will not come alive as a consequence of the fact that scholars are entombed in research libraries.

No one group can be blamed for the low ebb of literary achievement. Publisher, public, public-relations agent, critic, creative artist—all wrapped up in this package of spoiled produce. And mercenary notions are not solely responsible for the crests and troughs of literary endeavors.

Teachers of literature bear heavy burdens because of the decline of literature. In bypassing the mass media, some teachers treat the creative efforts of television and the films as beneath contempt, others with a shrug of superiority. Some are doing their level best to revive the declining literature of our time by using the movie or the television drama as a springboard to reading. Usually however, these uses of the media seek to foster a love of the classics; e.g., the film, *Hamlet,* as motivation for the reading of the play. Reading-readiness for *Hamlet,* it appears, is not necessarily appreciably assisted by the film. *Hamlet,* to be read with discretion and judgment, is understood better through a teacher's brilliance in adapting the concepts and kinds of man's universal hesitations to those of his particular students.

But the mass media do have vital uses in the teaching of literature. A film may handle both story and characterization better than its parent novel. It may be wiser, for example, to see and live with the movie, *Ivanhoe,* than to force the novel's antiquated descriptions on modern youth. A television writer may treat the mood of a problem-play better than the news-story from which it is derived. It may very well be the better course to view and to discuss a typical select sequence from *The Defenders* or *Ben Casey* than to subject the student to an extended examination of a news-and-editorial story. Such reporting at best remains emotionally superficial as contrasted with the television treatment. A film that transforms a novel or drama into a magnificent experience, as in *Billy Budd,* is great literature in itself and, incidentally, provides the healthiest motivation for the reading of Melville.

A great hero like Billy Budd is worthy of literature and man's devotion to literature. One of the tragedies of contemporary literature is that it has few real heroes. We also seem to be unable to discover heroes where they really are. A frequency count of occupation and character of heroes in the novel and the drama indicates an astounding result, that more than 70 percent are drawn from the shadow world of criminality and mental illness. Sympathy for the heel, the Pal Joey, and the Sammy Glick, demonstrates a fine compassion, but perhaps a bit too fine to grasp a genuine appreciation of man's intrinsic virtues.

If teachers and critics realize that literature is undergoing a desperate struggle for survival, they will enlist the active defense of students and public to the mass media. Thus, they may reduce the impact of infection from a hostile atmosphere and may bring the good germs of many a television and film program to bear upon a sick organism. We may not be able to make our time a gloried period in literature, but a bit of critical surgery at this time of the undue glorifications of our latter-day Millers and Williams may yet prevent the fall. We dare not spurn the legacy of literature bequeathed to us by television and films simply because we are print-bound. Let us not look a gift horse in the mouth. The heritage of Homer, Sophocles, et al. was transmitted to us through speech. A living literature awaits our attentive ears and disciplined sights. The survival of literature depends in great part on the recognition of the new literature, its incorporation in our most dignified columns of critical review, its repetition of performance, and its being made available for our private film-libraries at a cost approximating the book-in-print.

Literature and the Resumption of Self

Edmund J. Farrell

If no one promptly rises these days when one asks himself "Will the real me please stand up," the inertia is accountable. Bereft of most of the traditional means by which he defines himself—his work, his family, his symbols, his community, his knowledge, his values—the modern American in Prufrockian fashion prepares lots of faces to meet the faces that he meets and by long day's end can no longer distinguish the personae from the person, the masks from the man. More Madison Avenue *id* than healthy *I* in his identity, he frequently defines himself, if he's affluent, by his possessions—split-level home, color TV, two car garage, station wagon, washer and dryer—and nocturnally and ritualistically, if not religiously, he ponders over two martinis, preferably dry and with a twist, the depth of his discontent. If he's not affluent, he's apt to define himself by what radio and video hawkers and hucksters inform him he needs and doesn't have, no more salubrious a concept of selfhood than that formulated by the fat-cat suburbanite he wishes to emulate.

Time was when a man rooted part of his identity in his work. Not "Who are you?" but "What do you do?" is still the standard Midwest opener, to which the response "Not much" or "Nothing" is regarded as both ungracious and unsatisfactory, if not downright suspicious. Nevertheless, it is the response to which increasing numbers of Americans are being compelled as our cybernated society passes from birth pangs to maturity.

To give you some notion of the dramatic effects of automation on employment, allow me to quote some figures: in New York City alone, automatic elevators have displaced 40,000 elevator operators; in 1960 new equipment in the Census Bureau enabled 50 statisticians to do the work that had required 4,000 statisticians in 1950; the check writing staff in the Treasury Department has been reduced from 400 people to four.[1] In less than 15 years, 3,000,000 were replaced by machines in coal mines, over 130,000 were made surplus in steel mills, and only half as many man-hours are now needed to produce a car. A total of 14 operators preside at present over the glass-blowing machines that make 90 percent of our light bulbs.[2]

To give you some idea of how rapidly the computer, the heart of cybernation, is becoming the pulse of the society, allow me to quote some other figures: the first commercial computer was installed in 1950; by 1960, there were 5,000 computers; by 1970, there will be approximately 70,000 computers, each used by an average of ten people on a time-sharing basis and each, on the average, at least 1,000 times faster than it was in 1960—an increase in computer power during one decade of 140,000 times, with no apparent reasons for the rate of increase in power soon to abate.[3]

Already the computer is affecting the structure and performance of every major institution. It has been called upon to bookkeep, monitor underground nuclear explosions, control newspaper type, dictate how sausage is made, navigate ships and planes, mix cakes and cement, prepare weather forecasts, check income-tax returns, direct city traffic, and diagnose both human and machine ailments.[4] It has been used to store and retrieve knowledge; rule on the authenticity of authorship; prepare concordances; play checkers, chess, and war; help catch criminals and guide astronauts to the moon. It has even been used to pick out from records of talented individuals the records of those persons most suitable for presidential appointments.[5]

The consequences of cybernation's encroachment are that more and more unskilled, semiskilled, skilled, and middle-management occupations are being eliminated and that more and more boondoggling is going on—coffee breaks, shortened work weeks, extended vacations, sabbaticals, early retirements, even conferences—to keep as many as possible "gainfully employed" until a substitute for work can be found, if it can be.

What work does exist helps little in the search for self-identity: if one is a blue-collar worker, chances are he is alienated by machinery from the products of his labor; if white-collar, chances are that he is either shuffling papers in rhythmic compliance with Parkinson's law or being unwarrantedly polite to people all day in accord with the image of his profession—that is, until he can get home to bitch at the wife and beat the kids, a scarcely ennobling way to end one's day. If it weren't for those two martinis, familial homicides would dominate obituary pages.

Teachers, incidentally, are not exempt from the alienating strains of the forced smile and the pseudo enthusiasms about one's wares. Trying to motivate interest in grammar in a class of postpubescent boys has laid out many a schoolmarm on a psychiatrist's couch, while the prohibitions against violence and profanity in the classroom drive male teachers to talk in the faculty room like mule-skinning wrestlers who have just invented sex.

If one doesn't find himself in his work, then perhaps he can come to know himself in the loving confines of his family.

Alas, the sociologists tell us, no longer so. Left leaderless by father's and perhaps mother's daily exodus from home to the place of employment; left traditionless by the shipment of the elderly to antiseptic leisure worlds where they can't contaminate the young; left rootless by mobility from city to city and site to site; left fragmented by portable video sets—even "I Love Lucy" will no longer hold it together—today's nuclear family lacks continuity and cohesion. Rather than the place in which one finds the emotional warmth of common endeavors and a shared tradition, home has become the temporary boarding house of strangers, each of whom does his own (most often trifling) thing between TV dinners.

Time was when western man could partially find his identity in religion. As you know, however, that source of self was in good part lost when Copernicus displaced man from the center of the universe, from his God-favored position midway betwixt heaven and hell, angel and beast. Darwin's thesis that man apparently evolved over millions of years from lower forms of life further spelled the end for literal interpretations of the *Bible,* William Jennings Bryan notwithstanding. Now seen as an inhabitant of a small planet in one solar system in one galaxy in a universe of millions of galaxies, man has become an infinitesimal speck in the scheme of things, not even a mote in the eye of the Infinite, and the cross is no longer a transcendent symbol holding nations and people together. Recently a scribe for the *San Francisco Chronicle* reported that a man he knew, following the papal demotion of the saints, replaced the statue of St. Christopher in his car with a plasticized picture of Ralph Nader.

If the American is no longer as ready as he once was to crusade for the cross, he seems every bit as reluctant to rally round the flag. Patriotism as a source of self-identity has waned in fervor, particularly among many of the young who regard our participation in Vietnam as imperialistic and our leaders as hypocritical. Nor is hero worship, by means of which one identifies with and psychologically ingests the attributes of another, as popular a method of *becoming* and *being* as it was in the days of my youth. Now that we know what the white man did and is doing to the American Indian, the cowboy has lost his glamor, and the good guys don't stand out from the bad guys with that Ken Maynard radiance of old. Even the astronauts, those modern-day Galahads who bring back rocks in place of the Grail, sell their stories exclusively to *Life* instead of to eternity, and the moon dust turns out to be appropriately tattle-tale gray.

Gone also is that sense of community that enabled the wayfarer to know where he was going because he knew where he was from. Wilder's *Our Town* has moved from hit to myth, George and Emily don't dig that jive anymore, and the good country doctor has been replaced by a clinic and Medicare. We lock our doors at night, pull down the shades, and after a sleeping pill or two, hope that sleep's sweet sustaining balm will help us forget that other kind, which haunts our waking hours. We don't know the people we live with or those we are buried among, and Thomas Wolfe's description in *Look Homeward, Angel* of the infant Eugene Gant's loneliness in his crib is the existential description of the modern Everyman:

> And left alone to sleep within a shuttered room, with the thick sunlight printed in bars upon the floor, unfathomable loneliness and sadness crept through him: he saw his life down the solemn vista of a forest aisle, and he knew he would always be the sad one: caged in that little round of skull, imprisoned in that beating and most secret heart, his life must always walk down lonely passages. Lost. He understood that men were forever strangers to one another, that no one ever comes really to know anyone, that imprisoned in the dark womb of our mother, we come to life without having seen her face, that we are given to her arms a stranger, and that, caught in that insoluble prison of being, we escape it never, no matter what arms may clasp us, what mouth may kiss us, what heart may warm us. Never, never, never, never, never.[6]

Here are some more figures to overwhelm you. From 8,000 *B.C.* to 1650 *A.D.*, world population grew at a rate of 50 percent each 1,000 years; but from 1650 to 1965, the rate of millenial growth was 2,000 percent or 40 times greater in the modern age than in the premodern.[7] In the 50 years from 1968 to 2018, well within the anticipated life spans of our students, world population is projected to increase between 5.2 and 7.1 billion, with the medium increase 6.4 billion—an increase over one and one-half times greater than the present population of the world.[8] At the turn of the century about 60 areas in the United States would have qualified under later Federal definitions as being metropolitan. By 1960, approximately 113 million persons, 63 percent of the population, inhabited 212 Standard Metropolitan Areas.[9] According to the U.S. Department of Housing and Urban Development, by 2000 *A.D.* seven out of ten people will live in the 12 largest metropolitan areas of the country. The New

York metropolitan area alone will have a population of 24.8 million; Los
Angeles, 20.0 million; Chicago, 11.4 million; Delaware Valley, 8.4 million; San
Francisco, 7.7 million; Detroit, 7.6 million; Washington, 6 million; Miami, 5
million.[10]

Besides leaving in its wake such unresolved problems as poverty, pollution,
conservation, traffic, education, health, and welfare, the movement toward
urbanization, by cutting the ties which held rural people together in friendly
communion, has destroyed an important dimension of self. As a man daily
confronts impersonal institutions and is thrust among strange multitudes, he is
accompanied by feelings of impotence and alienation; and though he sees and is
in contact with ever greater numbers of people, the quality of his relationship
with them proportionately goes down. In comparison with friendships of the
past, the friendships he makes are trivial.

Dispossessed of work, family, symbols, and sense of community, the
individual can no longer even rely upon knowledge to provide him the sextant
by which to find himself and chart a course on a cosmic and unfathomable sea.
Grandmother's admonition to get a good education because they can't take that
away from you is today's bad advice. They can and do.

Allow me to bombard you once again. In 1750 there were about ten scientific
journals in the world; now there are 7,000 related to biomedical sciences alone.
In 1950, chemists were publishing 558 articles every two weeks in their journals;
in 1965, they were publishing 6,700 articles every fortnight. If Yale were to
continue using its obsolescent card catalogue, it would need eight acres of floor
space by the year 2040 for the cards alone.[11] More printed material has been
published since 1900 than during the previous five centuries, and relatively even
more is expected to be published during the next half-century.[12] At present,
colleges and universities double their library collections about every 16 years,
collections which now run to two million volumes and beyond in a large
university.[13] Our knowledge is estimated to be doubling every ten years, which
means that we are adding 65,000 words every minute, or 330 volumes every day,
to our store of information.[14] It also means that if one reenters a technological
field or a scientific profession after an absence of six years, most of his
knowledge is outdated.

In short, any literate person in the society who hasn't wanted in the past year
to scream, "Stop the presses!" just hasn't been visiting his local bookstores.

If information were pouring from presses alone, we would be sufficiently
overwhelmed to justify our receiving a sabbatical every third year to catch up
with our own libraries: the novels we bought and haven't read, the articles we
meant to get to and didn't, the poems and the plays stacked in dusty disarray on
nightstands, awaiting that forever receding rainy day. But it's not just print that
accounts for those hairballs of anxiety in the pits of our stomachs, the ones that
constantly remind us that we're faking, that we really don't know anything, that
it's only a matter of time until the principal, the kids, and the colleagues expose
us for the dunces we are. It's the books we should have read, plus the movies we

should have seen, plus the television shows we should have viewed, plus the records, tapes, and radio programs we should have heard that are responsible for the seeming vacuity of our minds and the tremors of our viscera. I don't know who I am because I don't know enough to know who I am, and by the time I know enough to know who I am, the enough will be obsolete, which is what I am now.

More figures. In late 1948, there were 36 *TV* stations and just over a million home receivers in the United States. By 1968 there were 635 commercial stations and 80 million sets, 14.6 million of them designed to receive color broadcasts. In 1950, Americans owned around 100 million auto and home radios and listened to about 2400 *AM* and *FM* stations; by 1968, they owned 282 million sets and listened to over 6,300 stations.[15] In dollar volume, phonograph records already outsell all tradebooks published in the United States, and tapes may soon outsell all textbooks.[16] The director of the Xerox-sponsored TV production of *A Midsummer Night's Dream* estimated that the video audience could fill the 1,426-seat playhouse at Stratford for 30 years.[17] The investiture of Charles as Prince of Wales was transmitted via satellites and relays 94,000 miles in nine-tenths of a second.[18] By 1968, the Beatles had sold 210,000,000 records.[19] Scenes of astronauts and the sounds of their voices came to us live from over 200,000 miles in space, and Mariners 6 and 7 sent us Martian pictures from 160,000,000 miles away.

Small wonder we feel media-stunned.

If knowledge won't serve, then surely precepts long-revered and values thought timeless will enable us to plumb the depths of our being, to locate the essence of ourselves in what we have held to be important to existence. Or at least some values and precepts might, since we have disposed of "Hard work pays off," "My country, right or wrong," "Blessed is he who has a family," and a few others en route.

Let's try our belief in the sanctity and worth of the individual through a pastiche of examples:

If a Vietnamese Honda driver is killed by an American truck, the United States pays his family a maximum of 4,000 piastres, about $32, and sends a letter of "friendship, sympathy, and condolence." However, a clause in the Foreign Claims Act prohibits payment for an incident "which results directly from action by the enemy or by United States armed forces engaged in armed conflict or in immediate preparation for impending conflict." The clause thus excludes payment if a guard, mistaking the Honda driver for an enemy, shoots and kills him, or if an artillery barrage or an air stike, bomb or napalm, is mistakenly directed at the wrong village.[20]

The life expectancy of an adult American Indian is now 42 years.

The net gain in world population each year is about 70 million persons, nearly 58 million of whom are being born in underdeveloped nations. One scientist has calculated that if all the food in today's world were distributed evenly among its 3.5 billion human inhabitants, every one of then would go hungry. At present, the world is spending $2,000 for military purposes for every $1 spent to control population.[21]

One-third of Mexican-American families exist on less than $3,000 a year.

New York City has stipulated that a poor family on relief can be given $30 for a couch, $12 for a dinette table, $33 for a bed (single). A woman is budgeted enough for one lipstick a year—two if she is employed—two pairs of nylons (75 cents a pair) and a $3 hat. She can buy a $5 raincoat every two years, and a $5 bathrobe every three.[22]

We are approaching the time when *in vitro,* or testtube births will be possible, when an individual may be cloned, or reproduced, from a single one of his cells, when drug and electrical alteration of the mind are practices acceptable to most citizens.[23] One psychologist has already called for educator, psychologist, and neurobiochemist to collaborate in basic research in order to produce a new expert capable of administering precisely unto the child, the psychoneurobiochemeducator:

Tommy needs a bit more of an immediate memory stimulator; Jack could do with a chemical attention-span stretcher; Rachael needs an anti-cholinesterase to slow down her mental processes; Joan, some puromycin—she remembers too many details and gets lost.[24]

The infant mortality rate in Harlem is three times higher than that in adjoining white communities.

For every person alive, there are now stored 28,000 pounds of *T.N.T.* equivalent, or 200 pounds of explosives for every pound of human flesh.[25]

So much for dignity and worth. Let's skip the sexual revolution and what it is doing to destroy traditional values having to do with fidelity and love and family, a matter already well-publicized, and examine instead our cherished notions about privacy.

As our records—tax records; social security records; health records; census records; military records; employment records; credit records; property records; birth, marriage, and divorce records; arrest records; school records—all become subject to storage in computer memories for easy access and manipulation, it becomes concomittantly easier for any interested person or agency to prepare a thick dossier on any one of us. Through remote control, it is already possible to invade both personal and national privacy without trespassing. Telescope cameras, concealed transistors, unobtrusive closed-circuit television, tapped telephone lines, two-way mirrors, helicopter patrols, stratospheric airplanes, homing missiles, satelites—many are the devices available to the outsider for seeing what was not meant for his eyes and for hearing what was not meant for his ears. According to one eminent professor of law, the technology will continue to improve, probably at a geometric rate, so that . . . by the year 2000 it will be possible to place a man under constant surveillance without his ever becoming aware of it. Moreover, since the culture will become cognizant of this advance, men will live with the constant possibility that they are under surveillance without even being able to be sure whether this is so .[26]

Well, how, then, with most of the traditional means taken from us, are we to find the allusive *I*, the dissolving *self?* Where else shall we seek, and with what chances of success?

I wish that I had a reassuring answer to my questions, one that was profound and that carried as well a lifetime, money-back guarantee. But I don't have, and to my knowledge no one else has either. All that I have is faith (in that small-*f* sense in which E. M. Forster uses it in his essay "What I believe"), faith that literature can help us in our search.

As you may recall, E. M. Forster asks himself where he should start in order to keep up his end in an age "bloody in every sense of the word," and he replies, "With personal relationships." He then observes that even though psychology has taught us that persons are not fixed entities, that they are ever changing, they can nevertheless treat each other with love and loyalty. In fact, Forster goes so far as to declare that if he had to choose between betraying his country or betraying his friend, he hoped he should have the guts to betray his country, adding that though such a choice might scandalize the modern reader, it would not have shocked Dante, who confined Brutus and Cassius in the lowest circle of hell for having chosen to betray their friend Caesar rather than Rome.[27]

If one in a mass age is to find his salvation, as does Goethe's Faust, out of his personal relationships with and devoted service to others; if he is to both feel and act upon Donne's declaration that any man's death diminishes him, because he is involved in mankind; if he is to find his way clearly on a plain more darkling than ever was Arnold's, then literature may provide a microcosm that will help him not only to cope with macrocosmic *life* but to enrich it with his presence. As the verbally ordered and artistic enactment of man, literature allows us unobtrusively but without immoral invasion to enter lives different from our own, to identify with them, to vicariously suffer through their tragedies, endure their ennui, and exult in their triumphs. Through the mind's eye, we can see vistas never beheld before; encounter alien cultures; witness acts of both supreme courage and simpering cowardice; come to know compassion, integrity, cruelty, insensitivity, loneliness, joy, fear, and the selfless love in which, paradoxically, self has most often been found and most lucidly expressed; and to know these not as philosophical and linguistic abstractions but as human behaviors which confirm our own humanity, which inform us that we are not alone in the universe since, we, too, have felt and experienced some of these things; and though we may never come to know ourselves and others completely, we shall no longer be hostile strangers, for literature will have introduced us.

However, if literature is to assist us in our search for self-identity, it must be appropriate to the times in which we and our students live. If our pictures from space have taught us anything, they should have taught us that we do, indeed, live on a globe and that there are no visible borders determining nations and separating peoples except the natural ones of water and ice. We must bring into our classrooms not only the literatures of English-speaking nations but the translated literatures of the world. We must come to see all men as common inhabitants of spaceship Earth, sometimes having different cultures, languages, and values, but all sharing the need to survive on a planet whose ecology is in grave peril.

Too, we must present literature to students not as a canon of the tried and true, a cultural heritage whose worth has been forever fixed by unassailable arbiters of taste, but as a body of works which one has every right to argue with, measure himself against, incorporate into his being, or declare dead. The greatness of an author flows from the works to the man, not conversely, and that greatness, rather than being fixed for eternity, must be reestablished for each age, including—and perhaps most especially—our own. The teacher as listener and questioner rather than as transmitter or teller, taught principally not for aesthetic purposes (though these surely should not be ignored) but mainly for the human end that one can come better to know others and, through them, himself—these are what the times demand.

Further, if we are to present ourselves to students as persons who inhabit the world they know, we need to broaden our definition of literature to include television productions, films, records, and tapes as well as books. A picture *can* be worth a thousand words, and a play heard can be worth a dozen read silently: who among us has been able to look at the photographs or the films taken of bodies stacked in the open pits of concentration camps without being forever changed, without puzzling thereafter what it is to be a child of this century? Who has heard the Old Vic recording of *Macbeth,* starring Alec Guinness and Pamela Brown, and remained unmoved by the anguish and loneliness of a husband and wife who have destroyed their potential for greatness and in the process lost each other?

Finally, so that literature becomes a passageway to life in all its complexity and not a substitute for it, we must provide means of translating the one to the other. As George Steiner warns in *Language and Silence,* the humanities *may* dehumanize: by absorbing our capacity for imaginative reflex and moral risk, ". . . the cry in the poem may come to sound louder, more urgent, more real than the cry in the street outside. The death in the novel may move us more potently than the death in the next room."[28] Discussions which explore the relationships between fictive and actual behavior, between ethical choices made in books and those made in life, between times past and times present, may guard against students' unhealthily making literature one with life. As the reports from Dartmouth of the Anglo-American Seminar in English suggest, even more important may be the imaginative use of literature to provide students opportunities for dramatic improvisation and role playing, techniques which help them experience literary situations, both internally and externally, as situations significant to human existence.

In the Spring 1966 issue of *The American Scholar,* there appeared the following statement by Jacob Bronowski, quoted from his book *The Identity of Man:*

I hold each man has a self, and enlarges his self by his experiences, that is, he learns from experience: from the experiences of others as well as his own, and from their inner experiences as well as their outer. But he can learn from their inner experience only by entering it, and that is not done merely by reading a written record of it. We must have the gift to identify ourselves with other men, to relive their experience and to feel its conflicts as our own. And the conflicts are the essence of the experience. We gain knowledge of our selves by identifying ourselves with others, but that is not enough—that only gives us the fantasies of sex and the parodies of power, the absurd strutting daydreams of Secret Agent 007 and *Butterfield 8*. We must enter others in order to share their conflicts, and they must be shown to have grave conflicts, in order that we shall feel in their lives what we know in our own: the human dilemma. The knowledge of self cannot be formalized because it cannot be closed, even provisionally: it is perpetually open, because the dilemma is perpetually unresolved.[29]

And though the dilemma remains unresolved and knowledge of self ever open, I have faith that literature is and will be the richest source for each man to enlarge his self through entering into the lives of others and feeling their conflicts as his own: it is the repository in which one finds most fully and deeply recorded the human experience; it is the place in which one can come closest to discovering what man was and is; it is the truest compass I know directing us to what man should and yet could be.

NOTES

1. Grant Venn, *Man, Education, and Work* (Washington, D. C.: American Council on Education, 1964), p. 4.

2. A. Barach, "Changing Technology," in William Brickman and Stanley Lehrer, eds., *Automation, Education, and Human Values* (New York: School and Society Books, 1966), p. 58.

3. Robert Theobald, *Dialogue on Poverty* (Indianapolis, Ind.: Bobbs-Merrill Co., 1967), pp. 110-11.

4. "Technology: The Cybernated Generation," *Time*, 2 April 1965, p. 84.

5. John W. Macy, Jr. "Automated Government," *Saturday Review*, 23 July 1966, p. 25.

6. Thomas Wolfe, *Look Homeward, Angel* (New York: Scribner's Library Book—(SL-9), p. 31.

7. Herman Kahn and Anthony J. Wiener, *The Year 2000: A Framework for Speculation on the Next Thirty-three Years* (New York: Macmillan Co., 1967), p. 150.

8. Philip M. Hauser, "Population: The World's People Will Nearly Triple in Number," in Foreign Policy Association, ed., *Toward The Year 2018* (New York: Cowles Education Corporation, 1964), p. 139.

9. Philip Hauser and Martin Taitel, "Population Trends—Prologue to Educational Programs," in Edgar L. Morphet and Charles O. Ryan, eds., *Designing Education for the Future #1: Prospective Changes in Society by 1980* (New York: Citation Press, 1967), pp. 29-30.

10. "Way of Living in Year 2000," *San Francisco Sunday Examiner and Chronicle*, Real Estate, 3 August 1969, p. 31.

11. "Education: Libraries," *Time*, 3 September 1965, p. 52.

12. Burnham P. Beckwith, *The Next 500 Years: Scientific Predictions of Major Social Trends* (New York: Exposition Press, 1967), pp. 193-94.

13. Harold B. Gores, "The American Campus—1980," in Alvin C. Eurich, ed., *Campus 1980: The Shape of the Future in American Higher Education* (New York: Delacorte Press, 1968), p. 286.

14. Dr. Murray Tondow, "Man and Machine-Machine and Man—The Individual's Prerogative," Symposium II: *Technology and Education in the 21st Century* (Washington D.C.: San Francisco State College's Center for Technological Education, the Collaborative Projects Fund and the Departments of Education and Design and Industry, 1967), p. 61.

15. *SDC* (Systems Development Corporation) *Magazine*, Winter 1969, p. 4.

16. Nelson N. Foote, "The New Media and Our Total Society," in Peter Rossi and Bruce J. Biddle, eds., *The New Media and Education: Their Impact on Society* (New York: Doubleday Anchor, 1967), p. 414.

17. *Time*, 7 February 1967, p. 81.

18. T. O'Flaherty, "Mightier Than the Sword," *San Francisco Chronicle*, 7 July 1969, p. 40.

19. Luman H. Long, ed., *The 1969 World Almanac* (New York: Newspaper Enterprise Association, Inc., 1969), p. 13.

20. Stephen Erhart, "$32 for Traffic Deaths," *San Francisco Chronicle*, 25 March 1969, p. 13.

21. Tom Wicker, "The Way to Oblivion," *San Francisco Chronicle*, 5 May 1969, p. 1.

22. "Welfare and Illfare: the Alternatives to Poverty," *Time*, 13 December 1968, p. 25.

23. See, for example, Gordon Rattray Taylor, *The Biological Time Bomb* (New York: World Publishing Co., 1968).

24. David Krech, "Chemistry of Learning," *Saturday Review*, 20 January 1968, p. 60.

25. R. Buckminster Fuller, "Vision 65 Summary Lecture," *The American Scholar*, Spring 1966, p. 218.

26. Harry Kalven, Jr., "The Problems of Privacy in the Year 2000," *Daedalus*, Summer 1967, pp. 876-77.

27. E. M. Forster, "What I Believe," in Robert Jameson, ed., *Essays Old and New* (New York: Harcourt Brace Jovanovich, 1955), pp. 233-45.

28. George Steiner, *Language and Silence* (New York: Atheneum Press, 1967), p. 61.

29. J. Bronowski, "The Logic of the Mind," *The American Scholar*, Spring 1966, p. 240.

The Lively Arts: Are They Literary, Too?

Samuel D. Wehr

Literature in English classrooms has been book-centered and book-oriented for so long that generations of teachers have completely forgotten that it ever existed apart from the pages of a book. And having forgotten that literature was once almost entirely a lively art, having its existence on the stage or coming from the lips of storytellers, troubadours, minnesingers, and traveling players, they

From Samuel D. Wehr, "The Lively Arts: Are They Literary, Too?" *The High School Journal* 52 (April 1969): 412-18. Copyright © 1969 by the University of North Carolina Press. Reprinted by permission of *The High School Journal*.

have come to regard anything except printed literature as a second rate, spurious, or merely as an aid in teaching. This notion that print is the only literature and that reading is the only bona fide and truly respectable literary experience has restricted the literature curriculum, enfeebled our teaching of it, and warped our very notions of what literature and the literary experience really are.

It may make clear what this article is all about to leave the field of literature and go to the lively art of music for a moment. I am fortunate to have as friends a number of musicians and music teachers and at some time or other, have engaged all of them in a discussion about which is THE music—that which I *hear* in Philharmonic Hall, or that which I *see* on the score from which the orchestra makes its music? It is a ridiculous question, of course, though the discussion has always become very serious. There are differing kinds of musical experiences; the orchestra playing the Pastoral Symphony is having one kind; I as one in the audience listening to them am having another. The conductor is experiencing quite another. There has always been agreement that the notes and notations in the score are not music but only the means of producing music. There was further agreement that the orchestra's performing experience is greatly enhanced, even changed, by the fact that there is an audience out there listening to them, and I have quite a different musical experience in the hall with a live orchestra from that in my living room as I listen to a recording of the same piece by the same musicians. These are all musical experiences, though reading notes is an intellectual exercise more than it is a musical one.

I have taken classes ranging from sixth grade levels through the graduate school to the theater. I am a theater addict and have sat in matinees surrounded by pupils and their teachers when the Old Vic comes to town or the National Repertory Theater makes its annual tour. The audience reactions and comments during intermission always make me feel that the audience is saying, if they are adults, "This isn't the real literary experience. To get that I should go home and read the play." If they are students they seem to say, "We'll get the literary end of this when we read it in school." Or, "We had the literary part of this last week when we studied it in class." The audience always seems to be saying, "If I could forget that this is supposed to be a literary experience, I would enjoy it more." Audiences said this almost literally when Bert Lahr played Bottom some ten years ago at which time this talented comedian made *A Midsummer Night's Dream* so enjoyable they forgot that Shakespeare had to be read if you were to be literary about him. "I never knew Shakespeare was so much fun," they said very sheepishly, as if they felt it was wrong to enjoy him so much.

Without deliberate attempts, schools have succeeded in making literature something which is between the covers of a book, something that is worthy of the exalted name of literature only in its printed version. Not only must it be in book form, it must be in a certain kind of book form. I have seen teachers confiscate "classic comics," treating them as though they were scatological and their readers as though they were scurrilous cheats.

Teachers have used recordings of poetry as an aid to teaching and some have even grudingly regarded a recording of the poet reading his own verse as being very close to the real literary experience. But pupils are nearly always forced to return to the printed poems as though only if the poems have been read silently are they really literature and only then will pupils enjoy a truly literary experience.

Recordings of plays are treated in the same manner. It matters not that the finest actors of the day have recorded the lines, we must not treat the recording as the play, or the delight of hearing Gielgud or Olivier reciting the soliloquies as a true literary experience. These things must be treated as ancillary to the printed play. Recordings of poetry and plays, particularly, are to be used as enriching devices only, else they are for those poor benighted youngsters whose intelligences are too meager to cope with ideas buried in the abstractions of print. It is quite unthinkable that two or three hours listening to a recording of *Hamlet,* in the comforts of one's own home, or in a niche in a library browsing room, or even in the decidedly less comfortable confines of a listening booth, should be the literary experience. We would not dream of such a record session's being the core of the literary experience, with frequent returns to the recording and to class discussion to sharpen understanding, and with occasional reference to the printed word to reinforce memory and to deepen perception. It is nearly always the other way round. The printed poetry or play is the experience. We go to recordings for some enrichment or to help pupils understand more precisely, but we must always return to the passive printed word.

And ditto cinema! Woe be the pupil who, having seen Zeffirelli's *Romeo and Juliet,* should ask, "Why do I have to read it? I have seen it." The answers are always the same. "You haven't experienced the play unless you have read it. The movie was all right for background, to make some things clearer, to help us visualize the play better, but the movie wasn't the play."

As for television! What are the arguments here? Too much has been omitted? The commercials have destroyed the continuity of the piece? Well, yes. Geraldine Page was marvelous in Truman Capote's Christmas story and Dylan Thomas' *A Child's Christmas in Wales* was beautifully done, but . . ."

"Ballet? Dance? Musical Comedy? Well, yes, of course . . . but . . . when you come right down to it. . . ." Yes, I have said them all myself, as you have. All these old chestnuts merely mean that the printed word's the thing, theater, cinema, recordings notwithstanding.

The staged readings of *The Caine Mutiny, John Brown's Body* (Is this a poem or a novel?), Hal Holbrook's reincarnation of Mark Twain, Charles Laughton's readings; Shaw's *Don Juan in Hell,* and many others. What about these? Did you feel these, fine as they were, were but versions of literature? That, finally, one had to go back to the printed form of these works for the genuine literary experience? "These great performances were fine as entertainment. Did you ever imagine anything as talky as Shaw's *Man and Superman* could be so entertaining? But isn't that what they are, really, entertainment? They're not literature, of course."

"Well, what of all this?" you ask. Simply this.

For years and years, because we have limited a study of literature exclusively to the printed word, we have shamefully limited the literary offerings in our schools. Not only have we limited the number of pieces of literature in our curriculum, but restricted these to students who can read the printed word. This is shameful. In many schools more than half the pupils cannot really read our great literature. Are they to be denied this literature when it exists all around us in the lively nonbook media? I have no objection to retaining (when it is done well) our traditional in-class, close-study of a few well-selected pieces of our vast literary heritage. In fact, for our more intelligent students this in-depth study is very desirable. But what about that vast heritage of literature that never gets read or studied anywhere at any level? Cannot something be done about this treasure house of plays, poems, novels that never gets read in school?

For example, our six Nobel Literature laureates are all represented in film, all in good, some in very fine films. Our Nobel laureates as great world figures in world literature have never been truly honored as the nation's heroes they really are. Should we not accord them at least equal recognition with our military heroes? Do they not merit equal honors with our great inventors? How many students can name our literary Nobel laureates?

Should there not be a course, elective for all who can read the printed word creatively, required for all who cannot read thus, in which the best works of our Nobel Literary laureates are the *pieces de resistance?* In August 1969, at Temple University we will honor them with a film conference festival. Some of the works of Sinclair Lewis, Eugene O'Neill, Pearl Buck, William Faulkner, Ernest Hemingway, and John Steinbeck have been made into film. At least one of the films derived from the writings of these honored writers will be viewed; other of their works will be discussed in the course. *Arrowsmith, Dodsworth, Ah, Wilderness!, The Good Earth, Intruder in the Dust, The Old Man and the Sea, The Grapes of Wrath, Of Mice and Men, For Whom the Bell Tolls*—these films and others based on Nobel laureates' works can be rented. They all do justice to their authors, and can stand as works of art. Some of our students can't read the books, and schools haven't time to teach all. Could there not be a well-organized course in which the films are the media, not books? Should we not handle such a course as a bona fide literary experience? We need not feel that word-reading will suffer because of "film-reading." Experience in our libraries proves that there is always a demand for a book after a well-made movie based upon it has come out. Such a course ought to be *de rigueur* in our schools.

A similar course could easily be organized around our Pulitzer Prize winners. Only a few of the Pulitzer novels are regularly studied in schools: Marjorie K. Rawlings' *The Yearling*, John Steinbeck's *The Grapes of Wrath* (though the latter is too controversial for any but our best and most broad-minded communities and schools), and Ernest Hemingway's *The Old Man and the Sea.* Movies have been made of the following Pulitzer novels: Booth Tarkington's *Alice Adams* (1922)[1]; Thorton Wilder's *The Bridge of San Luis Rey* (1928); Pearl Buck's *The Good Earth* (1932); Margaret Mitchell's *Gone With the Wind*[2] (1937); Marjorie Rawlings' *The Yearling* (1939); John Steinbeck's *The Grapes of*

Wrath (1940); John Hersey's *A Bell for Adano* (1945); James Michener's *Tales From the South Pacific* (1948), on which the movie, *South Pacific*, was based; Herman Wouk's *The Caine Mutiny* (1952); Ernest Hemingway's *The Old Man and the Sea* (1953). How many of these fine novels are taught? How many would we have time to teach? But all of these would be "read" via a good film course.

The Pulitzer Prize is also awarded for plays, and good films based on some of these winners have also been made: Thorton Wilder's, *Our Town* (1938); Robert Sherwood's *Abe Lincoln in Illinois* (1939); Tennessee Williams' *A Streetcar Named Desire* (1948); Arthur Miller's *Death of a Salesman* (1949); Rodgers and Hammerstein's *South Pacific* (1950) (from James Michener's stories, *Tales From the South Pacific)*; Frances Goodrich and Albert Hackett's *The Diary of Anne Frank* (1958). Only a few of these are regularly studied in our schools. What a film festival they would make! What a fine course they would build!

Shakespeare? There are *Romeo and Juliet, Julius Caesar, Othello, Macbeth, Henry V, Hamlet, A Midsummer Night's Dream, Henry VIII, Taming of the Shrew, Anthony and Cleopatra.* How many do we teach? How much richer could our Shakespeare's offerings be? If we add to such a film course, the many fine recordings of almost all the plays, and make listening sessions as well as seeing or reading sessions both respectable and desirable, how rich would we all be in Shakespearean experiences!

As for our great authors, American, British, and world wide, they are nearly all represented in films. There could be a Dickens film course with *David Copperfield, Oliver Twist, Great Expectations, A Tale of Two Cities.* Well-represented in film are George Bernard Shaw, the Bronte sisters, Jane Austen, Victor Hugo, Herman Melville, Sir Walter Scott, John Galsworthy, Mark Twain, and many, many others. There could be film courses based on themes, periods, biography, historical events, nations, or continents. The possibilities are almost limitless and the enjoyment, enlightenment, and broadening that would result is breathtaking in contemplation.

We will need to teach students how to learn from films and records as we now try to teach them to appreciate books. Viewing skills are as necessary as reading skills and fortunately more can learn to view with more skill than seem to learn to read with artistry. Besides, our cultural environment of movies, TV, and theater have prepared most of us in some degree to view both willingly and intelligently.

Perhaps the greatest benefit of film courses, record-listening courses, theater-going courses, TV sessions, would be the gradual raising of the general public's understanding of our lively media and an increasing demand for better fare on TV, in movies, and on stage. Would it not be all the reward schools and teachers could ask if Hollywood and TV networks someday realized they had to produce fare for 18 or 20 year olds, instead of 12 year olds as is presently their standard? Courses of these kinds in our schools may be the best solution to the problem of public taste and for raising the standards of the lively arts.

A number of questions will arise at once. Is the Zeffirelli *Romeo and Juliet* really Shakespeare's play? Don't the deletions and distortions in many movies and plays rather tend to destroy these pieces as literature? Would you ask the same question about Verdi's great operatic masterpieces, *Othello, Macbeth, Falstaff,* all derived from Shakespeare but not slavishly true to the bard.[3] Few Shakespearean plays are given uncut whether at Stratford-on-Avon or Stratford, Connecticut. In our lifetime there has only been one uncut *Hamlet* and that had to be broken up with a dinner hour.

As for distortion, who has distorted Shakespeare more than English teachers? Any classroom of students that has come to think Shakespeare is dull has had that distortion created by the very teachers who cry "Havoc" at stage and movie deletions and distortions. Every pupil has created in his mind his own version (distortion?) of the piece of literature he has read. In fact, the better we are as teachers, the more ideas we cram into any piece of literature we teach. So short and fine a poem as Frost's "Stopping By The Woods" has been taught from the extreme of a simple scenic description to a lyric about a death wish. Was *My Fair Lady* a distortion of Shaw's *Pygmalion*? Is *West Side Story* a desecration of *Romeo and Juliet*? Did Shakespeare distort Plutarch's *Lives* and Holinshed's *Chronicles* when he drew play materials from them? Hundreds of thousands of pupils leave school or are graduated from college thoroughly disliking poetry. For most of these, our teaching of this literary form was a gross distortion. It is unfortunate that there have been needless changes, deletions, and distortions in adapting pieces of literature from one medium to the other, but these need not stop us from using them. This argument is probably an attempt to disguise our unwillingness to accord artistic and literary merit to another art form, under a cloak of scholarliness that really is pedantry when closely examined.

There is also a question of cost. Undoubtedly film rentals cost money, often a great deal of money. Records cost money, too, though these, like books, can be used over and over again. If, however, one is willing to teach the kinds of courses proposed here, and let the film or the record be the medium, then the money that would have gone into books would go a long way toward many rentals. And I would venture to ask if schools can justify high rental film costs as an excuse *not* to use films when most of these same schools feel they need not justify the high cost of uniforms for an athletic band? Furthermore, our insistence upon books as literature has brought federal funds by the millions to help supply them. Would not a loud and long insistence upon films as media of literature ultimately bring forth funds for these too?

Lastly, much great literature exists only in print. Let's teach that to those who can read it. The great literature that exists in the lively art forms of film, records, living theater, recordings, and TV videotapes and video scopes, can be experienced through those media. When we put all these into our literature programs, we will be amazed at how much literature we will be teaching our students.

NOTES

1. The dates indicate the year the novel won the Pulitzer Prize, not when the movie was released.
2. *Gone With the Wind* is still shown commercially and is not available for classroom rental.
3. Operas based upon great literature would make another great course. There are the three operatic masterpieces listed above. One could add Gounod's *Romeo and Juliet*, now a Metropolitan Opera hit, Debussy's *Pelleas and Melisande*, Donizetti's *Lucia di Lammermoor*, Gounod's *Faust*, Mozart's *Marriage of Figaro*, Rossini's *Barber of Seville*, Wagner's *Ring of the Nibelung*, for example. All are literature as well as music.

An Integrated Approach
to the Teaching
of Film and Literature

John Stuart Katz

For many English teachers the teaching of film is an exciting idea. To demonstrate this, one need only point to the program of this convention, the work of such organizations as the National Film Board, the American Film Institute, and the British Film Institute, as well as the numerous articles on film in journals in the teaching of English. We have every reason to believe not only that film will continue to be taught in the schools, but that its use will increase. Teachers and other educators should, however, be wary of jumping on a bandwagon. There is still a great need in screen education for extensive research, curriculum development work, and the training of teachers. Those who wish to deal successfully with film in the classroom must understand the medium and why they are teaching it.

One can identify at least four current approaches to the teaching of film, each of which has its own rationale and educational implication. Although these approaches are not mutually exclusive, they do exemplify divergent attitudes prevalent in screen education. The first two approaches illustrate what I believe is a dysfunctional use of the medium. The third approach would probably do most justice to film *per se*, but seems impractical in many schools and for most teachers. The fourth attempts to integrate film study with the knowledge and

From John Stuart Katz, "An Integrated Approach to the Teaching of Film and Literature," *The English Quarterly* 2 (January 1969): 25-29. Reprinted by permission of the publisher and the author.

curriculum realities of both teachers and students without ignoring film's essential uniqueness.

Film has been used in the schools primarily as an audio-visual aid. Students studying Shakespeare are rewarded with, or subjected to, a filmed version of the play being studied or an "instructional" film on the Elizabethan theatre. In such cases film acts merely as a "handmaiden" to the material in which the teacher is really interested. It is unlikely that this approach to film has resulted in enhancing students' appreciation of the medium. In fact, it has probably done just the opposite.

Another approach to film study was spawned by McLuhan and his disciples, whose incessant bombardments are sometimes called the Marshall Plan, or McLunacy by those less generous. At its extreme, this approach manifests itself in attempts to inundate the students in media. Don't interpret. Don't analyse. Just fill the classroom with films, TV, records, strobe lights, and let the students react as they will. The teacher using this approach acts as a noninterfering anthropologist watching the *primitifs* perform rites which we outsiders from the pre-electronic generation can never fully understand.

Thirdly, are two approaches, cinema arts and film making, which I consider here as one, because they frequently are combined in the classroom and tend to treat film in a highly specialized way. The cinema art approach usually concerns itself with the history, aesthetics, appreciation and even the economics of film, while the film making approach deals with technique and production. Too often, however, these courses see film as if it had sprung full blown from D. W. Griffith's head and with no relationship to any other art form. Moreover, these courses find themselves under the rubric of English for what appears, to both teacher and student, to be no reason other than expediency.

The fourth approach integrates the study of film with the study of literature. It is this approach I find most viable. To me, film is an art form, like literature, and is worthy of study *in* and *for* itself. Paradoxically, despite its uniqueness, the study of film when integrated with the study of literature allows students to see how each medium works and to explore the similarities and the differences between the two media. When students study film and literature together, they are able to understand not only the meaning or message of a particular work of art, but also what each medium is forced to do, what it is able to do most successfully, and what it seems unable to do.

Let us, for a moment, look at some of the similarities and differences between film and literature which are worth pursuing with secondary school students. The relationships to be discussed reflect what has happened historically in the mainstream of film and literature—although recent films, like many recent literary works, have attempted to overcome these conventions and limitations. But even if one must use the exceptions to prove the rule, there is value in a comparison and analysis of the fundamentals of the two media.

In 1897, in his Preface to *The Nigger of the "Narcissus,"* Joseph Conrad said, "My task which I am trying to achieve is, by the power of the written word to make you hear, to make you feel—it is, before all, to make you *see.*" Fifteen years later, the film maker D. W. Griffith said, "The task I'm trying to achieve is, above all, to make you see." Griffith was not necessarily commenting on visual perception. He was referring to the same task as Conrad–that of enabling the reader or viewer to go beyond apprehending to comprehending, to go beyond visceral reactions to an understanding of the sense of the work.

Both literature and film are liberating arts; they are part of the humanities. They make the viewer or reader aware of outward realities and of his own inward life. Both, as Northrop Frye says of literature, develop and educate the imagination. Both film and literature present to us an artist's ordering of the chaos of human experience. With the possible exception of *"l'art pour l'art,"* the poet, the novelist, the film maker, uses the pen or the camera to express a particular attitude towards some aspect of human experience.

Literature and film are similar also in that both tend to be content oriented. With some exceptions of course, both media make extensive use of the narrative mode. Both require cognitive participation in order to have the reader or viewer understand them. Finally, both film and literature frequently offer some form of entertainment. These last two components, understanding and entertainment, are reminiscent of the *utile et dulce* of which Horace speaks in defining the function of poetry.

When exploring relationships between film and literature, one must also examine the basic differences between the two media. To state that words are the fundamental tool of literature and pictures that of film is to make, for all of its obviousness, an important distinction. Just as a picture of a horse is not the horse itself, so the picture is also different from that image evoked by the word "horse," no matter how many modifiers the word may have. The imagination educed by literature is qualitatively different from that educed by film.

Film, because of its immediacy and its appearance of concreteness, usually deals more successfully with actions than with thoughts. Literature, on the other hand, deals with thoughts and abstractions just as easily as with actions. For example, Meursault, in Camus' *The Stranger,* has a detachment and an inwardness which are reflected in the way he recounts his story. Although he quotes directly the words of others, the judge and the priest for example, he seldom relates to the reader his exact words to them. Meursault tells the judge *that* it was by chance he had the gun and returned to the spot in which the Arab rested and similarly tells the priest *that* he does not believe in God. In the films, however, Visconti must transform the essence of what Meursault tells us *about* into something we can see, hear, or both. Visconti's Meursault, therefore, enters the realm of action.

One further difference between the two media lies in their handling of time and space. Whereas literature tends to convey time by the use of tense, films tends to convey time by the manipulation of space. In film, everything, even a flashback, happens as we watch it. The filmed version of the Ambrose Bierce short story "Occurrence at Owl Creek Bridge" by Roberto Enrico has immediacy because it is presented to us on the screen in the only way it can be shown–before our eyes, always at the present tense. But, as we learn at the end of the film, it only *appeared* to be in the present and actually was a subjunctive. The short story, in contrast, is written in the past tense, with only the description of Farquhar returning home rendered in the present. Then the sudden switch to the past tense to describe his death creates the sharp contrast which the movie achieves by showing action as it happens.

As an example of this approach which compares and contrasts film and literature, I would like to describe briefly an experimental curriculum now being developed by the Ontario Institute for Studies in Education at the University of Toronto. The curriculum is a ten-week "unit" being taught this year in three pilot schools in Ontario to eleventh grade academic and technical students. The course integrates the study of film with the study of literature by investigating ways in which each medium handles a particular theme. The curriculum treats film as film and literature as literature while exploring ways in which each medium deals with certain aspects of the theme which we selected to work on this year—man's relationship to machines.

We approach the theme of man's relationship to machines in three ways. First, we consider works of literature and film which depict man in the absence of, or unaffected by machines, including some Utopian and pastoral works. Secondly, we consider those works in which the machine is praised or even apotheosized for the role it plays in man's existence. And finally, there are those works in which the machine is shown as the physical or spiritual destroyer of mankind.

The students are involved in three activities related to this thematic approach. They see films, discuss them, and write about them; they read books in an individualized reading program, discuss them, and write about them; and they make movies and discuss them. The films seen and the books read are in our judgement worthwhile works of art; no film or literary work is used only because of its theme.

The students begin the course by discussing how film and literature portray man in the absence of machines. They view short films such as *Sky, Nahanni,* and *Leaf.* At the same time they have available to them, for individualized reading, literature such as *Walden, Erewhon, Who Has Seen the Wind,* and nature poetry. The students write on the theme as well as on the ways in which film and literature deal with the theme. As a corollary to the writing, they are given 8 mm cameras, some technical instruction, and are set loose in a rural or natural setting to make a short film. The course does not attempt to make professional film makers of the students. We are more interested in the process than in the product of film making. But by making a filmic statement, the students are forced to consider some of the medium's basic aspects such as camera angles, lighting, perspective, and editing. They are, in short, as is the writer or the film maker, ordering the chaos of their experiences. They are learning to appreciate what is involved in making a coherent statement in either medium.

Students then consider works which take an objective or positive viewpoint towards machines. They view and discuss shorts such as *N.Y.N.Y.* and *Skyscraper* and features such as Robert Flaherty's *Louisianna Story* and

Eisenstein's *The Old and the New (The General Line)*. Simultaneously, they read and discuss such books as Saint Exupery's *Night Flight,* the poetry of Carl Sandburg, and science fiction by writers such as Ray Bradbury, Isaac Asimov, and Jules Verne. Again, the students are given the 8 mm cameras and film, and set loose, this time in the middle of the city or a factory.

Next, the students see films and read books which deal with the machine as the spiritual or physical destroyer of mankind. Included here would be the short films *Day After Day, 21/87, Very Nice, Very Nice,* and the features—Godard's *Alphaville,* Kubrick's *Dr. Strangelove,* and Theoeodore Flicker's *The President's Analyst.* Books the students might be reading at this time include *Brave New World, 1984, A Canticle for Leibowitz, Hiroshima, Octopus,* and *The Grapes of Wrath.*

As a final project, students are given the opportunity to work in a group on the production of their own 16 mm film, including the script writing, acting, directing, shooting, and editing.

We are now attempting to devise ways of evaluating the success of the program, and indeed, of any program in screen education. This model for a curriculum is still in the formative stages and will be for at least the next year. We are developing and testing a flexible approach which, I believe, will enable the student to "see" better, in the Griffith-Conrad sense. While it is only one approach to the study of film, it does seem to be a viable way of incorporating an important medium into the school curriculum.

The Literate Adolescent in an Age of Mass Media

Jack R. Cameron and Emma E. Plattor

A REDEFINATION OF LITERACY

Since the "literate" man has traditionally been defined in terms of print, reading education has attempted to give the child, and subsequently the adolescent, some competence in handling written verbal symbols both critically and imaginatively. Ideally, teachers attempted to strike a balance between the emotional *reserve* needed for factual prose, and the emotional *release* prompted by fiction. If the learner is an enthusiastic and creative reader of quality literature, he is not literate if he is unable to read the daily newspaper critically.

From Jack R. Cameron and Emma E. Plattor, "The Literate Adolescent in an Age of Mass Media," a paper presented at the International Reading Association, Kansas City. Copyright © 1969 by the IRA, Inc. Reprinted by permission of the IRA and the authors.

The youngster who critically reads the newspaper but is incapable of observing the world around him and responding creatively to good literature is not literate either. Unfortunately, large numbers of adolescents don't read either newspapers or quality literature. They are too busy actively responding to the stimulations of the mass media. Such present media developments as the motion picture, television, filmstrips, 35 mm slides, and electronic devices for sound and light provide the adolescent with dimensions of experience in sight, sound, and movement which we have only just begun to appreciate. Future media developments will provide dimensions of experience which we cannot begin to anticipate.

The traditional definition of "literacy" is thus too narrow to serve the needs of today. It is important to speak and teach in terms of oral, aural, and pictorial literacy. The mass media demand it.

THE CHALLENGE OF THE MASS MEDIA

Teaching students how to handle the mass media critically and creatively is a challenge few teachers have so far accepted. Since the electronic world of the media bombards us with an assortment of sensory stimuli, we no longer live in a world where adequate response to only one or two kinds of stimuli can be assumed to be sufficient for intelligent functioning. As McLuhan has put it in *Understanding Media:*

> Just as we now try to control atom-bomb fallout, so we will one day try to control media fallout. Education will become recognized as civil defense against media fallout. The only medium for which our education offers some civil defense is the print medium. The educational establishment, founded on print, does not yet admit to any other responsibilities.

Public education must reflect on the accusation that it is still rooted in a premedia print era. That teachers are probably sick and tired of being told this does not make it any less true. Teaching people to read is not enough any more. Telling them how language works without asking them to undertake a disciplined investigation of different types of media is insufficient, and language learning without such investigation is probably irrelevant.

The teaching of English at all levels of public instruction is having a hard time catching up with the electronic era. With some scattered and sometimes notable exceptions, neither the curriculum nor the methodology of English has been able to shake clear of the traditional dependency on the written page. If it were simply a question of English education being slow to adapt to the spread of television, things would not be so serious. But English is not only oriented to a pretelevision age, it is in a premotion picture, preradio era. Teachers have generally not only neglected the mass media, they have failed to exploit or even use at all some of the most commonly available electronic equipment in teaching language and literature. But at this point, some concrete suggestions for action are called for.

APPROACHING LITERATURE VISUALLLY

If the study of literature, for example, is to produce a "literate" man and thereby fulfill its principal function of educating the imagination, it is important that literary experiences stimulate the student's imagination as strongly and as frequently as possible. For a variety of reasons, much of the literature that is taught from textbooks fails to achieve such stimulation. Printed linguistic appeals to the senses are generally undramatic and uninteresting compared to the multisensory stimuli of the mass media. It is no wonder that a television program or a motion picture can easily woo the pupil from the printed page. Is it possible, then, for teachers to lift a piece of poetry or prose off the printed page so that it will attack the imagination of young people conditioned by the mass media? Is it possible, for instance, to excite and stimulate both learners and teachers who have come through traditional educational programs to read and write poetry with heightened powers of observation and appreciation?

Two current projects at the University of Calgary provide some answers to these questions. One project involves the use of poetry as raw material for the production of motion pictures. The teacher begins by asking his class about a selected poem: If we were going to shoot a motion picture about this poem, where would we begin? What is the first thing we would see? Would we try to depict the first line literally, or would we lead up to it by shooting more generally for atmosphere? Would we need close-ups? Would we need human figures? Why? Where?

As the "raw script" of the poem is gradually structured in terms of the visual, the collective imagination of the class is sharpened. Perhaps for the first time the students are forced to think hard about the visual and dramatic details of literature. In doing so, they are probably "studying" a poem in greater depth than ever before. This approach, of course, is also a stimulating way to look at a scene from a short story, play, or novel.

A further sensory dimension is added when an accompanying tape-recorded sound track is planned. What background music or sound effects should we use? When do we read the words and when do we keep silent? How do we use sound to change mood and tempo?

At Calgary, we have put together samples of the kinds of short 8 mm color films and accompanying sound tracks suggested above. We have used inexpensive cameras and avoided the use of sophisticated equipment. We have then said to preservice and in-service teachers: If we can do this with simple equipment and without previous experience, so can you. We have found that they not only can, they do. Teachers and pupils who have never held a camera in their hands have been making short films and sound tracks to illustrate poems which they have selected themselves. The teachers report that looking at literature as the raw material for class-produced motion pictures has been an imaginatively dynamic experience for them as well as for the young people in their classes.

FILMS AND HAIKU

In a related project, an attempt was made to encourage motion picture production with poetry which preservice teachers wrote themselves. We hoped that this technique might stimulate the imaginations and heighten the powers of observation of preservice teachers so that they might do the same with their pupils.

A specific type of poetry, haiku, was selected for this project, since it was felt that this form would lend itself well to a multimedia approach. Articles in professional journals attest to the value of haiku as a way of motivating the writing and oral interpretation of poetry at a wide variety of instructional levels.

The haiku form developed in seventeenth-century Japan. It consists of a unit of three lines containing 17 syllables: five syllables in the first line, seven in the second, and five in the third. Traditional Japanese haiku usually contained a word to suggest the season of the year, and thus is seasonal as well as being sensual—involving imagery and mood. Modern haiku is more concerned with everyday occurrences which evoke personal thoughts, feelings, and emotions. Haiku provides an opportunity for the writer of any age or ability level to draw on his own personal background to arouse a response in the reader through a disciplined yet simple verse form.

In this project, preservice teachers were introduced to haiku poetry, wrote their own haiku, and read them to their fellow students. Samples of the 8 mm color films produced as part of the project described earlier were then shown to them, as well as film clips made by the authors, to illustrate haiku which they had written or which they felt might serve as motivational material for the writing of haiku. The students were then told that the motion picture camera belonging to the Department of Curriculum and Instruction was available to them to make a film clip to illustrate a haiku which they might like to write. They were taught to use the camera (which is very simple to operate), how to pan, zoom, fade, etc. They were then free to take the camera anywhere they chose. Film and developing services were provided by the department. When all the haiku were written and all of the film clips completed, a session was devoted to showing the films, reading the haiku, and critiquing both the choice of the "raw material" in terms of the content of the haiku and the filming techniques.

The students filmed a wide variety of scenes and situations. Much of the camera work was, as expected, amateurish, but that in no way diminished their enthusiasm for the method. One boy focussed on a pile of burning leaves, then panned slowly up the bare tree to accompany this haiku:

> Once those leaves had life
> And gave life to that gaunt form
> Their time is past now.

Another student panned the interior of the library:

Captives, golden caged
Scratch dry print for meagre crumbs
Outside, free, birds jeer.

Zooming in slowly on a sewer grating (manhole cover) produced a striking medallion-like effect, and these whimsical reactions:

You could have been square.
Where are your four perfect sides?
Put up with your fate.

A round mind is good
Far better than a square mind.
You're ahead of me.

Finally, this charming haiku from a student who set a swing in motion in a deserted November playground, then turned on the camera:

You, Cold Winter Wind,
Chased all the laughter away
Now I swing forlorn.

Student reaction to this technique was extremely positive. Most students wished to use the technique in their student teaching, and, as a result, a unit was planned which was taught by a number of preservice teachers at both the elementary and secondary grade levels. In addition, the film clips shot by the authors were shown to pupils at these various instructional levels, and haiku were written to illustrate them, thus reversing the technique. Among the haiku were these, written by "literate adolescents" at the secondary level:

Oh what a weekend!
With all the dancing and tears
It should have been fun.

Curly hair is out
And skirts are getting longer
This is called progress?

Sit there, calendar
You truly know how to live
Each day in itself.

One student produced this striking paradox:

He is different
In many ways, except
He is a foreigner.

Future projects involve producing 8 mm films and 35 mm color slides to illustrate other types of poetry written by pupils, including limericks, ballads, and cinquains. Prose selections, both pupil-written and textual, will also serve as "raw script" for other multimedia projects.

The literate adolescent is turned on and tuned in—on all sensory channels. The mass media is today, and tomorrow, and the future. Not only are the mass media and electronic equipment useful, they are absolutely essential to a concept of literacy which is sufficiently broad to encompass all aspects of critical and creative communication.

Rock Poetry, Relevance, and Revelation

Helen W. English

Classrooms in English have been too long emphasizing subject matter that is impersonal and irrelevant. No wonder warm bodies deposited in those 36 chairs are tuned out, spaced out, and burned out. Many of our students are underachieving, filled with unbridled hostility, uninvolved intellectually and emotionally in what passes as a lesson in English classrooms. Students often wear a sophisticated facade which says, "All right, try to interest me! This lesson is bound to be the same old boring routine, so why should I listen?" They rush to open the windows so that they can feel the fresh air and hear the noise of the traffic to liberate them from the confining, oppressive atmosphere of Cell 14 and the droning voice of the teacher. Students, numbed by the lack of variety in teaching methods, are so tuned out to the voice of the teacher, the dancing linear page of the book, and so burned out with the read, analyze, and report technique of teaching the traditional past that it is no wonder we see them depressed, daydreaming, and dulled intellectually.

To keep archaic teaching methods while updating content is like riding the painted pony on the educational merry-go-round. It always arrives where it started—in the same groove. Likewise, a teacher who resists change in a changing world had better get off the merry-go-round. Content has to be relevant and meaningful; method must stimulate and motivate.

Why shouldn't the content of a course be related to things in which students are interested? This question was something I asked myself when our high school gave us an opportunity to revise the curriculum; we became involved with

From Helen W. English, "Rock Poetry, Relevance, and Revelation," *English Journal* 59 (November 1970): 1122-27. Copyright © 1970 by the National Council of Teachers of English. Reprinted by permission of the publisher and Helen W. English.

instructional innovations—a nongraded, elective English program. Any subject matter we would choose would have to be nine weeks in length, and able to adapt itself to tenth, eleventh, and twelfth graders of all levels of ability since there would be no tracking.

Having taken a class in modern music and poetry at a northwestern university, I was excited about trying what I called a contemporary poetry class. Why contemporary? Mainly because it is happening "now" and with subject matter with which students are concerned. This course involved the exploration of the new sounds in contemporary poetry and the study of the movement of the rock music and its major themes. I wanted the subject matter to be relevant, personal, and affective. I wanted students to be able to experience poetry as it happens—through an emotional experience rather than an analytical experience. Music and poetry appeal to us emotionally when we apprehend the feeling the artist has expressed, but it appeals intellectually when we understand how the artist manipulated his material. So I wanted the student to experience poetry and to enjoy it, not to dissect it or to disintegrate it. I wanted them to hear it, not to read it.

Too much and too often, we teachers of English approach poetry through analysis. This method might be fine for the college prep student, who is more capable, but this analysis is where the average student gets turned off. Not all students are capable of handling the analytical approach, but almost all of them "feel" a piece of literature in some way, even though they may try to mask those feelings with a sophisticated air as though these feelings did not exist.

Poetry's primary purpose is to communicate experience, the poet's experience. When we are objective about a poem, we lose all that is subjective about it. A poet doesn't write a poem in an antiseptic vacuum, void of emotion and feeling. Why should we look at his creation with such a sterile eye and probe it always clinically and scientifically?

All art, whether it be poetry or music, focuses and organizes experience to give us a better insight or understanding of life. If poetry communicates the poet's feeling or emotive experience, it has a liberating effect on the reader or listener. It releases the inner sea of feeling. Music does the same thing. Daniel Kramer, in his book *Bob Dylan,* quotes Bob as saying, "We must respond as we see fit, and let our insides out." Roger Sessions in *The Musical Experience* (Atheneum, 1950) says music communicates in this way:

> " . . . the basic ingredient of music is not so much sound as movement, . . . it embodies movement of a specifically human type that goes to the roots of our being and takes shape in the inner gestures which embody our deepest and most intimate responses."

Music played on a stereo record player is sound in depth; it reaches to the roots of our being and liberates us emotionally. Actually handling any artistic content in depth, whether it be poetry or music, excites and arouses the intellect and feeling and often produces an appreciation of the content.

Jonathan Eisen in *The Age of Rock* (Vintage, 1969) says that " . . . rock now must be seen as an art form like any other that arises and talks to the people in direct, charged, and organic ways." Rock music certainly speaks to this generation of students. It is a medium that communicates and humanizes. Wiley L. Housewright, president of the Music Educators National Conference, stated in the *NEA Journal,* May 1970, about rock music: "Music is a humanizing force that can heighten communication in any era when human relations cause so many problems." Students listen to rock music constantly on the radio. One of my students said, "This is the Rock Age and we are Rock children. Let us understand and learn about ourselves and our music."

My major aims for the contemporary poetry course were to get the student to learn how to listen, to appreciate the sharp impact of poetry, to break down his inhibitions and to release the inner sea of feeling, to write his own feelings, and "to swim alone in a sea of sound" (Nat Hentoff in *The Age of Rock*). A school purchased text was *The Poetry of Rock* edited by Richard Goldstein (Bantam, 1969), although it was used only several days for browsing because we did not intend to read the lyrics or handle them separately from the music. The students sometimes used the books to sing along with the music when the lyrics did not come through clearly on the record. We found the music was very necessary to the response to feeling gained from the lyrics.

If it were true that this generation of students of the seventies, which we are teaching, are so television oriented and stereo oriented and turned off to the linear page as Marshall McLuhan has indicated, then I would have to include in the course as much of the depth of sound as I could and as little of the linear page as possible. So I tried methods of teaching which I had never explored together before. I decided to use the stereo record player and the cassette tape recorder and to eliminate the books and the personality of the teacher as much as possible.

The history and background of rock music were taped in 12- to 15- minute lectures. Using the cassette enabled me to stop the lecture at any point without losing a word and illustrate by a song or poem on record or tape. I tried to show the progression of the history of the rock music from rhythm and blues and country western through folk rock into contemporary rock, including raga rock.

Some lectures illustrated influences on music by such rock poets as Chuck Berry, Bob Dylan, Paul Simon and Art Garfunkel, John Lennon, and Paul McCartney. Other lectures on tape were based on the protest themes found in the rock music. I illustrated them with songs and poems on record and my own taped readings of contemporary poetry which fit the theme. I used some of the poetry of Joseph Langland, David Ignatow, William Stafford, Rod McKuen, Leonard Cohen, Louis Simpson, Kenneth Patchen, Clarence Major, Barbara Gibson, and others. Some of the themes in the music were these: Youth as a Victim of the Generation Gap, Alienation, Loneliness, Love, Our Plastic Society, Drugs, Anti-War, Freedom, Racial Protest, Civil Rights, and Sacrifices of Our Environment.

After a period of several weeks, all responses from all students improved. It took the academically talented and the remedial student longer to break out of their shells and begin to feel. Of course, when the academically talented student did break out, he was extremely articulate about his feelings. One student said, "Not many parents can break down a kid's inhibitions and really get to his feelings, but I think this class does. It helps a student to get himself together and find something to dig besides dope."

The lesson each day with the lecture, interspersed by songs and poetry, would run about 35 minutes. Generally, four to five songs and about six poems would be used. Here is an example of one day's lesson on the theme of Racial Protest:

Taped Lecture:
A short, two-minute introduction of the theme, stating mainly that the best protest is the strong affirmation of what you believe.

Records:
"Society's Child" Janis Ian
"Black Boys, White Boys," *Hair*
"The Streets of Your Town," Country Joe and the Fish

Taped Poetry:
"The White House," Claude McKay
"A Moment Please," Samuel Allen
"The Chicago Defenders Send A Man to Little Rock, Fall 1957," Gwendolyn Brooks
"How To Change the U.S.A.," Harry Edwards

Records:
"Oxford Town," Bob Dylan
"Mississippi Goddam," Nina Simone

Taped Poetry:
"If We Must Die," Claude McKay
"Between the World and Me," Richard Wright
"Dark Testament," Pauli Murray

Record:

"We Shall Overcome," Joan Baez

Student Essay:
Which song or poem left the deepest impression on you? Discuss your reaction.

Some days I turned the lights off, closed the curtains, and we sat in the dark, listening to music and poetry with no distractions. The last 15 minutes of each period was used for the student to write his feelings about what he had heard. I did not wish the student to analyze what he had heard, but to discuss it subjectively. All questions were affective questions. I encouraged students to talk specifically about certain songs or poems rather than to generalize about them and to tell what their reactions to them were. I found it was easier for students to write their feelings than it was to express them orally. Many of them would not have felt free to say orally what they said on paper.

The response the first two or three weeks was varied. I found that the academically talented student and the remedial student were both trying to conform to what they thought the teacher wanted to hear. The academically talented student was trying to be totally objective, but then hadn't he been taught daily to be objective and never let his true feelings show? The remedial student would generalize and say either, "I don't like that music" or "I like that poem," giving no reasons. The student of average ability gave the best response. It seemed easy for him to feel, and his ability to express himself creatively was stronger. He let the music and sound of poetry take him where it would go. He gave the best feeling responses and good reasons.

After a period of several weeks, all responses from all students improved. It took the academically talented and the remedial student longer to break out of their shells and begin to feel. Of course, when the academically talented student did break out, he was extremely articulate about his feelings. One student said, "Not many parents can break down a kid's inhibitions and really get to his feelings, but I think this class does. It helps a student to get himself together and find something to dig besides dope."

Since the class was primarily a listening class, students were graded on listening, which was a new experience for them, but they were willing to go along with it. They were convinced that they never had to listen in any other kind of class. Listening in this class meant that they could not talk to their neighbors while the music or tape was on, or read a book, or do papers for other classes. They could, however, tap their feet to the music, drum on the desk, doodle on paper, look out the window, close their eyes, put their heads down on the desk, and take notes without losing listening points. These classes were the quietest and the most attentive of any classes throughout the day. One student said, "Students want different things happening in order to pay attention and this is what this course is doing." Before class and during the time the students were writing, I always played the most current records or the records that they liked the most. There was a wide range in taste in music, but the students learned to be open-minded about songs and poems that they did not think they liked.

Since the teacher's homework was finished when she came to class, she sat at the back of the room, observing students and checking on the listening. Outside of the teacher's voice on the tape, her personality was out of the way. As one student said, "I was able to keep an open mind very easily during these lectures. The reason is that the teacher tried to present an unbiased point of view towards each rock group or entertainer or poet. She let us form our own point of view." Another student looked upon the records and poems as the teacher: "The records we had were like a teacher; they taught us many things. They taught us to bring out our feelings."

There was early in the course a short resource paper about a poet, rock artist, or rock group. All tests were essay with three-fifths of the questions being affective questions. At the end of the course, a poetry notebook, a collection of the student's favorite contemporary poetry, centered around one theme, was due. This paper was graded on the student's artistically or intellectually creative effort.

One day a young poet, who had just published a book of poems and had worked with a rock music group, was invited to read his poems to the class. Many students felt this was worthwhile, and it encouraged some of them to try writing poems, although this was never a requirement of the class.

By the end of the course, much was revealed in the change that had taken place in the student himself as indicated by his final evaluation of the course. I saw why the course was valuable to the curriculum of any high school. For one thing, it allowed the student to relax from the other tensions he had, while learning to understand music and poetry. One student who was always oppressed by her other classes said, "In here, I feel free and relaxed; my other classes upset me." Another student who rarely ever achieved a passing grade and who usually put other teachers into a state of shock said, "Every day in here is a day to remember. It's not the same old grind; every day is different. Every day is meaningful. It's not boring like other classes." This student was now sitting in class interested, working at taking notes, involved in sound, taking an interest in poetry for the first time in his life, even writing a little poetry of his own. One of the college prep students taking the class observed this, "I've noticed that the students who are usually not interested in school (the potential dropouts) are trying. I think this is great! What more can one ask from a course?"

Each hour that the class was taught, there seemed to be five or six students—those who always seem to be in the halls—hanging about the door, listening to the whole lesson. One day one of those students said to me, "This class is up-to-date. It makes kids want to learn and hear more. When can I sign up for it?"

Each student had his reasons why he valued the class. One student said, "I believe that the most important thing to learn in life is how to relate to other people and feel as they do and to learn how to deal with oneself and one's emotions. This class has helped me do this." Another said, "Listening to music and the lectures has made me think more about me and my place in life, and about important issues." Another student said after the third week that he was changing his viewpoint and attitude about a lot of things. He indicated the difficulty of the course, "This course is harder than geometry. In geometry all you have to do is homework, but in here you have to open up from inside your shell." Since there was no daily homework to the course, except supplying the teacher with records to illustrate with, this made the course seem more attractive to students.

One sophomore said about the contemporary poems, "They help me express myself when they hit so close to the core of my own feelings." An English course should make one aware of people, their feelings and dignity, that is, if we are at all aware of being humanistic. But probably the best evaluation came in a very short sentence scratched in almost unreadable script, "This class is necessary because it makes our lives a little more beautiful." Isn't it about time some of our English classes make a student's life "a little more beautiful" instead of oppressive, depressive, and repressive? Isn't the beauty of art taught in the schools going to feed our souls for a long time after we have graduated?

TEACHER'S RESOURCES

Rock Music

Carl Belz, *The Story of Rock* (New York: Oxford University Press, 1969).
Jonathan Eisen, *The Age of Rock* (New York: Vintage Books, 1969).
Daniel Kramer, *Bob Dylan* (New York: Pocket Books, 1968).
Arnold Shaw, *The Rock Revolution* (New York: Crowell-Collier Press, 1969).
Stephanie Spinner, *Rock Is Beautiful* (New York: Dell Publishing Co., 1970).
Paul Williams, *Outlaw Blues* (New York: E. P. Dutton & Co., 1969).
Jazz and Pop Magazine

Contemporary Poetry

Berg & Mezey, *Naked Poetry* (Indianapolis: The Bobbs-Merrill Co., 1969).
Arna Bontemps, *American Negro Poetry* (New York: Hill and Wang, 1963).
Paul Carroll, *The Young American Poets* (Chicago: Follett Publishing Co. 1968).
Leonard Cohen, *Selected Poems, 1956-1968* (New York: Viking Compass, 1964).
Dunning, Lueders, Smith, *Some Haystacks Don't Even Have Any Needle and Other Complete Modern Poems* (Glenview, Ill.: Scott, Foresman and Co. 1969).
Reflections on a Gift of Watermelon Pickle (New York: Scholastic Book Services, 1966).
Paul Engle and Joseph Langland, *Poet's Choice* (Delta, 1962).
John Hollander, *Poems of Our Moment* (New York: Pegasus, 1969).
Walter Lowenfels, *The Writing on the Wall* (New York: Doubleday & Co., 1969).
Paris Leary and Robert Kelly, *A Controversy of Poets* (New York: Doubleday & Co., 1965).
Rod McKuen, *Listen to the Warm* (New York: Random House, 1967).
Lonesome Cities (New York: Random House, 1967).
Stanyan Street and Other Sorrows (New York: Random House, 1966).
Clarence Major, *The New Black Poetry* (New World, 1969).
Ken Noyle, *Here Today, Zen Inspired Poetry* (Rutland, Vt.: Charles E. Tuttle Co., 1969).

Poetry Records

Today's Poets, Vol. 3, Scholastic Records FS 11003 Vols. 1 and 2.
Selected Poems of Kenneth Patchen, Folkways, FL 9717.
Anthology of Contemporary American Poetry, Folkways, FL 9735.
For Lovers, The San Sebastian Strings, Rod McKuen, Warner Bros. Records, 1795.
Some Haystacks Don't Even Have Any Needle, Dunning, Lueders, Smith, Scott, Foresman & Co., 03393.

Comics as Classics?

Charles Suhor

The value of comics has been a subject of debate in America for almost three decades. In the 1940s parents and teachers fretted over the degrading effects of comics on American youth. In the 1950s psychologists and educators investigated the claim that comics might be related to juvenile delinquency. More recently the comics have been viewed as a charming and highly revealing expression of popular culture, and exegetes of modern society like Marshall McLuhan and David Manning White have commented on the role of the comics in shaping modern life.

But the comics have seldom been considered from a purely literary point of view. "Literary" evaluations of the comics have typically consisted of irrelevant comparisons to more complex genres, without reference to the structural qualities that are unique to comics. The practice of comparing comics to novels recalls the simplistic methods of many critics in the 1940s who set out to demonstrate the inferiority of jazz by comparing the form of a Beethoven symphony to the *Saint Louis Blues*—invariably to the disadvantage of the latter. But a genre is not defined in terms of the characteristics of other genres. A haiku is not accurately described as a bad sonnet, nor can a sonnet be seen as a watered-down epic poem. A genuine literary criticism of the comics must begin with the comic genre itself.

Comics must be judged by special criteria, since the cartoonist's skill is an essential part of the total impression created by any comic strip. It is also evident that different *kinds* of comics are subject to different standards of criticism, because structural limitations differ greatly in the case of the single frame comic, the two-panel comic, the four-panel daily comic strip, and the full length comic book.

The creative possibilities of the comics have not been, perhaps cannot be, realized in all of these comic forms. The single frame comic, for example is intrinsically limited by its rigid format, which from *The Yellow Kid* (the first

From Charles Suhor, "Comics as Classics?" *Media and Methods* 3 (May 1967): 26-29. Copyright © 1967 by Media and Methods Institute, Inc. Reprinted by permission of the publisher and Charles Suhor.

real comic) to *Toonerville Folks* to *They'll Do It Every Time* has consisted of a humorous action in the foreground, commented on or complicated by one or more figures in the background. In the two-panel comic, the second panel simply exposes the chicanery or hypocrisy of a character introduced in the first. The cluttered canvas of the single frame comic and the pat formula of the two-panel comic have produced little more than occasional witty satirical barbs.

The full length comic book, or "funny book," has given psychologists much to toy with, but seldom has it produced anything of literary value. The comic books of the Disney-Schlesinger-Lantz variety have been consistently wholesome since the early 1940s, but clearly they are lacking in literary interest. They have had considerable influence on American culture, but it is the airy and limited impact of a Hans Christian Andersen tale or a Strauss waltz—a genuine but profoundly unprofound grass roots pop art. The few full-length adventure comics that offered, by accident or design, a kid-sized *Weltanschauung (Captain Marvel, Superman, The Phantom, Buck Rogers)* might reveal something about popular fantasy-patterns and stereotypes, but this is hardly a literary perspective.

It is in the four-panel daily comic strip that most of the comics that can make any claim to literary quality have appeared. The viability and appeal of *Li'l Abner, Pogo,* and *Peanuts* may be attributed to an instinctively creative response to the possibilities of an extremely confining genre.

The limitations inherent in the four-panel comic are manifold. The four-panel comic demands a simplicity in form and content and discourages extensive use of dialogue and virtuoso art work. The comic is basically a visual art, an art of action in which the action itself must stand out clearly against a simple, uncluttered landscape. Unless the cartoonist consciously uses these limitations as a gimmick and an identifying aspect of his style (as in *Smoky Stover*), the use of excessive dialogue and overambitious art work can destroy the clarity and pace of a comic strip. (Perhaps it was excessive dialogue that killed Crockett Johnson's brilliant *Barnaby* strip.)

The limitations in content in the four-panel strip spring from the limitations in form. How can the writer hope for any significant development of character, plot, and theme when working with a minimum of dialogue? Moreover, attempts at subtle development of a character or at introduction of a subplot are virtually impossible when the artist must confront the reader with such minute units of story each day. Compression is necessary: characters must be utterly self-revealing. They must react in caricatures of human emotion if the story is not to be protracted to absurd length—a practice which would run counter to the reader's desire to enter into a world that is clear and highly animated in content as well as in form.

The comic strip, then, is unsuitable for treatment of "serious" themes and characters. Adventure and humor, both of which are compatible with stereotyped characters, are adaptable to the comic page. Attempts at creating "drama" (*Mary Worth, Judge Parker, Rex Morgan, M.D.*) result in a comic literature that makes soap opera look like high art. The gag, the quick quip set in motion in the first panel and brought to a peewee crescendo of renewed comic anticipation in the last, is the format most natural to the comic strip. And indeed, a wide variety of comic characters—many of the "classics" of the comic world—fall into this category: *Blondie*, so true to American family life of the first half of the century; those misplaced vaudevillians, Mutt and Jeff; *Smoky Stover*, overflowing with outrageous puns and zany irrelevancies; *Bringing Up Father*, which turned the comic art onto the age-old problem of the uneven battle of the sexes.

But these famous comics, however quaint and steeped in Americana, only fulfill the comic genre. They do not rise above it, as *Li'l Abner, Pogo,* and *Peanuts* do. How, then do the best comics transcend the limitations of the genre?

PSYCHOLOGY AND SATIRE

First, they do excellently what all good comics do. The art work bears the unmistakable stamp of an original cartooning stylist, and it is uniquely *expressive.* The successful cartoonist brings a sense of motion to every panel, drawing the reader actively into the four-panel sequence with a remarkable sense of presence and immediacy. Al Capp is superlative in this respect. Li'l Abner's huge feet seem almost three-dimensional as he struts good-naturedly through a panel; Mammy Yokum's violently clairvoyant trances are as throbbingly alive as the heartbeat of Poe's famous tale; the bizarre ingredients that go into Kickapoo Joy Juice seem to evoke visually a terrible stench as Hairless Joe and his Indian pal stir the cauldron.

Charles Schulz's artistic technique in *Peanuts* is understatement. In his own way Capp's equal in expressiveness, Schulz can portray a sheepish, guilt-ridden grin, a grimace of exasperation or a bad attempt at suppressing hostilities with little or no overt action on the part of his characters. Schulz can, of course, depict motion magnificently when the occasion calls for it. When motion comes, it is typically spasmodic and consciously overstated, as in Snoopy's ebullient dances or Lucy's cyclonic shouts of anger that literally cause Charlie Brown to do a flip backwards. But the basic artistic device employed in *Peanuts* is not gross physical action but an essential restraint brought hilariously to life with a few economical strokes of the pen.

Clever cartoon styles, however, are not rare in the world of the comics. The three comics under analysis have, in varying degrees, two qualities that finally lift them to the sphere of art; they employ a creative use of language and, most importantly, symbolic elements either in the basic structure of the strip itself or in episodic materials. These symbolic elements are the vehicle through which the comic artist exposes foibles and makes his comments on society.

The freshest use of language appears in Walt Kelly's *Pogo.* While Capp is more faithful to the dialect of his characters than his predecessors were, Kelly's language goes far beyond relatively familiar dialects to a unique Pogo-lingo, an ingenious, purposeful distortion of language for comic effect. (E.g., Kelly's delightful Christmas carol parody, "Deck Us All with Boston Charlie," or a recent comment by a Pogofenokeean: "In my country we leave no stone unthrown for justice.") This is not mere malapropism but a creative toying with sounds and words, much in the style that John Lennon uses in his book, *In His Own Write.*

Moreover, in Kelly the dialogue is part of the cartooning style; it has graphic value. Kelly makes extensive use of selected words and syllables printed (or rather, "drawn") in boldface or small print to depict the vocal inflections in his characters' speech—in much the same way as J. D. Salinger. Moreover, Kelly not only portrays the dynamics of conversation more expressively through the wide range of graphic techniques at his disposal but he playfully interweaves bogus dialect stresses and submerged puns.

Kelly enlivens his dialogue with visual devices that comment on the character of the speaker of the quality of the utterance. At other times the cartography of the dialogue directly complements the action in the panel.

Schulz's use of language, like his cartoon style, takes a different form from that of Kelly and Capp. The characters in *Peanuts* alternate between kid talk and the most improbable adult diction. Charlie Brown says "I don't pretend to be a student of prophetic literature"; Linus, watching an ant, observes that "He's grinning in a knowing way"; Lucy won't stop crying: "Why should I deprive myself of an emotional outlet?" Schulz did not invent anticlimax, of course, but who else has been able to use it so integrally and persuasively in a comic strip?

The most brilliant individuating device used by great comic artists is the manipulation of symbolic materials. With Schulz a simple overriding device—the play of adult psychology within the winsome children who move about the panels—is employed in a variety of situations as several adult personality types act and react under the innocent guise of children.

This unlikely device "comes off" in *Peanuts* because of the magical combination of the basic child-adult masquerade, the clever understatement of Schulz's cartoon style, and the skillfully manipulated language. Despite the wide acclaim that the strip has received as a perceptive critique of modern life, however, it is high comic art by virtue of its synthesis of formal elements, and not by reason of any striking originality in its intellectual content. Schulz's material in itself carries no new insight into the nature of contemporary anxiety.

. The social commentary of Kelly and Capp, like the dialect, is in the Huckleberry Finn tradition in American literature. Pogo and Abner are innocents, lovable picaros whose spontaneous responses to social institutions throw light on the pomposity, evil, and waste in contemporary society. Kelly, of course, is the less incisive social critic. His strip was at its funniest and most popular in the 1952 presidential campaign ("I Go Pogo"), during which he goodnaturedly and quite transparently satirized the political scene with a portable smoke-filled room, two pinko cowbirds that spouted Marxian cliches, a clock transformed into a walking "political machine," an elephant and a donkey who agree to take turns winning at badminton and to share the same balloons in their dialogue.

Capp's gift for satire is well known. Indeed, Capp hits so hard and so often and at so many targets—Vietniks, social workers, foreign aid, television, the welfare state—that he might well be dampening the effect of his more penetrating social criticism. Still, future scholars seeking out an index of social problems of the mid-twentieth century in popular literature will find few more thorough and more amusing commentators than Capp.

Capp's upbraiding of modern society has taken many forms, but his most memorable—and most prophetic—contribution is the shmoo. The shmoo, Capp fans will recall, is a pear-shaped animal that solves all of humanity's problems. It lays eggs, gives milk, tastes delicious, reproduces with incredible rapidity, grows whiskers that serve as toothpicks, and, best of all, loves to give itself to mankind.

But with the discovery of the shmoo (when it escapes from the Valley of the Shmoon) come the problems that are inevitable when a society is freed from the burdens of existence—millions are put out of work, excessive leisure begets indolence and self-indulgence, the economy is in chaos. Capp foresaw and expressed through the comic medium the pitfalls of a prosperity that liberates man from the familiar world of drudgery, only to place him in a vacuum of inactivity which he has no resources to cope with. While the shmoo is certainly not a symbol of automation and cybernetics, it created problems of abundance and leisure which automation and cybernetics are posing for contemporary society. What happens, Capp is asking, when the American Dream comes true and a society accustomed to toil finds itself at last provided with daily bread—but robbed of its daily labor?

Capp, Kelly, and Schulz inherited the four-panel structure from their predecessors. Their genius, like that of Louis Armstrong in jazz, lay in their ability to inform an apparently static structure with a bristling artistic energy. With *Li'l Abner, Pogo,* and *Peanuts,* the comic genre achieves not maturity but a healthy adolescence: it is still "kid stuff" yet it is earnestly at war with the fraud and pretense of the adult world. Perhaps it will never grow to full size, but the American literary tradition is rich in examples of profound juvenilia, from Twain to F. Scott Fitzgerald to J. D. Salinger. The comic is American mirth, democratic mirth, the mirth of a nation so bent on equality and self-improvement that it must use its popular arts as media for education and as an outlet for the creative energies of its people. The logic can be expressed in a paraphrase of Schulz's Lucy: Why should we deprive ourselves of an outlet?

War in the Classroom: Mass Media vs. Education

Louis Penfield

Like it or not, in the conflict between classrooms and commercials, the textbook is finishing last. With the average high school student spending more time in front of the TV than ever before, mass media represents the biggest challenge facing American education today. How can we as educators compete with the deadly soft sell of Madison Avenue?

At first the answer seemed to lie in a more integrated curriculum. At Mayfield High, we began experimenting with the concept of humanities over eight years ago. Our main objective was to teach students the interrelationship of art, music, and literature with social and historical phenomena. Faculty members mapped out a plan for team teaching, scheduling several English and history classes to come together in the auditorium for 60-minute programs.

During a history period on the Civil War, for example, an art teacher presented slides on Winslow Homer and Mathew Brady and discussed how their art reflected the atmosphere of the time. And when social studies classes took up the problem of urbanization versus overpopulation, the teaching team presented the paintings of William Hogarth, the photography of Gordon Parks, and the writings of Jonathan Swift. Students compared Hogarth's vivid portrayal of eighteenth-century slum life—notably in "Gin Lane," with its drunken beggars, rats, and crumbling brickwork—with Gordon Parks' outstanding photographic essay on life in twentieth-century Harlem. They examined Swift's ironic satire "A Modest Proposal," a bitter protest against English exploitation of the starving Irish masses.

The humanities approach worked well, as it helped our students see that the problem of communications is a universal one with parallels in all forms of human endeavor. But gradually, we began to realize that our curriculum needed something more. It occurred to us that we were concentrating too heavily on historical events, whereas we should be focusing on what is happening *now*.

"Contemporary ideas" evolved as a new study unit encompassing programs on photography, contemporary architecture, design, cinema, and television.

From Louis Penfield, "War in the Classroom: Mass Media vs. Education," *Scholastic Teacher* (September 22, 1969), pp. 14-15, 36. Copyright © 1969 by Scholastic Magazines, Inc. Reprinted by permission of Scholastic Magazines, Inc.

Under this approach, English teachers assigned their students reports on a variety of art forms, including topics from Renaissance painting to pop art. One student set up his own light show, complete with strobe lights, slides, and music. Afterwards, class discussion centered on psychedelic art as a new concept, a spontaneous audio-visual creation in which the viewer is immersed in a totality of sound, color, and movement. Students and teachers had an excellent opportunity to evaluate this contemporary phenomenon.

To further develop our innovative programs, we were granted federal funds to conduct "A Study of Contemporary Art Forms." We decided to add experimental study units to the tenth-, eleventh-, and twelfth-grade English and social studies curricula, rather than to the art classes taken by only 10 percent of our pupils.

Slides, films, and photographs familiarized students with the best of twentieth-century architecture, design, and cinema—the works of Frank Lloyd Wright, Buckminster Fuller, Alvar Aalto, Edward Weston, Gordon Parks, Robert Flaherty, and many others. To focus on the immediacy of the present, we showed news photos through an opaque projector. For follow-up research and reports, students gathered information from current magazines and books.

One highly effective experiment dealt with evaluating photography. We literally covered the walls of our English classrooms with photographs to create an intense collage effect. Photos were clipped from current news and magazines such as *Life, Look, Seventeen,* and *Holiday,* and we included mediocre shots to give the display a variety of quality. As their first assignment, students selected a magazine photo to add to the collage, explaining to their classmates why they considered it a good picture. During class discussions, each student showed his photograph through the opaque projector, thereby focusing attention on problems of photographic composition.

Students next viewed films on the lives of great photographers, along with Edward Steichen's "The Family Of Man" and Louis Clyde Stoumen's "The Naked Eye," These films explore photography as an instant and direct means of communication. Students discovered that photographs not only express a way of seeing but also explore every form of human emotion.

As their next assignment, The classes created a complete magazine article. Each class decided on a theme—ranging from earthquakes to miniskirts—then wrote the story, gathered photographs, and pasted up a layout complete with captions, headlines and text.

The final phase was completed over spring vacation. Students chose either to write a research paper on a famous photographer or select a theme which they themselves would photograph. More than 60 percent of one class chose to try their hand with the camera—the final proof, I believe, of our program's effectiveness.

As a follow-up to the photography unit, we explored the cinema—letting students lead the discussions. Some became so interested in motion pictures that they experimented and made 8mm color movies on their own, and one entire class became involved in making a film.

Later, contemporary architecture and design were incorporated into the English and social studies classes, enabling students of the "now" generation to evaluate a total environment. As Frank Lloyd Wright stated: "Whether people are conscious of it or not, they derive countenance and sustenance from the 'atmosphere' of the things they live in or with. We are rooted in them just as a plant is in the soil in which it is planted."

All in all, our "Study of Contemporary Art Forms" has proved itself a strong competitor with that educational poacher, mass media.

Suggested Discussion Questions and Activities

1. **DISCUSSION** What do you see as the major reason(s) for expanding the meaning of literature as offered by the authors in this section? With which of their beliefs do you agree or disagree?

2. **DISCUSSION** Explain why you do or do not believe the expanding dimensions of literature identified by Farrell will facilitate the adolescent's search for self-identity.

3. **ACTIVITY** Wehr makes reference to several films and records appropriate for a variety of English programs.
   a. Check any catalogues in your school and/or university media center to identify film distributors and costs.
   b. Write to these distributors requesting their most recent catalogue and information on special programs for schools.

4. **DISCUSSION** Review Katz's list of similarities and differences between film and literature. Do you agree with his observations? Can you think of others? What is your reaction to his ten-week unit integrating film and literature? Would such an approach be appropriate for the secondary school? What changes, if any, would you suggest?

5. **DISCUSSION** Could the Cameron and Plattor haiku 8 mm film illustration be applied to other English activities? If so, which ones and what procedures would you follow?

6. **DISCUSSION** Is it appropriate to include rock and comics in the expanding view of literature? Explain your position.

7. **ACTIVITY** Design an activity built around film, theater, records, television, rock poetry, and/or the comics that might accomplish the same objectives as an activity that you have done or are planning to do in the classroom. For both the original and the new plan, indicate the objectives, materials, methods, and evaluation plans.

8. **ACTIVITY** Penfield's article describes a program with a variety of activities and student involvement. How can an average school, without special funding and without inflating the regular budget, develop a program like Penfield's? Anticipating typical budget director refusals ("Film rentals are not worth the investment" or "Paperback books wear out too fast" or "Television belongs in the home"), develop a rationale for allocating monies to an English program of media study. (You may want to wait until you have read sections five to eight before attempting this activity.)

SECTION FIVE

Paperbacks

THE ADVERTISEMENTS PROCLAIM:

"A Vital New Educational Tool . . . ." (Dell)

"The World Is Shrinking . . . Shrinking to Paperback Size." (Scholastic)

"Guarantee the Success of Your Reading Program with These Outstanding Best Sellers . . . ." (Harper & Row)

"Explore! Discover! Excite! Stimulate! Through the Use of Book-Movie Tie-ins" (Popular Library)

"THE PRINTED WORD. It's alive and well in PAPERBACK." (Noble and Noble)

THE AUTHORS PROCLAIM:

"In Defense of Trash" (John Rouse)

"Slow Readers—A Happy Experience" (Laurence L. Hardman)

"Here Comede Paperbacks" (Robin Mudrick and Michael F. Kelly, Jr.)

"think of the kids, too" (R. L.)

139

In Defense of Trash

John Rouse

I wish to say a few words not only in defense of trash, but in praise of it. By trash I mean popular novels and cheap fiction, the kind of thing your high school English teacher considered unfit for frivolous young minds in need of serious fare. The kind of thing everyone has read but no teacher can praise, much less introduce into the classroom, without calling into question her academic purity. This includes everything from the works of Ian Fleming and Edgar Rice Burroughs to the latest books by Irving Wallace, James Michener, and Rod Serling.

One might think such stuff hardly needs defending given its popularity and steady proliferation. The health of popular fiction is largely illusory, however, since hardly anyone reads anything, the sales of books being accounted for by an increasingly small percentage of the literate public. I would defend popular fiction, then, against teachers who do so much to discourage reading by showing contempt for the books most people enjoy. And as for praise, I intend to maintain that popular fiction has more value and usefulness in the typical high school classroom than the books now generally taught there.

First, an account of the typical literature program and how it got that way. The sad story need not be long in the telling. It began when college admissions officials met in 1899 to set down for the secondary schools their requirements for entering freshmen. At this time they established a list of "classics" that has dominated literature teaching in most of our high schools to this very day, a list including such works as *Ivanhoe, Silas Marner, Idylls of the King, A Tale of Two Cities,* and *Julius Caesar.* With one exception, none of these represents the author's best work, none can be considered a classic today. What they do represent is middlebrow taste at the turn of the century. Subsequent updatings of this list have usually followed the middlebrow standard, avoiding accounts of

From John Rouse, "In Defense of Trash," *Media and Methods* 3 (September 1966): 27-29, 48. Copyright © 1966 by John Rouse. Reprinted by permission of the publisher and John Rouse.

contemporary life in favor of safe classics that only the brightest and most docile students will read.

Sometimes an effort is made to engage the attention of students by giving them easier books. These usually turn out to be either simple tales of rustic innocence, like *Old Yeller,* or abridged classics, perhaps *David Copperfield* or *Jane Eyre.* In either case the selections are usually remote from the interests of today's adolescents, who do not need easy books so much as they need books that examine, even question, life as they live it and see it lived.

Programs have been dominated, then, by the classics—and by those minor works of great authors that pass for classics with the middlebrow. I would hate, in these crass, materialistic times, to be accused of preferring utility over essence, but I doubt if many of these works have any real usefulness. Just what does *The Scarlet Letter* do for a sixteen year old, I wonder? Of what use are *Julius Caesar, Moby Dick, Treasure Island,* and *Great Expectations* to their adolescent readers? Such questions are irrelevant to many teachers, who apparently regard the classics as grand and good things in themselves, like war memorials. The reader is expected to come away from them, perhaps, with a sense of pious satisfaction for having done his duty. I'm afraid he more often comes away with a sense of personal inadequacy and a hatred of reading. It's a high price we pay in "passing on the literary heritage."

How can we account for the curious fact that books which have delighted and instructed thousands are often regarded by teachers as bad, whereas books that have bored generations of schoolchildren and turned them against reading are thought of as good? Such views are not taken as evidence of woolly-headedness, I am sorry to say. They derive from an abstract literary standard that treats books as ends in themselves, quite apart from any immediate interest or usefulness these books may have for the reader. It is this standard that produces classroom anthologies constructed on the principle that what's difficult or dull must be good, and lists of required reading drawn up as though every kid in the class was going on to graduate school for advanced literary training. It is acquired by apprentice English teachers in college survey courses, where they learn that good books are objects to be admired, not experiences to be enjoyed.

Suppose we try a different standard, and define as good that book which gives the student a meaningful emotional experience. Then only rarely will a classic turn out to be a good book. The pleasure that comes from experiencing ideas, attitudes, and emotions the reader recognizes as relevant to his condition is provided for most people by books of less than the highest literary quality, sometimes even by trash. Anything worth doing with literature in the classroom probably depends on finding books that give this experience. To see a student interested in a book and concerned about the welfare of its people is a fine thing, whether that book is *The Red Badge of Courage* or *Road Rocket.* occasionally one of the modern classics may prove to be a useful book, but we can expect to help most students find their place in the modern predicament only through popular works within their intellectual and emotional reach. Teachers who feel comfortable only with masterpieces will find this a tough assignment, but if we believe that literature ought to serve the reader by helping him learn how to be at home in his own time, then we must turn to the books he can read.

How popular literature serves in this way can be illustrated from any period since mass education created the best seller. For example, there was Mrs. Humphrey Ward's *Robert Elsmere,* the publishing sensation of its day (1888). This story of a clergyman whose faith could not withstand the "new" skepticism was pretty strong stuff to the popular audience of the time. The critics could dismiss the author as a poor writer already out of date, a writer who relived the controversial issues of her youth long after the literary world had passed them by, but they had no more influence on the great reading public than critics do today. Certainly Mrs. Ward was not avant-garde, and judged by some strict literary standard she was no doubt a poor writer whose work is unreadable today by any audience. But the problem of skepticism and loss of faith she dealt with in *Robert Elsmere* was obviously a vital issue to her many readers, just as the recent announcement of God's demise is of general concern today. The service her work performed, then, was to give its readers an organized emotional experience with the intellectual issues that had shaped their times, and so give meaning to those times.

Ever since science and technology began transforming the social structure and value orientation of modern society, reading has played an important part in educating the emotions for life in that society. Old patterns of thought do not always fit the new conditions, and popular fiction, by giving expression to common doubts and fears, gives anxiety a tangible form and so makes it manageable. So that's what the trouble is all about! a reader may say to himself with some sense of relief. What the trouble is about, judging from recent fiction, is, for one thing, problems of moral choice. For another, it is the problem of finding one's own identity in the mass society (the search for personal identity and personal freedom having become something of a national obsession). These are the concerns that sell novels like *The Embezzler, All Fall Down, Hot Rod, A Separate Peace, Fahrenheit 451,* to mention a few.

Think of teachers going on year after year as if such concerns and such books did not exist, assigning ten more pages in the anthology (next week, the Colonial Period) and collecting book reports on *Lassie Come Home* or *Two Years Before the Mast.* No wonder students are convinced that teachers live in a world of make-believe far removed from the things that count. The girl who is worrying about the conflict between what her friends think is right and what her mother thinks is not likely to believe that *Pride and Prejudice* is just what she needs. The boy who is beginning to think that maybe he really doesn't want to be like his father is not likely to enthuse with the teacher over *Moby Dick.*

If we are ever going to make readers of young people then we will have to turn to the fiction of contemporary writers. And this means not just the work of the best writers, but the work of popular writers of all kinds. Perhaps

More to the point would be *Pickpocket Run,* * the story of a boy whose only prospect after graduating from high school seems to be working in his father's gas station and helping him cheat the tourists on whom the family depends for a living. Or *Two and the Town,* a new retelling of the old story about the girl in trouble. Or *Dark Adventure,* in which that lost soul, the high school dropout, searches for his identity. These are books more apt to shape the average adolescent's thoughts and feelings than such teacher favorites as *The Scarlet Letter* or even *Huckleberry Finn.*

We can find classics—like those just mentioned—that explore subjects of concern to adolescents, but the trouble is that they deal with experience at too great a remove from life as young people know it today. *Huckleberry Finn* has been one of the most popular books in the schools—with teachers. It has everything teachers think a book for young people ought to have including humor, adventure, a good "message," some literary allusions to be explained—all this and status as a classic too. Yet *Huckleberry Finn* is an astonishingly difficult book to teach to adolescents. They seem unable to recognize in Huck's flights from civilization their own struggles with the hypocrisies of adults and the pressures for conformity. The barefoot boy on a raft floating down the Mississippi is a long way from the booted teenager tooling along the expressway. And the humor is quite beyond their serious, even grim approach to life. Not that they don't need to take themselves a little less seriously, but Twain is not an author who can help them do that—not yet. Anyone who missed *Huckleberry Finn* at 12 cannot read it until 20.

Young people need books in the modern idiom, then, to help them work through—emotionally and intellectually—the concerns they feel are important. And any book that helps them do this will be a good book, whether or not it is admired by the cognoscenti.

Unfortunately, many teachers select books to satisy their own needs and not those of students. For example, there is the need to spend time (*Macbeth* can take up weeks). And the need for academic respectability. And most important of all, perhaps, is the need to keep students at a distance. Any book that touches on the actual concerns of life is apt to arouse the powerful emotional energies students bring into the classroom, and some teachers fear these as they would a riot. They need a barrier between themselves and the discomforting questions, the unsatisfied yearnings, the hostile attitudes behind those bored faces. The classics make an effective barrier and have been so used for generations. The classic is preeminently the safe book.

I take it for granted, however, that English teachers are not in the business of teaching literature, but of influencing behavior. Why teach a book at all unless it

Hooked On Books, (New York: Berkeley Publishing Corp.) by Dan Fader and Morton Shaevitz, reinforces John Rouse's contentions. It describes how the "unreachables" have been reached by giving children the books *they* want to read. The absence of "name" authors in Fader's "500" list at the end of the books is enlightening.

promises to change the reader in some way that makes him a more effective person? It seems to me that as teachers we should value a book above all for the help it gives us in shaping the interior world by which the student interprets his experience and guides his impulses into action. I suggest, then, that literary analysis be abandoned as a major classroom activity and that instead we spend the time helping the student explore the experience a book gives him. This means, of course, a frank discussion of real attitudes and feelings.

Some teachers will argue that after all, an inferior book may very well give a superficial or even false impression of life and would, therefore, be harmful to the student, perhaps by arousing his worst impulses. We can count on the classic, the argument runs, to be true in some deep and fundamental way. The argument sounds better than it is. First, the difference between poorly written and well written books is very often one of degree and not of kind. The difference is not simply that one book is good for us and another bad, one true and another false. Both may say something worth hearing, although one may say much more. The great themes are not found only in the great books.

Also, this argument assumes that the teacher's function is simply to explicate the book—explain the hard parts—and the student's function is to "learn" the book (in preparation for a test, no doubt). This division of labor is typical of classrooms where the great books are taught to students not ready for them. I think, however, there is no such thing as learning a book. All we can learn is what our response to the book has been, and the teacher's job, then, ought to be to help the student find out what the book means to him, and to help him test this meaning against his whole experience. In the end the student must be the one to decide whether the book is true enough for him.

The success of such teaching depends, of course, on finding books that will interest young people and that deal with matters important enough to provoke them to discussion. This is not easy. Good trash is a difficult thing to find. But not quite as difficult to find as a good classic.

Slow Readers— A Happy Experience

Laurence L. Hardman

When I came to Fort Hunt High School in the fall of 1966, I was very happy and enthusiastic about the English program for juniors and seniors based on six-week elective units and open to all average and above average students. However, I found I was to have one junior class of slow readers along with four regular classes. This class was made up of juniors who: (1) had a record of failure in English, and (2) read from fourth- to ninth-grade level. This was called a traditional English class—one in which I was to have the same students for the year, and in which I was expected to bring about an improvement in reading. The class contained 20 students from all economic backgrounds.

I was very much at a loss. We had a standard literature anthology textbook. We had a very capable reading consultant. However, I could not feel my efforts were satisfying. The students had little interest and, I was convinced, they made little progress.

What I *wanted* to accomplish were the following:

1. That the students would *like* reading.
2. That the students would enjoy talking about books, would feel *free* to talk, and would be confident of their expression.
3. That the students would have the *time* to read a large quantity of material.
4. That the students would be able to talk to *me* about their books.
5. That the students could *expect* passing grades if they read and had a feeling of achievement.
6. That the students could improve their reading comprehension primarily but also their vocabulary and reading speed.
7. That the students would receive some understanding of themes and symbolism.

A tall order. Something new and perhaps radical was needed. The answer, I found, was in *Hooked on Books* by Daniel N. Fader and Morton H. Shaevitz, Berkley Publishing Co. I resolved to give it a try.

To meet my objectives I would need:

From Laurence L. Hardman, "Slow Readers—A Happy Experience," *English Journal* 57 (March 1968): 405-8; Copyright ©1968 by the National Council of Teachers of English. Reprinted by permission of the publisher and Laurence L. Hardman.

1. Hundreds of paperback books of all types.
2. Time to meet with each student for 20 or 30 minutes after he had read his book. (This could mean that during the year the student would get three to four hours of personal attention from the instructor. Most English students do not get more than 20 minutes of personal attention from his English teacher in the entire year.)
3. Time to allow study periods in class.
4. A way to adjust reading levels to individual abilities and yet allow competition for grades as an incentive.
5. Freedom to grade as I chose.

Fort Hunt High School, fortunately, has great quantities of paperback books. The elective English program for juniors and seniors encouraged the use of paperbacks. I resolved to make use of this resource.

From all my classes I spent two days attempting to get a pledge of three or more paperback books from each student. By bringing at least one book they could become a member of the paperback library in my room. I reminded them that people seldom read a book twice, and that 1,500 books are left in the lockers at the end of every school year. Many throw them away or let them collect dust for years.

I wanted three of any kind (except spicy ones which I said would become part of my own private library if they brought them in). I would accept all levels from *Tom Swift* to *The Dialogues of Plato*. I would accept any subjects from mysteries and westerns to Greek plays. I found classics and great literature were *most* often the contribution.

I quickly gathered 700 paperback books. Some students brought 40 or 50. All contributed at least one. My other classes changed every six weeks, so I was able to collect books from other students in the next term.

By contributing at least one book the students were permanent members of the paperback library. It saved them money, and the library was well used.

Then I was ready to start the remedial program in my one class of slow readers. Motivation was my first concern. I talked at some length on the importance of reading. I showed each student his reading scores, when available, and reminded him of his poor showing in English and in other subjects. I took an anonymous poll to see how many had read how much. Several had *never* read a whole novel! Most had not read more than three. Only two read three a year.

I told them of the reading experience of students in other classes and pointed out the obvious: this very lack of reading experience accounted for their poor reading and thus for their lack of success in English.

I then proposed the following:

1. They could read anything.
2. They would be graded on *quantity* of reading alone.
3. They would be tested by me *orally* in a session after the completion of each book.
4. The following grade policy would be in effect, for the nine-week period:

1800 pages = C
2200 pages = B
2600 pages = A

I emphasized that 1800 pages were a minimum. There would be *no* D's. They were shocked but impressed by my promise that I would, by their showing, flunk all of them or give all of them an A, if that proved to be what they earned according to the scale outlined.

They could, if the book was boring, give it up and thus receive no credit; or read it and earn a bonus of 100 to 300 pages depending on my decision. In this way I could motivate them to read more difficult material. This motivation proved to be quite adequate. Some were quite amazed that they, F and D students, could earn an A!

I added a bar graph of this program on the bulletin board. This made it possible for them to display their achievements. Extending his bar after completion of his book became an important act for each student. It always attracted attention and it was a source of pride. I kept a personal record of each student's books and the credit he earned for each. The grades were usually good.

Class time was to be spent in reading their book or browsing. No other activities were acceptable. If their book was boring I encouraged them to start another as a change of pace and to keep the old one or give it up, depending on the situation. They began to be quite possessive of this in-class reading time. While the class was reading, I quizzed orally any student who had finished his book. After quizzing the student I tried to draw him out about the book. We often strayed to other topics related to the book. Thus we spent 20 to 30 minutes in each session.

I found, to my surprise, that the poorest readers wanted *me* to choose their new book. I often asked, "What do you like to read?" The answer was often, "I don't know, I ain't never read before." I asked questions from the list, Questions I, concerning such books as those in Books—Level I (given at the end of the article).

When he seemed to be ready, after months in many cases, after weeks in others, I encouraged the student to read books from those on the list entitled, Books—Level II. I asked, then, many questions from Questions II.

The results on the Nelson Denny reading tests are satisfying. There was a 21 percentile increase in comprehension, an 8 percentile increase in vocabulary, and a 1.3 percentile increase in rate. All this is above the *expected* rise in reading ability due to completing one year of school.

Tests can hardly evaluate, however, the endlessness of the new relationships and concepts, subtle nuances, and even the new facts that all of us realize are to be gained from reading.

I feel the students like to read. This feeling is based on our conversations. Most students gained confidence in their ability to read, their ability to talk about literature, their perceptions about theme, symbolism, and author purpose. Our conversations often reached the point of mutual enjoyment, enthusiasm, and appreciation of the book.

In conclusion, I feel that the program was a complete success. What began as a year of groping and doubt for all of us has ended as one of mutual enjoyment and gain.

QUESTIONS I

1. Did you like the book? Why? Why not?
2. Briefly describe the main characters.
3. Describe briefly the plot.
4. What was the climax of the book?
5. What was the mood of the book?
6. Which character did you like best? Least?
7. What, when, where, is the setting?
8. How was the story told (in whose words)?
9. What seems to be the author's purpose?
10. What was the book about?
    I asked about a specific incident from each quarter of the book.
    What happened when?
    Who did what?
    Why?

QUESTIONS II

1. What was the tone or mood of the book?
2. What was the point of view used by the author?
3. What sort of sentences and words did the author use? Long sentences? Difficult words?
4. What was the climax of the book?
5. Which character did you like–dislike? Why?
6. What does the author seem to think of the characters? Why do you think so?
7. What is the author's purpose or message?
8. What is the main theme of the book? Why do you think so?
9. Do you think the author's message is true? Do you agree? Why? Why not?
10. Did you find any place in the book where the pace was too slow?
11. Were the characters and their actions believable? Why so? Why not?

BOOKS–LEVEL I

Many books by Ian Fleming, Agatha Christie, and Erle Stanley Gardner
The Cross and the Switchblade
Red Alert
The Good Earth
Studs Lonigan
The Spy
The Green Beret
The Story of Helen Keller
The After House
Kim

Big Red
Skip Bomber
Tortilla Flat
Those Magnificent Men in Their Flying
    Machines
Old Yeller
The Preposterous Papa
How To Murder Your Wife
I Was a Teen-age Dwarf
Abandon Ship!
The Life of Thomas Alva Edison
The Autobiography of Ben Franklin
On the Beach
Stories of Suspense
Goodbye, Mr. Chips
Treasure Island
Robinson Crusoe
The Quest of the Snow Leopard
Mutiny on the Bounty
The Caine Mutiny
The Birdman of Alcatraz
The Angry Wife

BOOKS—LEVEL II

Alas, Babylon!
Animal Farm
The Catcher in the Rye
Main Street
Black Like Me
A Separate Peace
Lord of the Flies
Too Late the Phalarope
Of Mice and Men
The Red Pony
The Pearl
The Grapes of Wrath
Green Mansions
The Old Man and the Sea
To Have and To have Not
Triumph
The Iliad
The Odyssey
The Lilies of the Field
To Kill a Mockingbird

NOTES

1. *See* Ann M. Jackle, English Coordinator, Junior and Senior Level, Fort Hunt High School, Fairfax County, Virginia, "Safe for Diversity: Another Approach to the English Curriculum," *English Journal,* February 1967.

Here Come de Paperbacks

Robin Mudrick
and Michael F. Kelly, Jr.

"Wow! Look at all those good books."
"Can we keep them here in the class?"
"Are we going to start reading them today?"
"I've got firsts on the surfing book!"
The first morning was chaotic. We laid the books on several desks so that overlapping rows of colors, illustrations, and titles created a mosaic of paperbacks when our fifth and sixth graders entered the classroom. The reactions were electric. Questions and excited exclamations bounced off the walls of the old, high-ceilinged classroom.

What was evident from the beginning was the overwhelming impact of the classroom library and its natural advantage over the system's agency, the school library. Educators like Dan Fader and Dave Sohn have been telling us for years that books *can* turn kids on. What our modest experiment indicated was that the right paperback in the right atmosphere effortlessly scored with the kids.

We were also anxious to see the reactions of our nonwhite children to the newly created titles dealing with characters from minority groups. We also wondered how our white students would react to these books. It was the end of September and reading habits and patterns were beginning to be formed. Would the voracious readers be able to influence the less willing? Would the popular lightweight paperback overcome the heavyweight reading problems our students have?

Initial reactions were all affirmative, some samples:

Susan, a good reader, seventh-grade level, commented, "There are so many I'll be reading all day. I love to read. I never seen so many books. I like the one about surfing."

From Marvin, who keeps an immaculate desk: ". . . to show you we appreciate it, we will take good care of them."

From Lynne, "I think they are very nice and great. I love to read them and I like to look at them."

From Robin Mudrick and Michael F. Kelly, Jr., "Here Come de Paperbacks," *Media and Methods* 5 (February 1969): 40-43. Copyright © 1969 by Media and Methods Institute, Inc. Reprinted by permission of the publisher.

Michael, an alert student, said, "I would like the one about the war. It looks very good. I can tell by the top." And read war books he did, every one in the group.

Cliff, not an enthusiastic reader, spied the surfing book, grabbed it with a flourish and then asked for more on the same subject.

All books related to TV or motion pictures had immense recognition value, although once reading had begun not all of them held the interest of the students. Without question the most popular of these books were the ones relating to the gothic soap opera, *Dark Shadows,* shown daily on TV. All the books in this series were quickly grabbed and subsequently read. They are great interest holders and the students consumed them at every opportunity in and out of school. The books were in constant demand by the other students who do not have them and certain groups, particularly girls, tried to keep the books within their private circle until each member of the group had seen or read them. They seemed to be nearly as popular with boys.

The taste of the classes varied on a great number of books, but some patterns could be seen. The boys were most interested in books dealing with action and adventure, and most strongly with books dealing with war, particularly WW II. In this category such books as *Four Stars of Hell, The First and the Last, Night Fighter, Suicide Submarine* and *Fail Safe* proved to be very popular and were read by many of the boys in the class. The majority of the girls were turned off by these titles.

The girls preferred books which dealt with either teenage romance, gothic tales or mystery stories. *A Present for Rosita, Karen, Rosemary, Melindy's Medal, A Tree Grows in Brooklyn, Crossroads for Chela,* and *Who Wants Music on Monday?* were read by a fair number of the girls in the class. They were not read by any of the boys.

Many books were of interest to both girls and boys. Most popular here and those which created the most activity and the widest range of reading, were the books related to the mass media. Books tied into television and movies received great attention. Among the more widely read in this category were: *Around the World in 80 Days, My Friend Flicka, To Sir, With Love, Dark Shadows* (entire series), *The Incredible Journey, Star Trek, The Avengers, Tarzan, A Christmas Carol, Half a Sixpence, Fail Safe.*

Animal books did not find much favor with either boys or girls and such books as *Tark, The Otter,* or *The Peregrine Falcon* were totally ignored. Raquel Welch may be alive and bountiful, but Tark, the Otter is dead.

Sport books generally were read by the boys, and all the books on sports were read by at least three boys in each class. Whether the book was a true life story such as *Go Up for Glory* and *The Jim Thorpe Story,* or fiction such as *Hard to Tackle* or *Fullback Fury,* the books were read and given positive reviews by the boys. Some of the girls showed interest in the sports books, but none was totally read by any girl.

One of the classes decided on a system for cataloguing the books and checking them out. They put consecutive numbers on the books before placing them on the book shelf reserved for the classroom library. The titles were recorded in a notebook by two assistant librarians and the prices were also recorded alongside the number and title. The class decided that if the book were lost by a student, he would contribute the cost of the book or submit a comparable title. Ironically, in the two months we read the books, only one of the approximately 240 titles was lost. The girl responsible was so upset that she brought 40¢ in the very next day to pay for it and no amount of forgiveness could make her feel any better about it.

In conjunction with the filing system, a card file was kept for recording each person's reading record. The reader selected a book, recorded the file number, title, and date the book was borrowed on the card bearing his name. When the book was returned, the borrower recorded the date again. This gave the teacher an idea how long various books take to be read, which ones seem to come back quickly, and which readers are hung up on Charlie Brown and can't get off the hook.

A metal file card was kept on the teacher's desk and there was a constant stream of traffic between the file box and the book shelf at the other end of the room. A general rule was that books could be perused and borrowed whenever a given assignment was completed by the individual, even though others might still be working. Reading went on just about all the time, though, with the more avid readers squeezing in a page or two between classroom assignments. When one card had been filled, another was stapled on the back to continue recording the books. No time limit was imposed, which really afforded the slow reader a comfortable margin.

A sample card would be like this:

Last Name, First Name

Book#	Book Title	Date Out	Date In
111	*Beany Malone*	10/7/68	10/11/68
90	*The 101 Dalmations*	10/11/68	10/14/68
24	*Almost Like Sisters*	10/14/68	10/18/68

It was easy to check on the reading being done and about once a week the cards were checked and conferences held with students who seemed to spend too long on one book. Often the conversation would reveal that the book was too advanced and another book on the same subject was suggested.

Science fiction attracted readers, but the quantity of available material was not sufficient or varied enough to fully show its impact. Among the titles on hand, *Star Trek* was most popular. One boy made the telling point that his experiences made it easier for him to understand science fiction books such as *Star Trek* than books written about past history such as *The Pioneers*.

Because of student interest, book reports no longer had the onus they used to have. Reports were aimed at other members of the class (not the teacher) and reading was done by the students for their own pleasure and information. Not every book read was reported on, and when a book had been returned to the library, it could easily be referred to again if a report was decided upon. The variety of reporting techniques also encouraged extra reading since artistic, musical, or otherwise talented students have found fascinating ways to share what they have read with others. Book reviewing instead of reporting was encouraged. Sixth-grade students went beyond relating factual parts of the story and became involved in critical analyses of particular books.

The lack of pictures, which was a negative aspect and drew criticism, at times proved useful as students expressed themselves through related activities, such as drawing illustrations for the book.

Other criticisms came to light in this analysis which indicated particular problems with paperback books. Among them were physical construction and the degree of difficulty in the vocabulary used. Among the comments made were that the books were hard to handle; students were not used to the size and were at times inconvenienced because they had been used to having their reading material placed flat on a surface.

This was true for most of their textbooks and other classroom reading material such as *Weekly Readers* or *Junior Scholastics*. The students mentioned that they could put the books down without putting a book marker in the page they were reading, and since they were not used to this, they sometimes lost their place. Another small problem in the physical make-up of the books that was expressed by some students was that if they were read by a number of students the binding on some of the books would weaken and some pages would drop out or become lost.

The print of the paperback book is generally smaller than that which appears in elementary classroom textbooks. To the slower readers this presented a slight problem. As they began their reading, they had some trouble following sentences from one line to another, but after continuing with the story they overcame the problem.

Along with the print was the problem of the vocabulary used in the books. The good readers in the class had no problem with words, but many students began books that they soon lost interest in because the words were too difficult. A prime example of this problem was seen in the use of the two copies of the Bill Russell book, *Go Up For Glory*. A boy, an above average reader, had some difficulty with the original version, and though he wanted to read the story very much (he is a basketball player) he became discouraged because he was having trouble understanding the words. Given the adapted version, he felt completely at ease and read it to its conclusion.

On the whole there were very few criticisms about the physical condition of the books and the students generally felt pleased that they could carry their paperbacks wherever they went.

Titles, attractive cover art, and the general make-up of a book played an important part in its selection. Students mentioned that they would purchase copies of the books they were reading if they saw them on newsstands (providing they could afford them). They were generally pleased with the variety of paperbacks they had and felt that the books that they could get in the library were not as new or as current as the paperbacks they had in the classroom libraries.

War titles raised another interesting issue. These books reminded the boys of regular paperbacks on store displays where the reading level was too difficult and type too small for their pleasure. When it was discovered that these war books were written so that they could understand them, the clamor for them was tremendous. One boy even counted all the war titles and proclaimed that there were enough in the collection for each to read one at the same time and the clamor died down to a mere argument over who would get *P.T.109* first!

The amount of reading generated by the paperback library was obviously greater than it would have been if we had utilized only the school library. One fifth-grade child, reading at the second-grade level and in a special remedial class, had completed six books by the beginning of December, equivalent, he claimed, to his previous lifetime consumption of "real books." He had read and reported on *To Sir, With Love* —a book certainly far above his tested reading level. When asked about how he managed some of the harder words, he explained how he would ask someone, and if he were alone, he would try and figure the words out.

One of the most amusing happenings associated with our classroom library was the election of a librarian to see to the cataloguing and general upkeep of the books. As often happens in a peer group situation, the child with the lowest tested reading level in the class, and the one having a great deal of trouble with spelling and handwriting, was elected to the post of librarian. It was a fair and square election, though, and amazingly that child has now read eight books in eight weeks. Can we surmise that being librarian has at least doubled the amount of books he would have read had he not been elected?

We feel the following generalizations can be drawn from our paperback experience:

1. There is a wide range of interests that pleases both boys and girls.
2. Most of the boys are attracted by war books, science fiction, sports, and action stories; girls by the stories about teenagers, romance, and mysteries.
3. Books relating to movies or television have considerable appeal, and they are generally read.
4. Thin books attract readers.
5. There should be more illustration in most books if publishers want to reach young readers.
6. Difficulty with the binding of paperbacks creates handling problems.
7. Smallness of print is sometimes a negative factor.
8. Paperbacks, per se, have considerable impact as a stimulus to reading.

"...think of the kids, too"

R. L.

Early one morning I received a note in my mailbox instructing me to "drop in" to the principal's office during my free period. The millenium had arrived.

"It has come to my attention that you are having some of your students read a book called *The Invincible Man.*"

"Oh yes, you mean Ralph Ellison's novel *Invisible Man.* My eleventh-grade students are reading it."

"You had them buy it themselves?"

"Yes, it's an inexpensive paperback which they unanimously agreed to buy."

"Is that a Regents book?"

"I beg your pardon?"

"Is it a Regents book? You know, the Regents exam in June."

"Gee, I really don't know; but it is artful, and it reflects many of the problems of selfhood our young people face."

"Did you consult your department head about using this book?"

"I mentioned that I was planning to use it."

"But did she actually approve it?"

"I don't think she committed herself one way or the other; she did say she had heard of *The Invisible Man* by H. G. Wells, but that's an entirely different book."

"The people of this community have given us the grave responsibility of educating their children. That, I'm sure you understand, is a big job. And it takes big money, taxpayers' money. You know, a lot of that money is budgeted for the purchase of books. Now if you have the students buy one paperback, and if the social studies teacher has them buy one, and so does the chemistry teacher, it can become a pretty expensive ball game for all concerned."

"I understand what you're saying, but it was a voluntary situation. I even offered to buy copies myself for students who might find the cost prohibitive."

"I've been receiving calls from parents who don't think their children should

From R. L., "think of the kids, too," *Journal of Reading* 12 (February 1969): 377-78. Copyright © 1969 by the International Reading Association, Inc. Reprinted by permission of IRA.

read this book. Now I'll admit that these are fairly conservative parents, but they are taxpayers, and when we get calls like this, after all, we owe it to the parents to find out what's going on in the classroom."

"Of course. What do these parents find objectionable about the novel, sir?"

"Basically, it's the obscene language and the subject matter."

"Did they mention any specific chapters?"

"Well, one parent I spoke to was shocked by the first chapter."

"So was I. I think the author wants us to be shocked. But if you examine it in the context of what happens and what is said, I think you'll agree it is both truthful and artistic."

"Can you imagine how much time would be lost if I sat down and read every book that every teacher used? But that's beside the point. This particular parent felt that if the first chapter was that bad, God knows how bad the rest of the book must be!"

"Don't you think that's a rather hasty decision—I mean after reading only one chapter?"

"And another thing. These kids are saturated with this civil rights stuff."

"What do you mean?"

"Well, they get it on TV, in the newspapers, in social studies classes, everywhere. Enough's enough, don't you think? Now I don't object to an occasional discussion, but when everybody emphasizes civil right, even in English class, I begin to wonder where it's all going to end."

"Well, sir, the novel explores more than social issues; themes like growing up, discovering who you are and who you aren't, and deciding what to do with your life. The novel does a lot more than protest for black people."

"How are you going to prove this to the parents? Can you justify teaching the book . . ?"

"I thought that's what I was just doing."

"But to eleventh graders? . . . . in this community?" (deadly silence)

"Well, I'll see what I can do. Perhaps a back issue of the *English Journal* might have . . ."

"You do that. Get some materials together, and just drop them in my mailbox tomorrow."

"Tomorrow . . . yes, sir."

"Oh, and . . ." (turning to leave)

"Sir?"

"I do believe in academic freedom, you know . . . to a point. We've got to be reasonable about it, though. I don't mind a little academic freedom, but we've got to think about the kids, too."

"Yes, I agree."

Suggested Discussion Questions and Activities

1. **DISCUSSION** Rouse's "defense of trash" is
   a. an excellent satire on modern reading
   b. not worthy of rebuttal
   c. right on the mark
   d. all of the above
   e. none of the above
   Your answer   Explain.

2. **DISCUSSION** Do you agree with all of the procedures suggested by Hardman? If not, what would you change and why? How successful might this program be with other than "slow readers"?

3. **ACTIVITY** What are some ways an English department can provide a variety of paperbacks to implement the Rouse, Hardman, and Kelly and Murdick suggestions?
   a. Write to several paperback companies and ask for their catalogues, information on special rates, and suggestions for starting a paperback store or club in a school.
   b. Consider the possibility of actually starting a paperback bookstore or lounge. Talk with someone in business education about the feasibility of a student-run paperback operation combining the interests and talents of students from both departments.

4. **DISCUSSION** What would you have done in the "think of the kids, too" situation? Do you think the situation occurs frequently? Besides the students and the teachers, who is involved—directly or indirectly—in classroom decisions, such as book selection? What is the best procedure to follow when a decision is to be made about a potentially controversial situation?

SECTION SIX

News, Newspapers, and Magazines

WHO: John H. Langer, Laura S. Johnson, Lurene Brown, Helen B. Wachs, Howard F. Decker, and Thomas N. Walters

WHAT: Educational suggestions for the study and use of news, newspapers, and magazines

WHERE: In and out of the classroom

WHEN: Now!

WHY: "When enough of our people make the comparison between what can be and what too often is, they may insist upon improvement.
JOHN H. LANGER

"I found the newspaper the means for getting these students moving again in reading, and I recommend it without reservation to the teacher who has people who say they won't read."
LAURA S. JOHNSON

"The cartoon, found in almost every periodical seen . . . represents the perfect teaching device . . . for training young people to see situations as they really are, to take themselves a little less seriously, and to appreciate another of the many kinds of communication."
LURENE BROWN and
HELEN B. WACHS

"I have used the newspaper for several years with both accelerated and remedial students in both sophomore and senior classes. The results have always been good." **HOWARD F. DECKER**

"'. . . While I cannot claim absolute success in carrying out this plan, the attempt was predominantly worthwhile and should be of interest to other teachers of English, concerned with the magazines published for and read by their students.''

THOMAS N. WALTERS

The News Media
and Social Science Teaching

John H. Langer

Today's emphasis on current events in secondary and elementary school classrooms requires that teachers provide their students with background and guidelines for understanding what is printed or broadcast as news. The general assumption that objectivity and accuracy in reporting can be counted on should be particularly suspect in the light of recent occurrences. Teachers should provide a healthy, critical skepticism, along with a set of criteria for evaluating the media and their messages.

There is fierce competition for the day's lead story, and yesterday's events are seldom recalled unless they can recreate excitement in the reader. Deciding which stories to headline or broadcast is done by a relatively small number of people in news wire service offices and editorial rooms of communications media, as Vice President Agnew has recently pointed out. The difficulty in making good choices from among the multitude of events requires a rare blend of experience, knowledge, and moral judgment.

The experienced, ethical news reporter or editor deals with facts as he finds them and tries to provide a report that is both logical and consistent with the facts. But newsmen are human: They work at a fast pace and do make mistakes. Anxiety about the consequences of error causes certain elements of the press to foster the notion that they alone must be judges of their conduct: Irresponsible journalists must somehow be exempt from personal responsibility. This attitude and reluctance to admit error serve us badly, for they put ethical, hard-working newspeople under a cloud. A generally accepted code of ethics for the news media is long overdue. Short-range solutions include holding individual reporters strictly accountable for the effects of negligent and inaccurate reporting, and

From John H. Langer, "The News Media and Social Science Teaching," *Phi Kappa Deltan* 51 (February 1970): 318-20. Reprinted by permission of the publisher and the author.

instituting special training programs for the beginning reporter and editor. Of course, as with attorneys and physicians, self-policing is eminently desirable and efforts are being made.

Serious distrust of news media has developed in recent years. Reactions to the Agnew speeches of last November point it up. It is significant that after the riots at the 1968 Democratic National Convention in Chicago the press was attacked from different sides for bias. Even though most commentators and news reports were critical of police tactics, 75 percent of the public reaction was in support of the police. The public, knowing that they were not seeing everything that was occurring, discounted reporters' opinions given as on-the-spot news.

Subsequent to the vivid TV coverage, news stories strongly suggested that there were in fact dishonest reporting and abuses of the public trust placed in licensed media. (Later investigations confirmed this.) Here are some examples:

Item: (William Chapman, *Los Angeles Times-Washington Post* News Service) A study by the National Commission on the Causes and Prevention of Violence said: "The media, particularly television, created the stage on which demonstrators [at the convention] planned to carry out their protests through confrontations and 'street theater.' " The report quotes police as complaining that the press intentionally or accidentally helped the demonstrators, and that:

> some newsmen 'faked' stories and repeatedly attracted demonstrators by their presence . . . Senator Gale McGee (D-Wyo.) is quoted as saying that he saw two girls led by a television camera team to a spot near National Guard troops. With the cameras rolling, the girls started crying, "Don't beat me! Don't beat me!"

Item: (UPI, in the *Indiana Daily Student,* January 7, 1969) "A government investigator said yesterday a marijuana party attended by Northwestern University students and televised by a Chicago station was 'prearranged for the benefit of CBS.' " The Federal Communications Commission investigated and found that there was poor judgment on the part of an inexperienced reporter in the case.

Item: (Tom Littlewood, *Chicago Sun-Times*) The President's Commission on the Causes and Prevention of Violence heard testimony from T. A. Foran, a U.S. Department of Justice attorney in Chicago, and an assistant, James Casey, that witnesses saw camera crews from CBS film events that witnesses believed were staged. In one incident "two girls dressed in nurses' smocks were tending a prone victim, who, Casey said, walked away after the TV lights were turned off." Comments by Federal Communications Commission members included observations that "broadcasters are concerned more with profitable speech than free speech," and, "the impact of television is an ingredient in many social ills."

How can teachers handle the problems of lack of confidence in news reports and the requirement that students use accurate data on which to base judgments, draw inferences, and develop conclusions? Some specific caveats may be helpful.

Provide an opportunity for students to learn the relative value of different news sources. Quotes in context from persons clearly identified as authoritative are more reliable than "informed sources." It is certainly legitimate for reporters to protect their sources; yet if the net effect of the news item is to give the impression of truth when in fact the news is based on hearsay or rumor, then it should seem more ethical to include it in a political "gossip column" than to report it as news or euphemistically as "analysis."

Students should be taught to find the facts in a news report. Yesterday's rumor may or may not be today's fact. Students can, by comparing a series of news reports on a single on-going event, discover how so-called facts change, are left out, or are revised in different newspapers and magazines.

Students should understand that columnists or commentators have the right to express opinions in print or on the air, but that opinion and fact differ, and opinion in print is often a substitute for facts not available. "There is speculation" may mean that many people are speculating, or that only the writer is doing it.

Students should know that there is, occasionally, careless or dishonest reporting. The New York Times reported that Dag Hammerskjold, the late U.N. secretary general, had arrived at a Katanga, Africa, airfield and had departed in a jeep for a meeting with secessionist leader Moise Tschombe. The next day the *Times* reported that Hammerskjold had never reached the airfield but had been killed when his plane crashed en route. A reporter had apparently cabled his story in advance of the anticipated meeting.

Students should understand that time may make more facts available; they should not expect the press to have or report them all. Often only one side of a story is available to the press. Good reporters try to indicate this somewhere in the report. Yet in an important event the fact can be lost in a long list of details. Robert Oppenheimer, the great nuclear scientist, was investigated as a security risk in the early 1950s. Long after being denied access to Atomic Energy Commission laboratories, he was awarded the nation's highest civilian honor for service to his country. The story that made front page news was suspicion of the man's loyalty, not his long and worthy service.

Students should be shown how press reporting of emotional responses of public persons can stimulate others to those same emotions. At least one member of Congress called for a nuclear attack on North Korea after the *USS Pueblo* was captured. The final disposition of the case was very different, of course, yet there was an immediate public response, which if translated into action, might have led to more bloodshed.

Long- and short-range effects of media news treatment, especially television, strongly affect public opinion. Sympathetic treatment of Japan and Germany by the media have helped install them as friends of our nation in the minds of the public since World War II. China and Russia, on the other hand, receiving a bad press since 1947, have become objects of deep hostility. The reverse was true from 1939 to 1946. France, receiving a bad press during the de Gaulle era, is now slowly recovering status in the U.S. public mind, though its policies differ only in degree from policies of the de Gaulle period.

Students must understand that the free press and broadcast media are profit-making enterprises. As is true in any business, they must please their advertisers and earn a profit to pay their employees and stockholders. The need for circulation provides a constant temptation to add "excitement" to win a wider audience, and to censor news items which may lose advertisers, readers, or viewers. The limited use of editorials on television and radio is directly proportional to the ease with which they, when compared with newspapers, are "tuned out" of the home.

A currently controversial issue has arisen regarding the role of the press in demonstrations. Lawful demonstrations are well served, it is urged, by objective reporting. But when the demonstrations become disorderly, violent, and so unlawful, the press becomes a vehicle for the spread of the disorder. News people have not yet satisfactorily reconciled the problem of being "used" or exploited by special interest groups whose only means of gaining attention is through the press. Press people usually disclaim responsibility for the effects of their presence, while still claiming the right to be on the scene as objective news reporters. Yet it has been demonstrated that at least some social disorder would not have occurred had the press been absent.

Can news media claim to be neutral when they are actually vehicles for the dissemination of the views of groups whose intention is to exploit the media's need for "excitement" to gain publicity? Certainly careful judgment must be exercised by news media, or their critics will insist upon external controls. The Urban League's Whitney Young commented, no doubt with some exaggeration, that Negro militant Stokley Carmichael's following consisted of 50 Negroes and 5,000 newsmen. Certainly the reasoned responses of black leaders are less frequently reported than the more bellicose utterances of militants. Reporters and editors seem to have a built-in bias for controversy: No conflict, no news. The emphasis in a story is usually on the problem, less often on its solution. When 50 people walk out of a gathering of 5,000, too often 45 seconds of TV time is given to the walkout and 15 seconds to the speaker and his message.

The ideal of free and honest reporting has certainly not been reached. Accurate information has always been essential to individual participation in the democratic process: the need is critical. There is no substitute for the media we have for reporting events. Therefore they must be made as effective as possible. Government censorship is no answer; but this does not justify censorship by reporter, editor, columnist, or publisher.

A widely accepted code of ethics for news media is long overdue. It can come only if the public understands the problem and demands a solution. The media themselves can be (and some are) helpful by making clear distinctions between news and opinion. David Brinkley recently complained of being recognized as a celebrity rather than as a newsman, evidence that the personality of newsmen may affect audience perception of a report.

Legal remedies against media for damage to reputation are difficult to apply. One solution might be to make the individual reporter personally liable for damage resulting from negligent reporting, and the editor for his editing.

Incomplete reporting of facts could be cut down considerably. Police reporters and headline writers would have much less leeway.

The above are only possible solutions, difficult to apply. A more certain long-range solution is for teachers of elementary and secondary social studies to make our future news people more conscious of the moral and social consequences of irresponsible reporting. If we can also educate the news consumer to distinguish more clearly between fact and opinion, he will soon insist upon more accuracy and honesty in media reporting. The public is only now beginning to develop awareness of the effects of inadequate, ineffective, biased, and inept reporting of the great events of our time.

Infrequently, the media do rise to greatness, as in the reporting of the landing on the moon. With this as a standard, teachers can make judgments upon the daily, routine reporting in our media in the teaching of current events and social science. When enough of our people make the comparison between what *can be* and what too often *is*, they may insist upon improvement. A democratic society must be served by a free press; but no news medium which has lost its integrity deserves to remain free.

The Newspaper: A New Textbook Every Day— Part I

Laura S. Johnson

A basic requirement in the ESEA Title III grant for the establishment of a Diagnostic and Remedial Learning Center in our school last year, was that it be innovative. My part in the program was to work, through language processes with emphasis on reading, on a one-to-one basis with 20 students (all except two of them being boys ranging in age from 16 to 19 years) who were having learning difficulties in high school. Their trouble ranged from underachievement to severe misbehavior, and their number represented only a small fraction of that much larger group also having trouble achieving academically. With these few individuals, however, I hoped to evolve a rationale for the selection of materials, and I hoped to work out techniques for using them which could be adapted to larger groups. I believed that maximum effective individualization of reading

From Laura S. Johnson, "The Newspaper: A New Textbook Every Day—Part I," *Journal of Reading* 13 (November 1969): 107-12, 164. Copyright © 1969 by the International Reading Association, Inc. Reprinted by permission of the IRA and the author.

instruction could be achieved through the types of materials constantly available to students rather than through the number of teachers constantly available to students.

When I began, some of the students, though conscientious and still willing to try, were very discouraged with their past performance; they had just about given up hope of ever having anything good happen to them in school. That they did learn to feel better about themselves and their ability to achieve was summed up by one of them near the end of the year when he said, "At the beginning the picture was pretty sad, but now things are looking up."

Others in the group seemed headed straight down the dropout trail, unless the pushout trail came up first because of their obnoxious behavior. One of them put it this way when he showed up: "There ain't a rule this school can make, that I can't think of a dozen ways to break."

Their economic and social backgrounds were varied, ranging from the bottom to the top of the occupational scale. One was Mexican-American; the rest were white. All had average and above-average mental ability. Most of them had attended "good" suburban schools during their elementary and junior high school years. They had been exposed to the advantages considered prime requisites for success in school, but few had "taken." For high school students, all of them were poor readers. On a Triggs Survey Test given when they entered the program, their scores ranged from third- to seventh-grade reading level; WRAT scores in arithmetic and spelling were correspondingly low. All of them could be expected to have difficulty attaining even nominal success in the structure of the traditionally elite-oriented secondary school; most of them were failing or ready to drop out.

The Detroit Tests of Learning Aptitude indicated perceptual handicaps for all of them. For most, the deficiencies were visual or auditory. Two of them had considerable disorientation. Two were physically immature for their age. And so it went on down the list. As our staff met and discussed the students individually as well as collectively, their problems became more complex the further we went into them because of the emotional overlay of years of failure and frustration piled upon years of educational neglect of their specific impairments. Our staff members became more aware, too, that we were hovering with less distinction over the fine line separating the semantics of Learning Disabilities from what we became more inclined to term Learning Difficulties. Finally our psychologist resolved the problem of identification by saying, "Look! These kids are in trouble. Let's see what we can do to help them and forget about what to call it."

So I did, and took my cues for what to do for them by listening to what they said as they introduced themselves to me the first week of school (it took that long for some of them to show up).

"Don't gimme none of this jazz about readin', unnerstan', 'cause I ain't takin' none of it, ya unnerstan'?"

"If this is some more of the same old hash, no thank you. I'm cuttin' outta this joint anyway—before the Dean throws me out. He says he's lookin' for an excuse; it ain't gonna take me long to give him one."

"Who needs to read? I say, Babe, keep your eyes and ears open, and you can get along."

"Read a book? Why should I? The good ones are made into movies and they're a whole lot easier on the eyes."

"My counselor is an old ***. She says I'm stupid 'cause I can't read."

"You want to know something? I'm going to slit that *** teacher's throat if she asks me again, 'Where's your book?' "

Innovate?

What else could I do?

Whatever happens, I thought, it must not look like school or sound like school. But it must open up again the chance to learn, and it must arouse a willingness to learn. I must understand the desperation, the boredom, the ignorance, the bravado, and the hostility which their words express about the school's impact upon them. What in it felled them, I wondered? Where, along the way, did proportion get lost? Was it the school or their dear families, or both, that failed to show them, like the elephant's child in the *Just-So Stories,* the fun and the fact in learning? It was too late now for this, but perhaps something else would work. So I plunged into the jungle around me and searched for what might help this yowly, scowly bunch lacking in manners and with their curiosity not showing.

I began with a local, tabloid-sized morning newspaper, the *Chicago Sun-Times.* It was right for this group for many reasons. For one thing, it did not look insulting. The students were not ashamed to walk down the hall with it under an arm or on top of a pile of books. It was not, as one of them said when he disdainfully pitched a workbook from another class into my wastepaper basket, "Kid stuff!"

This newspaper was good, too, because it looked fresh and easy to handle. It kept the reading process from seeming "too big," "too complicated," "dry," "boring," "stupid," or any of the other adjectives a high school person wouldn't be caught dead with. The day's newspaper appealed to them also because it was related to what they already knew. They'd got some of it from the ten o'clock news the night before; they'd heard Johnny Carson talk about it on his "Tonight Show"; their favorite DJ worked it in while he switched from The Cream to Jimi Hendrix.

Also, for high-interest, easy-reading, the staff downtown in the *Sun-Times* office could always be counted on to furnish that touch of professionalism the kids expected in every phase of their living, for television has brought them up on it, and they turn off on anything that doesn't come up to the same sleek standard. Also, where for four cents can you get such an unbelievable windfall? You think you must be dreaming. But what a dream! Stacked, bundled, wired—you find it waiting for you every morning you enter the school office and prepare to face your students that day. The only thing that bothers you is that this feast should be available for the hundred kids who need it rather than the few who will get it.

The newspaper we used always had at least one eye-catching picture on the front page; sometimes it had two. A big, one-inch headline slammed the main story right into the eye. Smaller, half-inch heads on page two kindled curiosity on other major news events. Clear directions led further into the paper when a story was continued, thus exposing the students to additional happenings.

Mike, caught by an item on Khe Sahn on page one, inevitably continues to "Story on page five" because his brother is in Vietnam. When he finishes this, he finds right next to it an article about the possibility of higher rates coming up for the tollway. Mike reads that too because he drives a car, and all the costs come out of his pocket. Abe follows the missile crisis on through "Report on page four" because his grandfather lives near Libertyville, and no one in their family wants an ABM site that close. This item ends just above another about an eccentric who has 23 cats, which brings a snort from Abe: his stepmother has three Siamese, and he hates all four of them. Sam, a guitarist, gets carried away by "See page 17," where he reads about the 50,000 persons who turned out the night before to hear the Jefferson Airplane in Grant Park. Sam's eye is pulled further on to a nearby column where he reads a social worker's complaint about the inadequacy of the welfare program. Sam sighs; he has been hungry too.

The newspaper stirs up a lot in these three boys as they range freely through it the first half of the period every day. Each boy avidly reads what appeals to him; he responds to it; and he moves on to read some more, to respond again—to awaken, he eventually realizes, to words, to thought, to organization, to communication—first with himself and then with other people.

Though each of these students needs some very elementary and repetitious drills for building up strength in his own perceptual weaknesses, none is motivated enough at this late point in his schooling to take them on. To present these bald exercises to them now would be to turn them off on what I might be able to stir them up to do for themselves. So I approach them through something they will take, and I adapt it to what they need.

They take to the newspaper because it appeals to them personally in its awareness of what is going on today and because of its ability to change when tomorrow comes. It is not dead or frozen or stuck or creeping. It is alive and jet-propelled. Television, speeds of 25,000 miles per hour, trips to the moon, pictures of life (?) on Mars—this is the perceptual level of newspapers and students today; both "feel" to *Apollo 11,* not the *Santa Maria.* Students do not even see or hear the blank look and the dull pace of the hard-covered textbook which is one, two, three, or five years old. Their time is now and tomorrow—not yesterday or last year.

So they will read, listen to, and look at what's new and up-to-date. It is only *after* they have accepted this, and *after,* they have some kind of "readiness" appropriate to their age and interest that they are able to start asking questions about what came before. It is only then that they will want to turn to the kind of reading which supplies in-depth answers, which gives them the relationships they as human beings instinctively seek. It is then that they find reading to be a way of life rather than just a subject taught with "package deals." Once they discover the thrill of making their own connections through reading, they will not stop. The path which begins with Ann Landers' daily column in the newspaper can widen into the broader expanse of *Mr. and Mrs. BoJo Jones,* and that can elevate to the vista of *The Scarlet Letter.* For the poor high school reader, a sequence like this is absolutely necessary, even as we recognize that he may never be able to go the whole way. But to begin with the book which should be the culmination is to ruin the entire thing.

The boys whose bag is sports know where to start. They begin on the back page of the newspaper. For them, what the president said yesterday is nowhere near as important as what big Lou scored last night on the basketball court. For the sports lover, the newspaper is customized reading right down to the last percentage point: readiness, motivation, and content are all tailored exactly to their demands.

When their favorite hockey player's jaw is busted in the game between the Hawks and the Canadians, the boys get a sustained look at the fracas through the photographer's blowup. With no outside prodding, the fellows jostle each other for a chance to read aloud the thrilling story. I never have to squeeze interpretive analyses out of this group: the phenomena simply exude.

"What a guy! His jaw is going to be wired shut for eight weeks."

"How do you s'pose he's going to eat?"

"They'll think of something. They sure as heck won't let a million dollar guy like that starve to death."

"You know what? I betcha he never misses a game."

"Good old Bobby! Ain't he the greatest!"

At first none of them believed that a newspaper was going to be their textbook. They were skeptical. They looked for the catch. They braced themselves for the yank of the rug. But by the end of the first week, the old-shoe comfort of a newspaper began to produce the relaxing effect they had to have to get on with the business of finding out what else they wanted (and needed) to know. Finally, and with nothing said about it, they knew there wasn't any catch. This was for real. The whole thing was just as good as it looked.

They liked the period in their school day when they could come into a room, sit down, pick up a fresh nespaper, and know it was theirs to do with as they pleased. They could read it, talk about it, write about it, cut it up, tear things out of it, take it home—such personal freedom with print existed nowhere else at school, and often not at home either—it was wholly theirs. When someone saw a news item that struck him as good, he'd say, "Hey, listen to this," and then read it aloud. When he came to a word he did not know, he spelled it out and someone told him what it was. I made a note of these words so that they could be written on the board for analysis and discussion after the reading was finished and the conversing had begun.

We did a lot of talking in these classes, for they were small, ranging in size from two to four persons. We discussed what they wanted to talk about. News stories usually triggered into the open some personal topic, for the boys were centered around themselves rather than the outside world. If this seems immature in view of their age, consider their years of lack of contact with the ideas of other people, ideas to be obtained mostly through reading which they have not done. These students have missed a great deal during their years in school; they are minus whole chunks of life because they lost out on the access to it back at the beginning, when they made their first contact with the school and their problems in learning were not identified.

So the high school student with a learning difficulty characteristically begins a discussion with a gripe—about the school, the principal, the Dean, the library, some "other" teacher, his father, his mother, a brother, a sister. Rarely, however, does he gripe about his job or his girl. At first I wondered what the reason was for this sharp division between what he liked and what he didn't like in his personal relations with people. As I listened to his increasingly articulate discussions, I realized that the difference for him lay in whether he could choose what he must like and work with, or whether it was thrust in front of him and someone said, "Baby, you take it."

So he gripes about the people he is stuck with at home and at school. He feels that tradition and structure lock him into places he can't get out of. He says one thing that would help would be more freedom of choice. When he can't have this, he feels the home and the school are not on his side, so he fights everything that comes from them. In areas such as girls or jobs, he can choose, so he is satisfied. Considering his position, I see that his independence of spirit can be tapped to advantage, so I resolve that at least in his reading class he will get a chance to choose what he will read.

It was amazing to see how helpful an inexpensive item like the newspaper was for those tied-up, poor readers. Title III paid for their papers during the year of experimentation. Next year's innovations at the Diagnostic and Remedial Learning Center will go in another direction. So the school administration stands at the end of the school year at the point where it needs to decide whether the newspaper is a worthwhile way of reaching and teaching students such as those I worked with. Should the school spend money for newspapers? It hasn't done anything like this before. Or should it spend money repairing washrooms that have been wrecked by cherry bombs? It has done this before. The answer lies, of course, in discovering the students' reasons for coming to us. What are we supposed to be doing for them?

The Newspaper:
A New Textbook Every Day—
Part II

Laura S. Johnson

Through an informal reading inventory I gave the students the first day they entered my class, I obtained an insight into their language background as well as into their reading interests. Most of them were as nonverbal and as hostile toward each other as they were to me. My first night after my first day with them was a busy one, but it resulted in a second day which found each student in a setting of newspapers, magazines, and paperback books strongly reflecting his personal interests. The girl who had stormed in on day # 1 saying nobody could make her touch anything to read walked out on day # 2 with a copy of *Ingenue* under her arm because she just had to try the hairdos on page 54.

A similar accepting experience occurred with the boy who would not even come in and sit down the first day. "I ain't readin', period," he said, and then he just stood in the door, looking at the clock out in the hall for the entire 45 minutes. Head stock boy in a large supermarket with its thousands of items, I knew he was bright even though he swore he'd never need to know more than how to read cans.

So on his second day with me he got an envelope filled with the cut-up pages of his company's weekly newspaper ads. I asked him to reconstruct the layouts. To prove how well he knew his stock, he did the whole job in record time, right down to the last can of pears.

We went on from this to become friends, and by the time school was out, he had read enough in the newspaper about campus riots and other school problems to present on videotape a pointed analysis of how schools can fail some children, notably those like himself. His statement should be required listening for those people who wonder what makes some high school boys act the way they do. The answers are there, but they will probably not be heard by the right people, for as this boy said, "Nobody ever listens to us."

Because our classroom was small, I had no trouble surrounding these nonword people with words. The effect was dramatized, of course, but as

From Laura S. Johnson, "The Newspaper: A Textbook Every Day—Part II," *Journal of Reading* 13 (December 1969): 203-6; 240-45. Copyright © 1969 by the International Reading Association, Inc. Reprinted by permission of the IRA and the author.

someone once described Walt Whitman's technique, "Sometimes a person has to shout if he wants to be heard above a whisper." So though none of my students ever got to all of the print around them, it was always there and they couldn't miss the feeling that there was a lot for them to find out when they got ready to do so.

They could choose from the newspapers on their desks; they could select from the magazines strung on wires running around the walls of the room; they could pull out books from racks and bookcases; they could even take them off piles on the floor. We had so much to read around us that the students had literally to stop, look, and move printed matter if they wanted to sit down. And always they were surrounded by the odor of print, for ink and paper were everywhere. For many of them, this experience was unique. Whether they came from a home where English was a foreign language or one where a $1,500 TV set plus *Look* and *Better Homes* were all of the media, my saturation effect was bound to be something different. Some of the students were staggered; none were indifferent.

To show them what the reading process was, I approached them through something they could see and work with, something they could touch. They were bright and alert in their own way, capable when their capabilities were tapped. The girls were adept at making clothes; the boys could scrounge parts from old cars and put something together that would get them to the Friday night dance. Because these students responded to how things work, I showed them how reading works.

I pointed to the weather report in the newspaper. Someone read it. I printed on the board:

WEATHER

I said it again because repetition is important. Then I printed underneath the word:

XFBUIFS

and asked, "What does this say?"

Their answers just bordered on tolerance:

"That's not a word."

"It doesn't look right."

"Are you trying to be funny?"

I told them there was a relationship between the two words, and then I asked, "Can't anyone figure out what it is?"

When they couldn't, I gave each one a slip of paper on which were typed in sequence the letters of the alphabet. With this in front of them, they soon spotted the fact that X is the first letter after W, F the first one after E, B the first after A, and so on. Then I asked, "Who can explain the system I used for writing the second word?"

All of them could do this; they said it was easy and it made sense once you knew how to do it. Continuing to copy the weather report so that they could practice using the system they had just figured out, I wrote the following and asked who could decipher it first:

SBJO UPOJHIU

The game was on. We went rapidly from "Rain Tonight" to

DPPMFS BOE DMPVEZ UPNPSSPX

As they worked out the message, I said, "This is a very simple substitution cipher. Would you like to make up others that are not so easy and then select a partner to whom you will explain your system so that he can 'read' a message you send him written in it?"

It sounded like fun, and it was fun. As they worked out "hard" ciphers, they talked about the secret messages they had sent friends when they were in grade school. They talked about military and commercial uses of codes and ciphers. We defined and discussed such terms as cipher, encipher, decipher, code, encode, decode. We stayed with this exercise for about a week, taking first sentences and then paragraphs out of the newspaper for materials to encipher. These "dumb" students quit only when their systems got so complicated that a class period was not long enough for working them out.

There were two reasons I did not give them homework. During the time when they were so hostile toward school, they would never be caught taking any of it home with them. If I had asked them to do homework, that would have lined me up with what they were against. I wouldn't have been able to work with them if they had felt that way. Also, I knew that most of them had regular jobs, for they were in the cooperative work program our school operates in conjunction with firms in our area. So they just didn't have time for a lot of homework. I did not want them to feel obliged to do something for my class, and then feel guilty—and thus hostile again, when it was beginning to lessen—for not getting it done.

So when the ciphers became too long to finish in class, we went on to something else. But as we left that phase of reading, the students had the message. They had an insight into what the reading process consists of. They understood that their performance in it depended on how well they learned the systems for deciphering and decoding the words. Armed with this knowledge, their resistance was lowered toward some of the drills on blends, digraphs, prefixes, suffixes, and roots on which they worked too. Eventually they became more proficient in attacking the unfamiliar words they encountered in the newspaper and in their content subjects.

The newspaper was a great help in vocabulary building because it supplied the words we worked with, and it presented them through a popular medium in an interesting context. As a student read silently, he underlined words he did not know. When he finished reading, he listed some of them in a spiral notebook. He did not list all of them because a large number would have been too discouraging a prospect for him to face. So he listed only a few, and I wrote them on the board. He checked them in the dictionary for syllabication and definition. He selected the meaning as it was used in the newspaper item. If the word had more than one meaning, we talked about this and gave examples. The student practiced pronouncing the word and spelling it. We tried, through many forms of repetition, to make it a part of his working vocabulary.

Along with expanding vocabulary, we worked at improving comprehension. On some days the students took turns summarizing orally news items they had read. Other days they would write summaries. Most of them had trouble initially with organizing and retelling in their own words what the item was about. But after they discovered how the opening sentence (s) gave the *who, what, when, where, why,* and *how* of a piece—and that they did need to concentrate on remembering these essential items even to the point of writing them down as they came to them—when they had the answers to these six things, they could reconstruct the outline of the story. Then having the outline, they could recall some of the details, and by filling them in have a reasonably accurate account of what they had read.

Once they caught on to this system, they were able to find the plan in what they read. Then summarizing and remembering became easier, not only for newspaper reading but also for everything else they read. Another slant on this was SQRRR. This was expecially helpful to them when they applied it to reading their content subjects. By applying the SQRRR to a news item, they could come up with something like this:

Survey (Headline and photograph): "A Mideast Warning by Nixon"[1]
Question (Subhead): What is meant by "He Also Softens Nuclear Stand"?
Read, Recite, Review (Who, What, When, Where, Why, How):
Who: President Nixon
What: His first press conference
When: Yesterday
Where: Washington, D.C.
Why: People want to know how he stands on the mid-East crisis and the arms build-up
How: Comments by Congressional leaders on what he said

By combining these techniques, the students learned to use simple analytical tools which helped them to read to remember, regardless of the kind of content.

When a student said he could summarize orally but not in writing, he would dictate to me and I would write down what he said. Then he would read it back, thus being able to see that he could express himself in writing. Convinced that he could succeed, he became more willing to try to write without going through the medium of dictation. When he gave his oral summary, he found himself using some of the words that he had read in the newspaper. To write, he could see that all he had to do was put these same spoken words down on paper. This showed him how his system for reading fed into this system for speaking; and that it in turn fed into his system for writing. By following this process through again and again, his total language experience of using all of these systems began to take the shape of being a very useful tool for communication. It began to mean something important to him. He could see how improving one part of it would improve its other parts. This insight, added to the appeal of the material he read, gave him the momentum he needed for moving out of the ruts of frustration and hostility in which he had been stuck for most of his years in school.

Near the end of the term we tried to bring these experiences together for each student. Each one chose a topic of particular interest to himself, and he set about to compile a book about it. His materials were to come from newspaper clippings relevant to his topic and from written and oral reports he would do himself.

Don's project illustrates the language experiences involved in an exercise of this kind. His achievement also illustrates the progress possible through free reading when a student is allowed to follow his own interests. Seventeen years old and entering high school for the third autumn, he was still classified only as a freshman, for in all that time he had earned only three credits. Asked why this was so, he said, "I didn't like school, so I cut a lot."

He chose prisons for his topic. His interest in them had been stimulated by a field trip our classes had taken earlier in the year to Cook County Jail in Chicago (and perhaps this was an unconscious reaction to what school had always been to him). When Don first selected this topic, he said he would collect items about crime, criminals, and prisons. But after a few days of going through newspapers looking for these accounts, he saw that his topic was too broad. He found too much, so looking at his stack of clippings, he narrowed his idea down to items about Cook County Jail. Fortunately (or unfortunately?) for him, a jail break occurred during his period of reading, so he was almost overwhelmed again with materials for even his limited subject.

To learn more about the purpose for his book and its probable effect on his readers (the other students in my Title III classes), Don checked forewords, prefaces, introductions, and tables of contents as well as other elements of a book as he found them in the paperbacks in our classroom. He discovered that his book would be more interesting to his readers if they knew why he had chosen the topic, how the items he had selected represented his point of view, and what he hoped his readers would learn from using his book.

He wrote several drafts of a foreword before he was satisfied with the version which became final copy. He then analyzed the contents of his clippings so that he could write brief but informative titles for his Table of Contents. He mounted the clippings on unruled sheets of looseleaf notebook paper and enclosed them in a folder appropriately titled and illustrated. He chose one news story and wrote out several questions based on its contents. The questions would be given to another student for answering after he had read the account. Some of Don's questions were to have factual answers; some were to be interpretive. Don was interested in the relative values of the different types of questions, and he commented on the methods of questioning used by teachers in some of his other classes. Obviously, newspaper reading was opening up critical thinking for him. He began acquiring an insight into how to weigh one idea against another.

From this he went on to a consideration of ideas relating to jail. He wanted to view them as theme topics, one of which he would develop and write. Some of his topics were these:

1. What kind of person should a warden be?
2. A chaplain's day at Cook County Jail
3. A prisoner's defense for slugging and robbing a bus driver
4. How does a man in prison feel?
5. Thoughts on solitary confinement
6. A prosecuting attorney's plea for the death penalty for a murderer
7. Capital punishment, pro and con
8. What are some things, besides violent crime, for which a person can be put in jail?
9. What reforms are needed in prisons today?
10. An experiment in rehabilitation in a California prison

Don chose the last topic for the theme he would write because it represented the culmination of his interest in his topic. He had worked up to this through discussions in class which began with "How does a person get into jail?" and ended with "What does he do after he gets out?" Along the way he had asked such questions as "Will people trust him? Can he get a job? Is anything done to help him before he gets out so that he won't commit another crime and get back into jail again? What is the word for helping a man while he is still in prison?"

I gave him the word—rehabilitation—and then he wanted to know how he could find out something about it, for the newspaper did not have anything on this. Here, of course, came one of the high points of our work with the newspaper, for this was the place from which we took off, the point from which we would go further into other kinds of reading.

We went to the library, to the *Reader's Guide to Periodical Literature.* Don had not used this reference work before, so he was excited about discovering something so helpful for locating information. He read down the column of titles of articles on rehabilitation of criminals and selected one about an experiment in a California institution. Almost unbelievingly, he followed through with me the process for obtaining the four-year-old magazine from the stacks, checked it out, and then turned to see if the article really was on the page the *Guide* said it would be on! He took the magazine back to our classroom, read it, and made notes on facts he needed for his theme.

After writing the theme, he wanted to read and review a book related to his topic. I suggested Bill Sands' *My Shadow Ran Fast,* and when Don had finished it, he said, "That was the best book I ever read." Two years earlier, in his freshman English class he had been exposed to Dickens' *Great Expectations.* When I referred to this in connection with his interest in prisons, he said he thought *Great Expectations* was dry and unbelievable, expecially that part about Miss Havisham. We discussed some of the similarities between Dickens' symbolic, nonfiction account. Don then had a clearer understanding of what Dickens, as well as Sands, was trying to say about the effect of being in prison, and of how many kinds of prisons there are. He saw how two authors working with the same idea would handle it in different ways. He saw that the level of which Dickens wrote was more abstract, which explained why that book was more difficult to read than Sands' book. The reference to abstraction brought us to a discussion of levels of language meaning, and I showed him Hayakawa's Abstraction Ladder. These discussions went on, of course, in the presence of other members of the class, so they benefited from Don's work just as he benefited from theirs.

For a slightly different slant on prison but one still related to his topic, he wanted to read *The Loneliness of the Long Distance Runner*, for I had mentioned it as a possibility to him earlier. But he did not have time for this second book then because he was near the end of the school year, and he had some history reports to get in. Just feeling responsible for getting a credit in history, though, was a big achievement for him. Here again was one of the anticipated by-products of individualized reading instruction for students in the Title III project.

One of the other boys in the class had read Sillitoe's book, after seeing it as a movie on TV (said viewing stimulated by our remarks earlier), so he gave Don a thorough review of it. This is another example of how the students had developed to the point of being willing to help each other, which was in marked contrast to the way they had been at the beginning of the year.

When Don's book on Cook County Jail was finished, he had something which showed how he could develop through his words and those of other people an idea of special interest to himself. What he had done had led him through all kinds of oral and written experiences; it had made connections for him which had been missing; it had taken him into areas of reading he had not entered before. He had brought all of these things together because of his own interest in them and because of his planning how to organize and expand it. This project proved to him that he could do things on his own at school. It made him feel that he could repeat the process not only in a Title III class but also in other classes such as history, English, and science. As the year ended and after his history reports were in, he embarked of his own volition, on another reading project, stirred into existence by newspaper stories.

At the time of General Eisenhower's death, Gettysburg was frequently in the news. Don had visited the battlefield there while on a summer vacation with his parents, so the reference to that place turned his thoughts toward the Civil War. The last day I saw him, after finals were over in June, he was reading *Across Five Aprils* and looking forward to tackling Sandburg's *Abraham Lincoln*.

This seemed to me the most fitting evaluation we could have of a student in our innovative reading program. He showed dramatic improvement on all of the posttests we gave him, too, but the evaluation that will really count is the one we will not be in on: what will he do with reading when we are gone and the project is concluded?

Books similar to Don's were compiled by my other students. Each was different, and all of them were interesting. They illustrated vividly the importance of diversity and individualization of reading materials for students having learning difficulties in school. In most instances, these difficulties can be traced to poor performance in reading; and until the reading improves, the other school work will not improve. Like any skill, reading will not improve except with practice; and practice won't come from these older students until they initiate it. They are willing to do this when they like what they are doing, and when it seems to be accomplishing something for them.

So when we get these students, we need to prime them into action again just as we would pour water into a hand pump, dry and unresponsive from disuse, if we would get the stream flowing. I found the newspaper the means for getting these students moving again in reading, and I recommend it without reservation to the teacher who has people who say they won't read. They will, if you give them a newspaper, because they just can't resist it. It's that good!

NOTES

1. S. I. Hayakawa, *Language in Thought and Action,* 2d ed. (New York: Harcourt Brace Jovanovich, 1964), p. 179.

Cartoons in the Classroom

Lurene Brown and Helen B. Wachs

Ski tracks mark a snowy mountainside. They come to a tree, bypass it one on either side, and go on together. No caption is needed.

Two cavemen, clubs beside them, ruefully survey their surroundings, the huge interior of a man-eating animal. One says, " 'Don't worry,' you said; 'he won't bother us,' you said. 'He's a vegetarian,' you said."

From a tenth-story scaffolding, a precariously balanced workman looks down at a little old lady, frantically signalling from the ground. The caption: "But Mother, I *can't* brush after every meal."

We look; we laugh. But if we, as teachers of English, do no more than that, we are missing a remarkably good teaching opportunity that involves student perception, comprehension, evaluation, and composition. And best of all, it introduces students to a life-long delight in the innocent merriment of the comic cartoon and an appreciation and understanding of the seen-at-a-glance sketch which satirizes, symbolizes, or caricatures.

From Lurene Brown and Helen B. Wachs, "Cartoons in the Classroom," *English Journal* 57 (May 1968): 662-64. Copyright © 1969 by the National Council of Teachers of English. Reprinted by permission of the publisher and Lurene Brown and Helen B. Wachs.

We may well begin our teaching with these—the three dictionary terms *satirize, symbolize,* and *caricature,* explaining what a cartoon is and does—and with the related words like *irony,* for instance. Cartoons shown on the overhead projector to the whole class demonstrate the meaning of *satire, symbol,* and *caricature* and are especially effective if they are selections made by the teacher for demonstration purposes. Later, student choices can test the ability of the class to understand the first lesson. Clearly, the picture of the important-looking executive kneeling by his bed and saying, "Harrison J. Endicott speaking," exposes the folly of becoming too self-important and falls under the heading of satire; while the little dachshund, smugly looking at his huge, magnificently distorted image in a trick mirror, symbolizes the universal desire to be bigger than we are, the "Mirror, mirror, on the wall" appeal. And hardly a newspaper lacks its cartoon of emphasis on a physical characteristic—the exaggeration of the size of nose or ears or mouth; the identifying forelock; or the pictured stress on a mannerism—in short, the caricature.

Probably the most general division of the cartoons which teachers and students can share is made up of those which are done strictly for the humor they represent—the comic strip, for instance. We could hardly include *Peanuts* here because of the sometimes serious undertones and the usual revelation of human weakness, but sometimes the series is just fun. "Henry," for example, in which the main character never speaks, is usually pure humor. One-picture cartoons, as well as the picture series, can also come under the just-for-fun heading.

Sometimes the humor is the result of a play on words, as in the sketch showing the huge boiling pot beside which a cannibal is reading a book called *1001 Ways To Serve Humanity*; or the slightly more subtle cartoon in which a wife, preparing for a masquerade, looks up at her husband, who is dressed as a court jester, and says, "Try not to make a fool of yourself tonight." A student may need to consult his dictionary or his thesaurus here, or the teacher may see just the right opportunity to introduce words like *denotation* and *connotation* and to explain the importance of context.

Occasionally no words are needed to explain the picture. Two birds on the branch of a tree lie on their backs in paroxysms of laughter at the lopsided birdhouse the man standing below has built for them. ... The man who has mistaken the back of a whale for an island suddenly finds that the "island" has a malevolent eye. ... On a cliff overlooking a roadway marked "Drive carefully. Children at play!" a sadistic-looking little boy is poised, ready to push a huge rock over the next car that comes by.

We all feel wonderfully complacent and superior when the cartoon shows someone in a position where we know what is going to happen and he does not. A woman bearing a lighted birthday cake calls gaily to her husband in the next room, "Darling, I have a surprise for you!" and *we* see that her next step will be on a rolling pin. ... As the sun peeps in the window, a disgruntled woman sits up in bed, glares at her sleepy husband, and says, "You certainly made enough noise coming upstairs last night!" We see what she does not—an interested-looking horse standing in the bedroom door. . . . Or outside a room where dignified guests are politely sipping their tea, one little boy, cymbals in hand, prepares for a deafening crash and says to the other boy, "Watch!" Students especially delight in the feeling of superiority.

They will also enjoy seeing someone "put on the spot" as is the smoke-ring blower whose girl catches one of the rings on her third finger, left hand, and coos, "Why, Harold, what a clever way to propose." Or they may enjoy imagining consequences as in the sketch showing bank staff members opening the vault and being greeted by a disheveled and angry executive who says, "Good morning! I trust you all had an enjoyable weekend?" They will appreciate the exaggeration of situation in a series of pictures showing the greyhound on the side of the bus, loping along until the bus stops for a red light and then sitting casually down to wait. And the ironical understatement of a wife's "Fred! People are staring!" will hardly be lost on them when they look at the man pointing a revolver at his temple as he stands in a crowded stadium.

Most of all, perhaps, they will appreciate the cartoon which reminds them of something which has happened to them. One such picture shows a sneaker-clad teenager in a low-cut formal, the hem of which her mother is carefully pinning. Her father is shouting, "What does it need? What does it need? I'll tell you what it needs! It needs a tee shirt underneath!"

It's fun to have fun in a class, but because life is often serious, as high school students already know, they will be interested in cartoons which make them think. For instance, during a recent well-publicized trial, the artist who pictured the judge studying a veritable mountain of testimony and saying, "Is there a Diogenes in the house?" did double duty. He used his talent to call attention to the lack of truth, to present a thought-provoking point of view, as an editorial might; and at the same time he taught a new allusion.

No student who has seen Mauldin's grieving Lincoln, which appeared originally in the *Chicago Sun-Times,* can fail to realize the potential of the serious cartoon for revealing an emotion. This picture which has become the classic symbol of the assassination of President Kennedy, illustrates forcefully the superior power of the picture over the word. Finding other symbolic representations will reinforce the awareness of the emotional power of the cartoon.

And last there is the caustic or satirical sketch, often political, often a caricature, and frequently the province of the history or government classes because of its special emphasis. Yet if we are to study the cartoon in depth, we cannot overlook the exaggeration, the ridicule, the expose of human weakness which can be found here. It may be the Wallaces, Ronald Reagan, and Lester Maddox in the roles of *Alice in Wonderland* characters; or it may be President Johnson in cowboy boots and ten-gallon hat saying to reporters, as he walks his dog, "War? War? What war?" Whatever it is, it assumes significance as it teaches, and it deserves study.

Ways to use the cartoon, this briefest form of communication, are numerous. Through its use we have all the ammunition we need to teach quotation marks—single and double—as well as the punctuation of direct address, terminal punctuation, capitalization, spelling, and literary allusions. How do we do it? There are several ways, two of which have proved to be especially successful. One is to let the students select pictures, mount them, and then explain briefly beneath why the cartoon is amusing or what they think the artist was trying to say. The second way is to have the teacher remove the captions. Then the students write their own and later check to see how well or how poorly they guessed what the artist had in mind.

Moving from the brief comment to the full-length theme is easy and natural in such a study. Discussing the various types of cartoons provides material for the same clear-cut organization we find in James Harvey Robinson's "Four Kinds of Thinking" or Wolfgang Langewiesche's "The Three Secrets of Human Flight," for example. Furthermore, such a theme provides an opportunity to show the importance of supporting an idea—this time through the use of specific illustrations.

The cartoon, found in almost every periodical seen, and usually interpreted at a glance, deals basically with human nature. Because this is true, it represents the perfect teaching device, not only for presenting mechanics in a relatively painless manner, but also for training young people to see situations as they really are, to take themselves a little less seriously, and to appreciate another of the many kinds of communication.

Five Dozen Ideas for Teaching the Newspaper Unit

Howard F. Decker

Teachers, not students, too often have a mental block against using the newspaper in the English classroom. The complaint I have heard most often is, "It sounds like a good idea, but I really don't know enough about newspapers to teach them."

But teaching the newspaper itself is not the purpose. Instead, the newspaper should be used as a tool to teach vocabulary, reading improvement, and

From Howard F. Decker, "Five Dozen Ideas for Teaching the Newspaper Unit," *English Journal* 59 (February 1970): 268-72. Copyright © 1970 by the National Council of Teachers of English. Reprinted by permission of the publisher and Howard F. Decker.

composition. When teachers approach the newspaper unit with this idea in mind, their fears often evaporate.

I have used the newspaper for several years with both accelerated and remedial students in both sophomore and senior classes. The results have always been good. Never have I heard a single student complain that the unit was boring or irrelevant or "the same old thing I had last year." To borrow a phrase from current adolescent slang, I have always found that every student was definitely "turned on."

Surprisingly, very few students know anything about newspapers. They read the sports section, they glance at the comic pages, and a few search the classified ads for bargains in the "Automotive—Used" columns, but most of them will be exploring virgin territory when you introduce the unit.

To help teachers present the newspaper unit, I have compiled a list of 60 ideas which I have found to be practical. Not every idea will work in every classroom, but surely enough of them can be adapted that it will be difficult to dismiss the newspaper unit on grounds of not having enough information about teaching it.

INTRODUCING THE UNIT

1. Call your nearest daily newspaper and arrange to have enough copies of the newspaper for each of your students sent to your school every day for one or two weeks (or even the whole semester). Some newspapers furnish copies to schools free of charge, and others sell them for as little as five cents each.

2. Show filmstrips or movies about newspapers. Numerous companies offer worthwhile audio-visual programs about newspapers. To find a rather complete listing of such materials available, consult the *Index to 35 mm Educational Filmstrips* and the *Index to 16 mm Educational Films,* both published by McGraw-Hill and compiled through the efforts of the National Information Center for Educational Media.

3. Point out the "masthead" of the newspaper, and show students that in it the newspaper announces its management and lists its subscription rates.

4. Point out that a "by-line" is simply the word *by* followed by the name of the reporter who wrote the story. Have students find by-lines in the newspaper.

5. Point out that a "dateline" is the name of the city and state where a news story originates. Local news stories carry no datelines. Have students note which stories are local and which are not.

6. Point out that the letters AP and UPI are the initials of the two major wire services—Associated Press and United Press International.

7. Give your students a half-hour to read the paper leisurely. Then have each student tell which item, news story, column, editorial, he appreciated most.

8. Clip several headlines from the newspaper and show them to the class, assigning students to write down the section of the paper in which they think the story probably appeared.

9. Have your students keep a scrapbook in which they include examples of dateline, by-line, cutlines, streamer headlines, local news story, wire service news story, syndicated news story, local columnist, obituary, etc.

IMPROVING VOCABULARY

10. Assign each student to find five words in the newspaper which he does not understand. Then each student should look up the words in a dictionary and use the words in original sentences.

11. Find numerous examples of abbreviations used in the newspaper (CIA, FHA, UAW, NATO, etc.). Have students circle these initials and then find the proper name for each set of initials.

12. Before class, find several words which you suspect your students might not be able to define. If your students have difficulty explaining the meanings of these words, show them the sentences in which the words appear and point out that words are almost always easier to understand when they are in context.

13. Assign your students to turn to one particular section of the newspaper and make a list of the words used more frequently in that one section than in any other section of the newspaper. In sports, for example, they will find such words as *inning, pennant, coach, gridders, referee, league, overtime, score,* etc.

IMPROVING READING ABILITY

14. As a weekend assignment, tell your students to read the Sunday edition of the newspaper and make a list of the differences they notice between the Sunday paper and the weekday issues. Then conduct a class discussion on the subject.

15. Assign the class to read the comic strips for 10 or 15 minutes and then conduct a class discussion on the types of humor; slapstick, wit, irony, satire, sight jokes, puns, etc.

16. Before class begins, write down 20 or 30 questions about the contents of the newspaper and assign the students to find the answers (e.g., What is tonight's weather forecast? When was Joe Smith born? What is showing this week at the Rialto? How much are Early American sofas at Ward's?).

17. Choose a dozen or so news stories and clip the headlines off. Then challenge your students—particularly slow readers—to match the stories with the correct headlines.

18. Clip a feature story which contains several examples of a reporter's interpreting or editorializing. Assign your class to identify the passages in which the feature writer exercises a freedom of expression denied to the writer of straight news copy.

19. Clip several news stories which contain errors overlooked by the proofreaders. Assign your students to find these errors.

20. Many daily newspapers feature a weekly news quiz. If your newspaper does publish such a news quiz, assign your students to take this quiz.

WRITING ASSIGNMENTS

21. Type several examples of news stories which have errors in spelling, punctuation, and factual information. Assign your students to act as copyreaders and find the errors.

22. Have your students read the editorials for several days. Then assign them to write an editorial of their own on any topic they wish.

23. Assign your students to study the stories of weddings and engagements on the women's pages and then write an imaginary wedding or engagement story about any two of their classmates.

24. Write a classified ad, using an abundance of words. Assign your class to rewrite the ad in as few words as possible without eliminating any information.

25. Assign each student to choose an advertisement from the classified section and write a letter in answer to it.

26. Assign the class to write a letter to the editor of the daily newspaper or the school newspaper, stating their beliefs on any topic of interest to them.

27. Write a news story in which you insert numerous examples of editorializing. Assign your students to rewrite the story, eliminating all editorial comments.

28. If your newspaper carries such advice columns as "Dear Abby" or "Dear Ann Landers," instruct your classes, as a composition assignment, to read the questions in the letters and then answer as if they were the "expert."

29. Assign your students to choose a news story and use it as a source for writing a poem or a short story.

30. Assign your students to interview another member of the student body and then write a feature story about him. Their stories should include many quotations, background information, physical description, and interesting facts.

31. Assign your students to write a "how-to-do-it" feature story. Similar to a demonstration speech, a how-to-do-it feature can discuss such topics as "How to make a tea ring," "How to ride horseback," "How to treat a victim of shock," "How to make paper flowers," etc.

32. Clip several news stories, cutting off the headlines. Then assign your class to write headlines for each story.

33. Pretend that you are a news source and have your students hold a "press conference" in which they interview you. Then they must write a news story.

34. After your students have written the news story as described above, tell them to exchange papers. Now they are copyreaders and must find the errors in their classmates' work.

35. Assign your students to cover a news story in your school. Make up a list of possible news sources so that each student has a different assignment: club sponsors, club presidents, coaches, committee chairmen, administrators, etc. Your school activities calendar should help you to find ideas.

36. Choose a well-known piece of literature such as "The Highwayman" or

Spoon River Anthology and assign your students to write a news story based on the literary work.

37. Pretend that you are a "legman" and "call in" a news story to the newsroom. Have your students act as rewrite men and take notes. Then assign them to write the news story in polished form, ready for publication.

CLASS DISCUSSION

38. Have your students search through the newspaper, noting stories which they feel were either phoned in by readers or sent in as news releases rather than being written by staff reporters. In class discussion have them explain their reasoning.

39. Telephone the local newspaper office and ask that the newsroom save several samples of the wire service news copy from the AP or the UPI so that you may show them to your classes. Then discuss with your students the many interesting features of wire service news copy.

40. From your school's newspaper sponsor, borrow copies of newspapers mailed in from neighboring schools. After your students have examined several other papers, conduct a class discussion in which you compare your school's paper with the papers from the other schools.

41. Ask the faculty adviser or the student editor of your school's newspaper to participate in a question-and-answer session with your class.

42. Call the editor of the nearest daily newspaper to see whether one or more members of his staff would be willing to speak before your class.

43. Find examples of news releases from large organizations and have your class discuss the merits of such publicity releases. Are they newsworthy items? Or are they merely advertising disguised as news?

44. Give your students dictionaries and find the page which lists proofreader's marks. Discuss these marks with your class.

45. Ask the editor of a nearby newspaper whether he can provide you with any interesting tools or materials which you can show to your students: mats, slugs, galley proofs, press plates, etc.

46. To illustrate the differences between big city dailies and small town weeklies, bring samples of both types to class and discuss them with your students. Later let the students spend some time on free reading with both types of newspapers.

SPECIAL PROJECTS

47. Take your entire class on a tour of the nearest newspaper plant.

48. As a one-week assignment, have students clip all stories from the newspaper which they think will be historically important in 100 years. In class discussion, ask them to explain their choices.

49. As an extra-credit assignment, ask your more artistic students to draw political cartoons suitable for the local daily or for the school newspaper.

50. Early in the newspaper unit, assign your class to keep a scrapbook in which they follow a current news topic for the entire unit. Help them to choose a news topic which will "keep" for several days or weeks (e.g., a political campaign, a court trial, a world crisis, a drought or flood, etc.). To conclude the assignment, each student should write a report.

51. After explaining the stock market listings, assign the class to pretend to "buy" a few stocks and to follow the market every day, computing their gains and losses at the end of the unit.

52. Acquaint your students with the school library's resources regarding newspapers: microfilm copies, current subscriptions to daily newspapers, biographies of famous journalists, journalism career books, journalism fiction books, etc.

53. Assign your students to produce their own classroom newspaper, which you can produce using a ditto machine, Xerox copier, etc.

54. On any given day have students make a list of the news stories which they think will be continued the following day. On the following day, have them make a checklist, noting which stories were continued and which were not. Conduct a class discussion on why some stories were continued and why some were not.

55. Assign students to find various types of feature stories: news background, biographical sketch, filler stories, how-to-do-it (or advice) features, and historical features. Then have the students trade clippings and identify the types of feature stories they are given.

CONCLUDING ASSIGNMENTS

When the newspaper unit is finished, have your students write briefly on one of the following topics:

56. What have you learned from the newspaper unit?

57. What do you think the value of importance of a free press is in a democratic society?

58. What effect would a nationwide newspaper strike have on our citizens?

59. Why is editorializing in news columns regarded as a bad thing?

60. What is the value of having a school-sponsored newspaper?

Teaching Values in Magazine Reading: An Approach

Thomas N. Walters

Recently, at the end of a junior class magazine sales project, my home room juniors, through their sales record, had won the opportunity to select a magazine of their choice to be sent regularly to the home room. I was pleased with the home room's spirited performance and even more pleased at the prospect of having some student-selected current writing in the room. Democratically, I left the selection strictly up to the class. Later, I learned that the vote had been in favor of a magazine singularly limited in value for the high school classroom. Due to a lack of direction, and the large number of girls in the class, the selection had been a periodical devoted to hair styles of the month. Helpful, perhaps even necessary, it was; but worthy of a place in the classroom, it was not.

I could not help but feel this to be a somewhat typical example of the twentiety-century American's affluent means and hard work bringing him no real intellectual return. All that work and cooperation had netted the boys nothing and the girls only pictures of a passing, narcissistic interest.

This mistake was mine, and I assumed its responsibility. While the incident did not initiate my concern for the magazine reading habits of my students, it did solidify an intention to try to effect a meaningful change in those habits.

During a previous semester at Duke University, Professor Stephen Dunning had assured me that the area of student magazine reading was a subject needing attention, but he had further warned me that such a unit of study was nearly impossible to organize and execute well. He was right, of course, and while I cannot claim absolute success in carrying out this plan, the attempt was predominantly worthwhile and should be of interest to other teachers of English concerned with the magazines published *for* and read *by* their students. Should my approach appear perhaps dogmatic or biased, or should it in some other way fail, the concerned teacher can surely correct the flaws within its flexible frame.

In arrangement, this unit suggests objectives and evaluation methods; then it gives a brief, ten-day sentence outline along with an expanded description of

From Thomas N. Walters, "Teaching Values in Magazine Reading: An Approach," *North Carolina English Teacher* 25 (April 1968): 15-24. Reprinted by permission of the publisher.

three crucial days, and finally it provides three brief bibliographical listings, items of which may be used as cross references in formulating a particular teaching approach to such a study.

The two-week unit of study involves the reading and attempted evaluations of four readily available magazines: *Saga, True Confessions, Holiday,* and *The Atlantic.*

The first general objective was to arrive at serviceable criteria for use in evaluating any magazines. The second broad objective was to improve student skills in expression, both written and oral, through having them develop their evaluations in papers and oral reports. The third over-all objective was to increase student enjoyment and intellectual reward, through better understanding of purposeful reading of magazines.

From these general objectives, the movement was to such specific objectives as these:

1. Lead the class in discussion, comparison, and evaluation of the magazines.
2. Improve students' skills in inspection, comparison, and evaluation techniques.
3. Improve students' abilities in self-expression through their participation in discussion and through their giving oral reports.
4. Improve students' abilities in composition through writing assignments.
5. Reinforce and improve students' letter writing skills through assigned writing of a letter to an editor.
6. Lead the class in arriving at criteria with which to evaluate the magazines. Some suggested questions concerning standards, which the class might or might not wish to incorporate, are listed here:
   a. Why am I reading? Instruction? Enlightenment? Pleasure? All?
   b. What does the purpose of the magazine appear to be?
   c. Does it fulfill this purpose?
   d. How does it fulfill it?
   e. What seems to be the level or appeal made by the publication?
   f. What seems to be the publishers' estimate of you as a reader?
   g. Do you agree with that estimate?
   h. Does the magazine appear attractive? Tasteful?
   i. Does its price seem justified?
   j. Is the photography and art work good?
   k. Is there a good, easily located index?
   l. Are there editorials?
   m. Are there both fiction and nonfiction articles?
   n. Is the content both rich and varied?
   o. Does the fiction reveal perception, or is it of a formula type?
   p. Does the nonfiction contain reliable and relevant information?
   q. Does the magazine initiate new ideas in the reader?
   r. Are the advertisements in good taste and aimed at a mature reader?
   s. Are there cartoons? Other humor?
   t. What type person does the editor expect to laugh at the cartoons?
   u. Does there appear to be bias in the articles? Editorials?

Some suggested methods of evaluation of students that were found helpful, were these:

1. Have written a short, in-class, paper of 150 words evaluating *Saga* using two or more of the criteria.
2. Have written a 500-word paper following these instructions:
   Write on just one of the four topics, remembering to document your composition by using the criteria, as they appear on the mimeographed sheet given you the second day of class in this unit. This paper is being assigned you on the sixth day and will be due on the eighth day. Your papers will be marked and graded and returned to you on the tenth day for review, discussion, and correction.
   Topic 1. Using the criteria, give a full description of the magazine to which you would most like to subscribe.
   Topic 2. Which magazine that we have studied would you send to a foreign student if you wanted him to have an idea of the interests of our English class? Give several criteria as reasons.
   Topic 3. Compare any two magazines we have read, making specific use of the criteria as they apply to both magazines.
   Topic 4. Pretend you are the editor of one of the studied magazines. Tell in your paper what you would change about your magazine, or what, and why, you would not change a part or parts.
3. Have oral reports given lasting three to five minutes. Students must objectively apply the criteria to a magazine not studied in class, and read outside class.

Of much value to the teacher in improving the approach was the student evaluation of the unit. Students were asked not to sign the mimeographed sheet. They were requested to be candid in answering this question list:

1. Do you think the magazines we studied were the best choices to use in learning to evaluate magazines? Yes or no.
2. If your answer to the above was no, list two or more magazines you think would be better to study:
3. Do you feel that you increased your skill in expressing yourself through the writing assignments in this unit? Yes or no.
4. Do you feel that you improved your ability of expression in fulfilling your oral report requirement? Yes or no.
5. If one of our written and oral requirements could be dropped which would you suggest:
6. Do you think we could have accomplished the same objectives by using only two magazines? Yes or no.
7. Which two of our four do you enjoy reading most?
8. Do you feel that we should have done more writing in this unit? Yes or no.
9. Do you feel more confident now in selecting magazine fare? Yes or no.
10. Any general comments on how you would improve the unit:

To give some idea of time allotment that was found necessary, the following ten brief outlines of daily activities should serve as guides:

Day 1. Introduce magazine unit. Outline proposed objectives. Mention that there will be oral reports, a letter, and two written papers, one short in-class paper, and a longer one as homework. Have class discuss and agree upon criteria for evaluation. Introduce *Saga*. Assign home reading of *Saga* in preparation for class discussion and in-class paper tomorrow. (This day is described below in detail.)

Day 2. Pass out mimeographed sheets of criteria agreed upon in class yesterday. Discuss *Saga*, utilizing the criteria. Through class discussion, draw expressions of student evaluations from class. In last half of period have students write short paper stating their evaluations of *Saga*. Students are to develop papers by using two or more criteria in their writing. Take up papers. Introduce *Holiday*. Assign home reading.

Day 3. Give advance assignment of short, three- to five-minute oral reports to be given on a magazine read outside class. Students will report in alphabetical order, with first half of class reporting on seventh day and remainder on ninth day. Have class read excerpts from *Holiday* aloud in class. Discuss in terms of criteria. After discussion, introduce *True Confessions*. Have students read aloud from magazine in class. Short discussion. Assign home reading of magazine.

Day 4. Return in-class papers written on day 2. Finish reading aloud by students of excerpts from *True Confessions*. Discussion in terms of criteria and foregoing evaluations of *Saga* and *Holiday*. In class, have students write letters to the editor of one magazine of their choice, referring, if they have to, to the letter writing section in grammar text. The letter must be in good form, and should mention a pleasing feature, or take issue with some aspect of the magazine. Take up letters.

Day 5. Return annotated letters. Comment. Students then make necessary corrections and mail the letters. Lead discussion in how magazines may affect us today, how they affect our reading habits, our school work, our social lives, our jobs, our families, etc. Introduce *The Atlantic*. Assign home reading of magazine. Give advance assignment of 500-word paper to be due on day 8. Hand out mimeograph sheet giving description of assignment.

Day 6. Have students read excerpts aloud from *The Atlantic*. Full discussion bringing in previous evaluations and comparing. Remaining class time spent with students working in class on their 500-word papers. Teacher will work closely with students during this time, helping with individual problems and answering questions. Also, ask if there are any questions concerning the first half of oral reports due at next meeting. (Detailed description below.)

Day 7. Begin oral reports. Make note of suggestions or comments to be made for improvement and encouragement to the students in later conferences. After oral reports, hold discussion. Then announce that each student should copy a short quotation, that he feels to be typical of a studied magazine, in preparation for a game to be played at next meeting. Announce teacher's availability after school for anyone having difficulty with 500-word paper due tomorrow. Select a student good at public speaking to explain the game to be played.

Day 8. Have pre-informed student introduce identification game to class. Call for volunteers to read their "typical" selections for identification by class. Full discussion of the differences encountered in the four different magazines. Take up 500-word papers. (Described in detail below.)

Day 9. Continue and finish oral reports. Make notes for improvement and encouragement. Discuss, ask, and answer questions regarding the criteria as applied to outside magazine reading.

Day 10. Have students fill in unsigned mimeographed sheet evaluating the magazine unit. Return students' 500-word papers. Review the papers, touching on notable points. Have students note and correct marked errors. Question, answer, and summary. Introduce next unit to begin at next class meeting.

Since there are, I feel, at least three days that are "crucial" to the success of the unit, they are here described in more detail. Here again, of course, the details may be changed somewhat, but the main steps prove important to the over-all success of having the students arrive at improved magazine selection.

On the first "crucial" day, drawing attention to previously prepared bulletin board display of magazine covers of the four magazines the class will study, introduce the magazine unit to the class. Outline and explain fully the proposed class objectives, telling students what they may expect to *derive* from the unit. Then outline the unit's requirements, asking the students to make notes, on what they may expect to *contribute* to the unit's work. Mention the three- to five-minute oral reports which are to be given on days 7 and 9, explaining that this will be more fully explained on day 3. Point out that the class will write letters to the editor of a magazine of their choice, and that the letters will be checked, suggestions made on them, and returned for rewriting and mailing to the magazine. Then mention the composition assignments, the short one in class for the following day, and the longer 500-word one to be assigned on day 5 and due on day 8. Ask if there are any questions at that point concerning required work. Answer any questions, making certain that everything is clear.

Returning then to the four magazines, ask the class if they have any ideas on how to objectively and critically read, and evaluate in some way, the four magazines. Try to evoke from the class the idea of setting up some criteria by which to judge magazines. Lead the class by suggesting broad ideas to consider, such as physical appearance of magazine, its content, the quality of its writing, its variety of style and subject matter, etc. As the students get this idea and begin to contribute to the list, have a student write out ideas on the blackboard. Should the class have difficulty arriving at points of criteria, have a suggested beginning list which should get the class started in making thoughtful additions to the list on the board. This should require the major portion of the class period, because this is a crucial point in the development of this unit. Inform the class of the importance of getting the best possible ideas, the good concrete points from which we will work.

Once the class feels there are adequate criteria on the blackboard, pause in this interaction and introduce class copies of *Saga* magazine. Give a short introductory statement for the magazine. Assign home reading of it, stressing that the students should read keeping in mind that they will be required tomorrow to write a paper in class evaluating the magazine using the criteria. Tell the class that tomorrow they will be given mimeograph copies of the class's criteria list, and that there will be space at the bottom of the sheet for any additional ideas that they might think of overnight.

On day 6, the students will have read, as homework, *The Atlantic*. Ask if anyone has a question or comment on the magazine at first. Ask pointed questions concerning how the class feels this magazine bears up under the criteria. Try to create as much student involvement as possible in this discussion. Have read aloud in class excerpts from different articles, sections, and even advertisements in the magazine. Have a student write some of our class evaluations of *The Atlantic* on the board and discuss these thoroughly. There should be varying ideas and it would be well if these discussions became heated enough to generate classwide interest and excitement. Summarize briefly all four of the magazines and our evaluations of them, ending with a summary of our comments on *The Atlantic*.

During the remainder of the class period, have students work in class on their 500-word compositions, so that they can be helped immediately with any individual problems. This provides a chance to make timely suggestions, give aid, and also preview what the general approach of most of the class is going to be to the requirement. Just before class ends, announce teacher's availability after school for any further help needed. Remind the class of the first half of the oral reports to be given at next class.

On day 8, the last "crucial" day, the students for their previous night's assignment will have each copied down a short passage he feels to be typical of one of the studied magazines. One of the more capable public speaking students has been requested to introduce the identification game to be played. He outlines the procedure of the game as follows: volunteers will read their selections and call on someone to try and tell which studied magazine the quotation would best fit in. If the correct answer is given then the student answering gets to ask his question. If the first student queried cannot identify the correct magazine, the questioner asks someone else. Mediate this exercise and see that everyone participates in some way. After everyone has read and had his selection identified, hold a quick humorous mock election to see who the class "magazine expert" is. Then wind up with a detailed discussion of all four magazines. Call for the 500-word compositions to be passed in.

For examples of the approaches of three other teachers to this area of study, see C. A. Brown's "Meeting Reality in the Classroom" in the March 1960 *English Journal.* It is an account of Mr. Brown's study of his students' magazine reading habits and his subsequently teaching them the art of selectivity. He and his class arrived at these criteria: cover art, index, cost as related to values received, stories and articles by qualified authors, poetry, advertising, illustrations for stories and articles, jokes, cartoons, and special features, in that order.

Another related article appearing in the March 1962 *English Journal,* F.S. Kiley's "Magazine in the Classroom" is a short survey of the responsibility of a magazine to the public (*Time* is used as main illustration) and how that responsibility is not always lived up to. Mr. Kiley advises the teaching of students in responsible and selective magazine reading. This article should prove especially valuable to the teacher interested in working exclusively, as earlier suggested, with the news magazine format.

Finally, in this my no means exhaustive suggested list, there is a bulletin by V. D. Moseley entitled "Studying the Current Magazines." Available for ten cents from Northern Illinois University Educational Bulletin Service, DeKalb, Illinois, it advocates the study of current magazines for their ability to arouse interest with today's youngsters.

As a final argument for attempting to teach a unit promoting purposeful magazine reading, I should mention that I have lost count of the number of students—and adult non-students—who have asked me ingenuously, "What magazines are worth my reading?" As always, the best solution to this situation is to produce informed persons who can select wisely for themselves, ultimately not having to depend on the teacher for guidance. I am convinced that such responsible and rewarding selectivity can be taught. In an age of proliferating and oftentimes empty printing, we must find a way to do it.

Suggested Discussion Questions and Activities

1. **ACTIVITY** For each of Langer's caveats, create an activity that might accomplish the understanding he identifies. Consider a variety of methods and materials.

2. **DISCUSSION** What are the major strengths and weakensses of newspapers as information sources when compared to radio and television? Do you believe most people rely more on any one medium for information? Is it really necessary to train students to understand the difference between fact and opinion, how to read cartoons, etc.? If so, why?

3. **ACTIVITY** As Decker suggests, the local newspaper can become an

integral part of the classroom. Call, visit, or write to local newspapers asking

a. if they have a newspaper in the classroom program
b. if they have special rates or delivery procedures
c. whether any of the staff is willing to visit the classroom
d. if they have arrangements for plant visits by school groups

4. **DISCUSSION** Do you agree with Decker that "Teaching the newspaper itself is not the purpose. Instead, the newspaper should be used as a tool . . ." Does it have to be an either . . . or situation? If not, what activities would aid the study of the newspaper as a medium of communication? Did Johnson suggest any in her articles? Which of her many suggestions did you find most interesting?

5. **ACTIVITY** Compare and contrast Walter's approach to magazine reading to McLaughlin's ideas in "A Recipe for Triggering Relevance." Consider the suggested and implied objectives and methods. Would you use either approach, both, or a combination of the two? Briefly outline how you might approach the reading of magazines in your classroom.

Television

The following scene is a dramatization. The names and comments are real although the situation is contrived. The scene is a hurriedly called English department meeting to discuss recent emphasis on television in the classroom; the meeting was requested by a small group of parents.

PARENT: I'd like to know why my son, who watches TV all the time as it is, has to talk about it and watch more in school. I didn't send him here to be entertained!

STENGEL: We are undertaking a great many classroom activities related to home viewing. We're trying to improve selection in the home. . . . We are helping to make students aware of their obligations to mass mediums in their role of intelligent audience.

COFFEY: The "traditional" television program has been viewed and discussed in classes attempting to develop good taste in TV viewing. As literary works, there are some good examples and some extremely bad ones but the student can begin to decide for himself.

PARENT: But my daughter is too immature to decide for herself. Why do you think I'm sending her to you? Teach her something! She can decide for herself at home!

MONAGHAN: If we are truly interested in developing standards which are intellectually defensible, we must begin with the viewer's own experience and point of view. We need to know what programs mean to him and how he compares one with another, rather than imposing standards upon him.

PARENT: Are people watching too much TV today? We watch a lot of TV, but not *everything*. Why the fuss?

MEADOWS: I've quit lying to my students about my television viewing habits. I watch television like a hawk. This medium brings me some of the finest art of the twentieth century—and some of the worst. I think I can tell the difference. The trouble is that my students often can't.

What is the High School Teacher of English Doing about Television?

Stuart Stengel

When a few years ago I was first asked the questions so often put to teachers these days—"What about television? What's it doing to students? What are you doing about it?"—I was at a loss for an answer. My inclination was to answer (apologetically), "I'm afraid I'm not doing anything about it—just yet." Since then, countless studies have made it possible for us to prove whatever we wish: that television has dropped the spelling proficiency of students "umpteen" percentage points or that it has stimulated interest in a thousand classroom activities. We are excited at the thought of a medium which permits us to sit at dinner with a president—and frightened by the future envisioned by Ray Bradbury in his story *The Pedestrian,* a story in which a lonely man walks the deserted streets in the suburbs of a great city: "and on his way he would see the cottages and homes with their dark windows, and it was not unequal to walking through a graveyard where only the faintest glimmers of firefly light appeared in flickers behind the windows"; he is picked up by the police and sent to the Psychiatric Center for Research in Regressive Tendencies because he, you see, is not televiewing with his fellow citizens.

From Stuart Stengel, "What Is the High School Teacher of English Doing about Television," *English Journal* 43 (March 1954): 120-24. Copyright © by the National Council of Teachers of English. Reprinted by permission of the publisher and Stuart Stengel.

But in the last two or three years we teachers have been coming to grips with the problems of television. Many of us have purchased sets of our own (with time-plan assistance, of course!), and we can no longer be TV snobs and sneer, as someone once did at the "really stupid people, sitting on TV stools, nibbling TV snackies, stretching the seats of TV loungie-jamas." We know that television brings each week to our homes a wealth of cultural and educational opportunity.

We are undertaking a great many classroom activities related to home viewing. We're trying to improve selection in the home, through aids such as the very fine *Lookables and Listenables* or Los Angeles' own *Radioways to Learning*. We are helping to make students aware of their obligations to mass mediums in their role of intelligent audience. We're evaluating techniques being developed in the discussion programs which are so prominent on TV and using them to improve classroom discussion. We're working constantly to improve students' ability to sift fact from opinion and truth from distortion in that which comes to them through all the mass mediums. We are doing many things.

But I wish to isolate what seems to me the most crucial problem which television has placed in the laps of English teachers. The problem is this: mass mediums so bombard us today that our students have little opportunity for the creative contemplation which is necessary before vicarious experience becomes a part of us. Our students—perhaps we, ourselves—are sated by an excess of vicarious experiences improperly digested. It makes little difference that we may in our livingrooms see marvellous productions of Shakespeare, listen to Toscanini, or be present at a presidential inauguration, if we as a result feel no emotional reaction or are not changed.

If Shakespeare's Henry V had lived in our day, he might not have been so envious of the common man:

> the wretched slave
> who with a body filled gets him to rest,
> cramm'd with the distressful images of
> half-a-dozen television shows

and who next morning rises with a vacant mind, eager to consume yet another dozen shows, none of which he digests in such a manner that his individuality grows as a result of that of which he has partaken.

Sometimes I feel our classroom children sit before us, "little pitchers waiting to be filled," as someone has said. But many of them are the reverse of the magic pitcher which pours endlessly: into them we can pour endlessly, and nothing bubbles over; there is no ferment of ideas taking place.

Why is it? It is not because the experiences—whether in the classroom or at home—are less rich than they once were. Rather, I think, it is because they are so overly abundant that our children move from one to another without ever really responding creatively to any experience. The wealth of our age has brought to our schools and our homes such a tremendous feast of drama and music and art as to make any other age seem impoverished by comparison. And yet I can't help recalling Edward Horn's incisive couplet, which summarizes a dilemma:

Daily, daily I grew thinner;
Did I dine or was I dinner?

Are we really dining at the festive board provided by television, or is our ability to respond with wonder and with understanding being consumed?

Not so long ago I was rereading Robert Penn Warren's first novel, *Nightrider*, a novel, by the way, well worth your reading. In one scene Percy Munn remembers:

> sometimes on Sunday afternoons, in winter, when he was a child, he had lain on the floor with the stereoscope and the stack of picture cards, each with its duplicate scene. Through the lenses, the card would show a rich, three-dimensional little world . . . with light falling over the objects there and casting shadows, as in the real world, with distances and depths like the real world, and recesses more secret and fascinating. Sometimes, pressing his forehead into the wooden frame until it ached, he had felt that if he could just break through into that little world where everything was motionless but seemed about to move, . . . he would know the most unutterable bliss. Then, slowly, he would take the frame from his eyes and remove the card from the clamps. He would inspect it: the flat, dull, fading picture printed in duplicate, the frayed, yellow edges of the cardboard. No life would be there, no depth. He would look about him at the familiar furniture of the room; at the fire failing now in the grate, perhaps; at the pattern of the carpet on which he lay.

Thirty years later Percy Munn remembers vividly the experience with that comparatively primitive instrument. In the last month, how many of us have seen on television fine dramatic presentations which we will not remember because we did not take the time to live with them a while before we allowed some other program to "consume us"?

I am not saying that we should go back to our grandmother's parlor and the stereoscope. But we must be aware of what happens if we open ourselves to a constant reception of impressions from various mediums and rarely digest that which we have received.

E. E. Cummings . . . said in one of his so-called "nonlectures" to Harvard students:

> You haven't the least or feeblest conception of being here, and now, and alone, and yourself. Why (you ask) should anyone want to be here, when (simply by pressing a button) anyone can be in 50 places at once? How could anyone want to be now, when anyone can go whening all all over creation at the twist of a knob? As for being yourself—why on earth should you be yourself; when instead of being yourself you can be a hundred, or a thousand, or a hundred thousand thousand, other people?

And then Cummings goes on to say that every art "was and is and forever will be strictly and distinctly a question of individuality." That, of course, is no new concept to teachers in our democracy. We have always been concerned with helping our students to become individuals who have an awareness of their uniqueness and the responsibilities which that uniqueness engenders. The processes by which that awareness is achieved, however difficult to define, are a primary concern of all teachers, and perhaps particularly of English teachers.

How does a child integrate the experiences—real or vicarious— which make up his life into a unique and desirable individuality? Psychologists elaborate for us in technical terms, but I prefer the vernacular of Mr. Shults, a character from Wright Morris' book *The Inhabitants*. Listen:

> A kid is a kid because he's what he is in little pieces. He's all broken up like a jigsaw loose in its box. He's just what we make of him and we never make more than we can use. . . . All the pieces left over nobody sees, he don't know they're there. . . . How's he to know that every kid is born with the whole of a man somewhere in him, but that half of him is never fitted, he don't know there's more. How's he to know livin' on earth that heaven is really a part of him—not somethin' he gets when he's gone, but has while he's here? How's he to know when the men who should fit him are just half-men? They weren't fit when they were kids and they only know their own pattern. They don't know that fittin' kids is what a man's for. An' they don't seem to know that a kid is more than a man is. They forgot that he's the sum of the whole darned works.

Well, if a kid is a kid because he's what he is in little pieces, what I am saying is that our modern mediums, and perhaps most of all television, are adding to the number of unfitted pieces. And it's our job, as teachers, to try to fit our kids so that they may really be "the sum of the whole darned works."

Now, how do we go about it?

We teachers have talked a great deal about the proper selection of programs, and we have complained because hours spent in viewing cannot be spent reading or doing homework or engaging in some other activity we desire. But are we failing to develop in students an understanding of what it is *really to see*—with an intensity which makes the *see-er* (and I purposely use that word with its connotation of participation, rather than the passive *viewer*) feel: "I don't want to see any more just now; I want to think about what I have seen"?

Joseph Wood Krutch says in his . . . *Desert Year*, "The rare moment is not the moment when there is something worth looking at but the moment when we are capable of seeing."

Recently Sam Levenson (who, by the way, is an English teacher who did something about television—he joined it!) told one of his warm stories of family life in which he pokes good-natured fun at his parents. He describes his father towing six or seven small Levensons, chained hand to hand, through the museum. Suddenly, in irritation at the slowness of their progress through the halls, the father says, "Look, kids, if you're gonna stop and look at everything, you ain't gonna see nothin'!" If we look shallowly at a great deal, we are apt to remember very little.

"Really to see something once or twice a week," says Mr. Krutch, "is almost inevitably to have to try . . . to make oneself a poet."

I am not saying that we should try to **make** every child a poet. But what I am saying is that we must try to help children find that depth of emotional response which will make them realize that to be "viewers"—to turn from *Hamlet* to the opera to the United Nations without pause, however fine each of these may be; to turn without pause for personal response—is to condemn one's self to shallowness and to a search for novelty and a spurious kind of stimulation.

I should like to suggest that one way of helping children find that depth of response is through poetry. Poetry, with its careful form and its ability to create an emotional response, is in a sense an anthithesis to the formlessness and the dulled response evoked by television. Because, however much form any single program may have, the total effect of watching many programs is formlessness.

Louise Bogan, writing in our *English Journal* earlier this year, pointed out that "there is no way of reading as one runs, or looking as one runs, when it comes to the examination of any highly developed art. We must move slowly through a book of poems, as we move slowly through a gallery of paintings, or as we give time and attention to the hearing of music."

This very necessity for moving slowly and thoughtfully, for listening carefully, for analyzing the imagery and theme, helps give students an approach to vicarious experience quite different from that of sitting passively while streams of images pass before them on a screen and fade to nothingness. Students are apt to remember Winfield Scott's *Swedish Angel* long after the Christmas television programs of this year are forgotten. . . . "Dispensing of all the brought light a total larger light"—isn't that a wonderful description of what we hope takes place in our students as a result of their experiences? And this simple poem, too, may help children to see that one may be moved by a simple daily experience as well as by the studpendous, the supercolossal, and the epic.

Once again, let me remind you that I am not saying that poetry should be substituted for television. What I am saying is that someone who has experienced the emotional response which can be created by a poem will be more apt to respond in kind to televison and might, perhaps, after seeing NBC's very beautiful annual Christmas presentation of *Amahl and the Night Visitors,* be inclined to shut off the set and let the music and the poetry become a part of him.

I have been suggesting that one of our major responsibilities as English teachers is to build an awareness that no television program, however fine, is going to give us growth unless we take the time to live with it and to understand its implications for our own lives. We have said that really to see, and not just to view, requires something of the sensitivity of the poet and that it is possible that developing the kind of active response which must be brought to the appreciation of poetry may help develop in children a more creative response to television.

I should like to touch upon one more outgrowth of the superficial viewing in which we engage when we "look at everythin' an' don't see nothin'." It is the desire on the part of some of our youngsters to have everything labeled for them and to be spoonfed their attitudes. Earlier this month *Time* magazine reported the results of a classroom survey on television taken by a Rhode Island teacher.

One student said bluntly that he preferred television to books because "books give you an idea of how to get into trouble but they never tell you how to get out of it!" For this student the process of making judgments for himself is just too difficult—he has been brought up in a never-never land of comic strips and pulp magazines and soap operas, where black is black and white is white, and gray is inconceivable.

And I'm afraid this student is not atypical. When one wishes to go "whening all over creation" continuously, it's pretty annoying to have loose sleeves of thought hanging out of your luggage. It's much nicer to have those disturbing thoughts neatly folded into place for you, with the bad man properly killed and the heroine properly married.

Haven't all of you had the experience of reading a problem story to a class and, when you have finished, hearing the class groan, "Is *that* the end of the story? What happened?" Children who live by stereotypes in which, as Bernard De Voto says, "thugs have hard voices, private eyes have menacing voices, and old ladies have old, old ladies' voices" need a great deal of classroom work in thinking through the best of literature: that which describes life and demands that the reader make his own judgments.

Contemporary short-story writers are giving us abundant material of this sort with which to work, and students love it, in spite of their groans. Once they are able to cope with the kind of story which demands an active response on their part, they begin to select on television a similar kind of material available on television, although such programs may not top the popularity ratings yet.

Wasn't there an art critic who once claimed that one reason the Venus de Milo is universally beloved is the very fact that her arms have been lost—and that each of us must create for himself a completed image of their position? At least it is true that the deepest enjoyment and understanding of any art form comes when we respond to it with creative contemplation, rather than half-listening or passive viewing.

"A kid is a kid because he's what he is in little pieces," said Mr. Shults. "He's all broken up like a jigsaw loose in its box." Our mass mediums bring to our kids an infinitely greater number of pieces of life than ever before—and as a result our children may either become increasingly disorganized or else gain an infinitely more complete personality. Which will it be?

A Chronicle of Television Use at Alhambra High School

H. Lavern Coffey

As the visitor walked down the corridor he noticed that one room was darkened. Upon opening the door and looking in he saw that the class was watching television. Not educational television as we generally consider it, but a videotape replay of a commercially produced television program that is common to all TV viewers every night of the week. Such a situation is not at all uncommon at Alhambra High School. Our English department makes frequent use of our television equipment. As a matter of fact all departments have made use of this equipment since its installation a little more than a year ago. Teachers of math, physical education, foreign languages, social studies, business, music, science and counselors, as well as English teachers, have used TV in their classrooms. Frequently the equipment is used all day by the various people and on one day (October 15, 1968) camera and videotape machine were in use from ·8:00 in the morning until 10:00 that night. However not all of our English teachers have used TV in their classrooms, but 10 of our 29 have, and some of these have made frequent use of television.

Our equipment consists of a videotape recorder, Ampex Model 5000, a Panasonic camera, and 14 TV receiver sets (23-inch screen). These TV sets are capable of receiving closed circuit video (cable television) or commercial programs by way of an antenna (RF). The school has one TV antenna in the instructional materials center that provides a source for all our sets. All our English classrooms are wired for cable television directly to the center so that a teacher who wishes to show commercial programs has only to turn the set on and select the channel. We can receive channels 3, 5, 8 (educational television from ASU), 10, 12, 21 (UHF) and our own program source originating within our high school. If a teacher chooses to use a program that has been prerecorded, he simply tells the instructional materials center to play a certain tape and he can view that on his set as often as desired while other teachers may be using a different channel. Each time the teacher uses the TV equipment he

From H. Lavern Coffey, "A Chronicle of Television Use at Alhambra High School," *Arizona English Bulletin* 12 (February 1970): 48-50. Reprinted by permission of the publisher.

must request the specific items needed on a printed form, and this printed form becomes a log of TV use. Comments are made by the teacher after use and this log has become a valuable guide for all persons interested in TV usage in the classroom.

Television is a versatile medium for it has a variety of uses. It has provided background information for a piece of literature being read in class. For instance, in my freshman English class, the class was reading the book *Kon Tiki*. *National Geographic* produced an excellent hour program entitled "Polynesian Adventure." This program gave good photographic coverage of the South Pacific area where the raft Kon Tiki landed as well as interesting information about the formation of coral islands. The program was broadcast at night and recorded on our videotape recorder. During the next weeks four teachers used the tape during their class periods.

Another teacher used a montage of news programs to compare the various treatments of news by TV stations. The daytime news programs from three different channels were put on one tape making it possible to see in just one period how the different stations treated the same news. This provided students a chance to observe how the placement of the news items can affect its relative importance. Focusing on a particular news item may give that item an importance not given by another channel.

The TV program has at times been the piece of literature under discussion. For instance the drama "People Next Door," presented on October 15, 1968, was recorded at night and played the next day in class. The play was discussed just as if it had been read by all the class from a book. In December the *Hallmark Playhouse* was recorded and used in class. This has made it possible to use good drama from contemporary sources in the classroom. Students had been told about the two drama presentations mentioned but very few of them had viewed these programs on their own.

Our television has also served as a vehicle for student research reports. While studying mythology and ancient Greece a group of students decided to present their material on the Greek wars by way of TV. These students recorded on videotape their presentation using pictures, charts, chalkboard material plus their own speeches. Unfortunately, when played back to the class the TV equipment did not function well and added nothing. Had the presentations been really first class the tape could have been profitably played for later groups or used as resource information for the next year. This experience though proved that considerable technical skill was needed to make a good presentation. Another teacher, however, had more success with a similar project. Her students showed more originality and produced a newsreel entitled "Beautiful Downtown Olympus." Another mythology report presented on TV was an interview with the cyclops. Other teachers have used the television to make dramatic reports. A senior English class was reading the novel *1984* by Orwell. They dramatized one scene from the book. The students wrote their own script form the book and produced the scene as they visualized it. This type of book report demands that students visualize what the author is trying to get across to his reader.

Besides being a vehicle for reporting research by the students, the television has been used often as an evaluating tool. Before a forensic competition the speech teacher taped one of the student's performances. When replayed, this provided a valuable opportunity for the student to evaluate his own performance and make improvements before the contest. In another case, a student teacher and her cooperating English teacher taped their classroom teaching for evaluation and comparison. First, the student teacher was videotaped and replayed in private. After watching herself on videotape, her comments indicated that she was unaware of her use of slang in front of the students. Also, she felt that she was too immobile in the classroom and should move more freely. The cooperating teacher then taught a lesson in front of the camera. The student teacher then could see ways of improving her own performance.

The commercials on television have provided a wealth of information and experience. They have been shown in class as examples of propaganda techniques. All the terms that exist only as words in a book become meaningful when the students see examples of testimonials, bandwagon, generalities, etc. Commercials also provide some of the best examples of dramatic effect. Commercials can compress into 30 seconds a tremendous effect. The students can see that the writer of commercials must condense into a sentence or two of writing and one scene that the essayist spends several pages doing. These commercials have provided some interesting experiences for the students.

The "traditional" television program has been viewed and discussed in classes attempting to develop good taste in TV viewing. As literary works, there are some good examples and some extremely bad ones but the student can begin to decide for himself. He has seen both of the extremes in class and knows how to decide on the basis of reason. He has developed an appreciation of good TV and can be selective in his viewing.

Television is not the only teaching tool at Alhambra High but it is one that offers promise to teachers for motivating students since this is one of the most familiar devices in the lives of high school students. Of course television is expensive. A videotape alone costs $60, or about $1 per minute. However, this tape can be reused frequently. Our students, though, have witnessed in class the inauguration of a president of the United States and the Apollo 11 moon flight. These events can awaken the students to the fact that high school can be related to their lives outside of the school walls.

Get Smart: Let TV Work for You

Robert Meadows

I've quit lying to my students about my television habits. I watch television like a hawk. This medium brings me some of the finest art of the twentieth century—and some of the worst. I think I can tell the difference. The trouble is that my students often can't. They think viewing's a passive process; and they sit there sopping it up to the point of saturation. Then it just sloshes through them, having little impact, raising little response. I search for ways to put them back in touch, to give them critical tools, to make them realize that art is somehow an interactive process, that creation and appreciation cannot exist apart. Art is always a dialogue, and it is as effective as are the participants' communication skills. Here is a simple six-step activity which encourages dynamic television viewing while it offers valuable experience with almost every communication tool we hope to sharpen in the English classroom. The steps in order are: (1) committee organization, (2) student television observation, (3) script writing, (4) rehearsal, (5) production, and (6) evaluation.

STEP 1: COMMITTEE SELECTION

First, I divide the class into five-member committees, each of which elects to watch a specific show. An average class might select *Beverly Hillbillies, Bonanza, Bullwinkle* (ah, yes), *The Dick Van Dyke Show,* and *Get Smart.* This is most important: any show they enjoy will do the job so long as it features a consistent cast of characters from week to week. I want the process to be *fun* for them.

STEP 2: OBSERVATION

Watching the show, each committee member takes notes, asking himself specific questions about the show in general and the character he has agreed to observe. Characterization comes first. Just how does that character

From Robert Meadows, "Get Smart: Let TV Work for You," *English Journal* 56 (January 1967): 121-24. Copyright ©1967 by the National Council of Teachers of English. Reprinted by permission of the publisher and Robert Meadows.

communicate? What are his speech patterns? His diction, phrasing, intonation, and stress are all important here. Further, how does he use his body? What gestures, facial expressions, and general physical mannerisms does he rely upon to make more sense of his sounds. Are there any recurring patterns which mark the character? And what about the other elements of form? The typical plot situation, the locale, the tone. Is there an obvious gimmick, such as the cultural contrast in *Green Acres* or *Beverly Hillbillies?*

STEP 3: SCRIPT WRITING

The observer must be on his toes, because in class the day following the viewing he must be ready to compare notes with his cohorts; and, together, using the recorded data, they must begin to construct a drama—an actual script—based upon the simple plot structure of *Little Red Riding Hood, Goldilocks,* or some other common tale. Here is where their "homework" will pay off, if they have observed keenly and recorded accurately. Script-writing sessions are lengthy and uproarious—and profitable for many reasons. The students have only a story line. Everything else they hammer out through compromise—the casting, the dialogue, the blocking, the technical effects. Every participant sees the possibilities of his own character; he sees the adaptation, its problems, and the solutions in a different way. But the show must go on. Compromises must be made. Every idea, every detail is subjected to meticulous criticism by the committee of peers. There is no better lesson in selection of detail than this, because it is based on concern for a respected audience rather than upon the teacher's criticisms. As he watches his students interact, hammering out compromises during the script-writing session, the observant teacher can learn a great deal about the social structure of his classroom, can begin to know his students as individuals, can discover their strengths and weaknesses, and can cultivate a climate in which students feel safe enough to take risks.

He also acts as a resource person, helping students resolve arguments, helping them make choices. He does *not* make the choices for them, but he *does* help them frame the issues: "Talk it onto paper! Get it down onto paper in concrete form. Then there can be no equivocating." Frequently students can't make choices simply because they cannot *see* the alternatives clearly. The teacher must understand his role here. He does not make choices for his students; he tries rather to show them an orderly process by which wise choices might be made.

But writing the dialogue—*hearing* it correctly—is only one problem. There is much more to a script. What about the movements? The lighting and sound effects? Costuming? Makeup? Everything must be heard, visualized, and put down in black and white. At this point, many students ask for the first time the vital question: "Just how *is* that done?" Many students are so naive about the techniques they have previously *slept* through in hours of viewing that they do not even have an idea what effects they—the students—can create. They have no idea what their possibilities are, or what is feasible within the limitations imposed by the classroom facilities. Frustrated, they go back to the television set and, for the first time, really pay attention. We got 'em now. Television never looks quite the same to these students again. And so they begin to write and understand. Slapstick and absurd plays on words are the rule, but no less eminent an artist then Robert Frost spoke of creativity as "the *wild* part of our nature." The students *are* wild. They *are* divergent. Enthusiasm runs high! This is *not* a quiet activity. The committee members gallop all over the room demonstrating their ideas. They argue, shout, and laugh, expressing approval or disapproval. And their material is wild also. But they *are* making a beginning. They begin to recognize the easy effects: the cheap appeals to sentiment, the cliches, the stereotyped characters, and the rigged plot sequences. Perhaps they are also beginning to recognize and cultivate a respect for the difficult effects that mark the finest art. I'll never forget the day an enthusiastic and insightful student athlete said to me, "Good art's like excellent basketball. The better it's played, the easier it looks. You have got to try it yourself to appreciate it." He was one youngster who got the point. Some don't get the point, I'm afraid. Nevertheless, they are participating actively, some of them for the first time, in an artistic endeavor. All we can do once we get them doing that is gamble and hope.

STEP 4: REHEARSAL

Tough as it is, the composition period is only the beginning. Even the finest script is a bundle of unsolved problems. Drama is the ultimate fusion of communication skills. All the speech skills are there: memorization, enunciation, intonation, emphasis, and whatever else a performer uses of himself to project meaning. The production staff aids the performer in countless ways with his communication problems. The setting, the lights, the costumes, even the lines meticulously drawn on his brow, are all a part of the performer's effect, his meaning. And there are so many production categories, offering so many opportunities for creative expression, that every student can find a satisfactory outlet that meets his needs, interests, and skill level. The poor writer may be the skilled light technician; the reticent performer may be the makeup artist or the sound effects man; and so on it goes.

STEP 5: PRODUCTION

So far the process has taken, perhaps, four or five days. The length of time it takes to put the thing together depends upon the students, their needs, and their skills. Every teacher will recognize this fact. Ultimately though, the students perform for the class; that's when the fun really begins.

Because I urge them to set whatever tone they wish when they're constructing their adaptions, the performances are usually highly imaginative and rollicking, combining as they often do cornball humor and characterization shifts. Maxwell Smart cavorts as an amorous wolf. Bonanza's supposedly urbane, masculine Paw skips guilelessly along to Grandma's. Baby Bear Dyke discovers the empty bowl, the broken chair, the tousled bed; and Baldilocks, played by bumbling, pun-cracking Morey Amsterdam, darts out the window for home. Most important, the movements, the spoken lines must approximate the form typical of the television character selected.

"Now just a cotton-pickin' minute here," says Baby Bear Dyke, as he discovers his empty bowl. Ellie May, in the same role, discovers her broken chair, and tousled bed "full o' critters."

"Vun moment, Boris Dahlink," demures Natashalocks, as she bombs Bullwinkle Wolf out of Grandma's bed.

"Would you believe three clouds, a dead sparrow, and a falling star?" queries Maxwell Smart, as Chicken Little.

The process satisfies the students' voracious appetite for corn. They recreate it, perform it, spoof it. They continue to enjoy it (intellectual snobbery does not constitute growth!). The important thing is that they see the mundane for what it really is—a thin veneer hoping to pass for solid, artistic material.

STEP 6: EVALUATION

The technique puts the student on the spot somewhat, but it offers him a chance to have fun. The informal atmosphere, the enthusiasm of his peers, the affirmative climate, and the subtle direction of the teacher, encourage even the reluctant or limited-ability student to risk exposure. In return for his risk he receives valuable experience in observing and recording, in assembling artistic elements skillfully, in performing before a group sufficiently well to bring the drama to life. There is hardly a communication skill which is not employed somewhere in the process. And I cannot underscore too emphatically the fact that the process is the important thing—not the product. It's what the students learn, what they *discover* in a process that really concerns me as a teacher. Products are nice; products make us proud. But there are shortcuts to products. We encourage students to cheat when we emphasize the product rather than the process. Math teachers have long since learned to evaluate the process and leave the product alone; they go so far as to print the answers right in the text! English teacher, too, must begin to think about what happens during the process and place the major emphasis there. Understand this vital point. Evaluation is not an *end* product, nor is it solely a teacher activity. By virtue of their making comparisons, making choices, the students are evaluating constantly. For his part, the teacher evaluates throughout the entire activity. He cannot help but see the students sharpening their critical skills, polishing their communication tools. After the activity, I ask the students to select a show and evaluate it. They respond in writing. One student said: "Last night I watched *Gunsmoke* again. Dillon did exactly the same things, said the same things, and so did Doc. Kitty is a cardboard character; she never changes. The show begins with the same quick draw every time, and the plots never vary." I ask the students to watch a noon soap opera. They talk later about the sentimental appeal; they see now bathos rather than pathos. Such responses are typical. I've never gotten beyond my student athlete's statement: "You've gotta try it yourself to appreciate it."

I say again, drama, the entire process from comparison to performance, is the ultimate fusion of communication skills. But there is another vital consideration—critical observation. Television *is* here to stay, and no one can say for certain what its impact will be. It will in all probability give our culture a common language experience, a basis for common understandings. This heartens me! However, the tremendous impact it can have upon a noncritical audience *frightens* me. I want my students to interact dynamically with television. I want them to make intellectual judgments about what they see. This will protect them. But I want them to make aesthetic judgments as well. Perhaps then they will discover the fine art in television, and through that art begin to discover themselves.

A New Way to Evaluate Programs

Robert R. Monaghan

There are many possible standards for evaluating radio and television programs, but most of them are not being used. Professional critics have failed to offer adequate leadership. One can read the critics for a long time before identifying what standards they impose on radio and television programs. When one can comprehend a critic's dimensions, he is likely to find that they are sloppily defined, cliché-ridden, and often personal and emotional. Furthermore, they may be inconsistent. And the critics do not agree among themselves.

Yet we all would benefit if standards for evaluation and criticism of radio and televison could be established. Educators particularly can contribute along these lines since they come into day-to-day, face-to-face contact with the public and are able to exert influence to an unusual degree.

The purpose of this paper is to describe a rationale and method for establishing critical standards which may be immediately and economically used in the classroom by any high school teacher. These procedures are easily demonstrated in the classroom, and out-of-class projects may then be assigned. It

From Robert R. Monaghan, "A New Way to Evaluate Programs," *The Bulletin of the National Association of Secondary School Principals* 50 (October 1966): 90-95. Copyright © 1966 by the National Association of Secondary School Principals. Reprinted by permission of the NASSP.

is recommended that the reader privately try the procedures on himself in order to become fully aware of how the system works.

Let us first return to the critic for a closer examination of his problem. Typically, a critic makes his judgment according to two criteria: (1) Does he like the program? and (2) Does he consider it good for the viewer? Just for visual illustration let us suppose we were "sighting-in" on a few television programs through the crosshairs of these two standards. We could then portray programs such as A, B, C, and D as in figure 1.

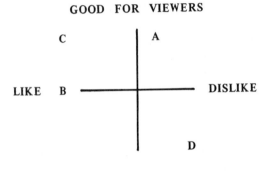

GOOD FOR VIEWERS

C   A

LIKE   B ———————+——————— DISLIKE

D

BAD FOR VIEWERS

FIGURE 1.

Program A, then, is considered good for the viewer, but neither high nor low in the critic's personal preference. Program B is personally enjoyable, but considered neither good nor bad for people to watch. Program C, of course, fits both criteria ideally; Program D, on the other hand, would be soundly panned.

To the extent that this visual representation generally reflects the usual dimensions of criticism some important basic questions may be raised:

1. *By what means do we determine our program standards?* Presumably, we want the best possible standards. However, we have freely imposed standards without bothering to evaluate the standards themselves.
2. *Should we consider the standards illustrated in Figure 1 sufficient?* Other standards may yet be invented by which programs can be meaningfully evaluated.
3. *How do we know our standards are most appropriate for the audience to which the program is directed?* If a program is judged according to whether it is good or bad for viewers, we need to know of what viewer we speak. If the critic judges a program by standards not relevant to its intended audience, then he has missed his mark.

There is a danger that we might arbitrarily set up a procrustean bed which we insist all programs, and therefore all viewers, should fit. How we decide upon a particular set of standards is somewhat of a mystery. When we insist that programs should be "for the good of viewers" we may mean for the good of *other* viewers.

I have yet to meet a critic who will admit that he himself has been damaged by certain kinds of programs. It is always someone else that he is worried about. We sometimes are concerned about an unspecified person who we claim is not really able to assume responsibility for his own choices. We tend to evaluate programs according to the effects we *imagine* the programs to have on others. We easily confuse the fancies of our speculation with solid knowledge and then make important decisions about program content on the basis of our confusion. Often we resort to premature judgments based upon personal bias and speculation.

If we are truly interested in developing standards which are intellectually defensible, we must begin with the viewer's own experience and point of view. We need to know what programs mean to him and how he compares one with another, rather than imposing standards upon him. It is not enough that the critic has his heart in the right place. He must understand the meanings the program has for the viewer as the viewer's frame of reference selects them.

The remainder of this article outlines one way of developing standards for the evaluation of radio or televison programs. It is a method which can, with a short explanation by the teacher, be understood easily and employed by any high school student.

THE RATIONALE

It is appropriate to explain first the rationale behind the method. If I say, "This is a beautiful day," I imply that I have experienced other days that are to me somehow similar to this day, and that this particular day belongs with those that I consider beautiful. Otherwise I could not make such a statement.

Or, if I identify a certain creature as "a dog," I could hardly do so without a more general concept of dogs. Although dogs vary widely in size, shape, and breed, I can identify a particular dog as a dog by associating him with a conceptual set we call dogs. Within this set, there are subsets of different kinds of dogs, all belonging to the universal set of dogs. Such conceptual sets are the essence of mathematical set theory.

Let us suppose a viewer is exposed to a number of television programs. To him, this total exposure represents the universal set of television programs. He structures television programs in the same way that he makes sense out of days, dogs, and the rest of his world. Certain programs belong together. Other programs are associated with still other programs.

Some television programs belong in set A because the experience the viewer associates with one member of set A is similar to the experience he associates with other members of that set. Other programs which are not members of this set are identified together in set B, and the experience associated with set B is distinct from that of set A. Still other programs may be identified as set C, and so on. Certain programs may represent a mixture or union of two or more sets.

However, it is still possible to make meaningful distinctions between subsets. Visually, sets of television programs might appear as in figure 2.

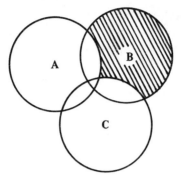

FIGURE 2.

The way we think and act is by nature economical, or at least we aspire toward economy. We seek the most practical and meaningful explanation of our world that we can find. We search for the smallest number of meaningful sets and subsets to account for the greatest amount of variation in the world around us. The mathematical set concept reflects this pattern of human behavior, and can be applied to the task of developing program standards.

A METHOD FOR DEVELOPING STANDARDS

Let us suppose we ask a television viewer to list the names of several different kinds of television programs, some that he likes and some that he does not like. There is no need to use the word "subset" in our request, although essentially we are asking him to identify his particular subsets and to give us the names of programs most representative of them. When he gives us the program titles, we proceed as follows:

1. We list each title on a separate card or piece of paper.
2. Then we rotate various pairs of these titles. For example, if he gives us the names of programs A, B, C, D, and E, we can pair off programs A and B, A and C, and so on.
3. We ask him to compare and contrast the programs in various pairs and tell us what important characteristics he can distinguish between them. In this way, we determine what dimensions or criteria he tends to use. That is, by a series of such comparisons we can identify a number of standards he employs.
4. We can follow this procedure for any number of persons. We then simply tally up the criteria which correspond. Various persons may use somewhat different words to mean much the same thing.

We could vary this procedure by taking the same list in three's instead of two's. That is, we could rotate the programs on our viewer's list and ask him to tell us which two go together, which one does not belong with the other two, and why. We can ask him to make such comparisons four at a time, five at a time, or in any quantity he can measure at one time. For example, let us suppose he gives us 20 titles. We can ask him to tell us which ones belong together. He might place ten in one pile and ten in another, and be able to explain to us his criterion for separating the two piles.

Or, of those 20 titles, he might place ten titles together, five other titles in another pile, and the remaining five titles in a third pile, and then tell us why he separated them as he did. This procedure can be followed not only for any number of programs, but also for any proportions within that total number.

There are many possible modifications and applications of this technique. In each case, we are following the kind of model shown in figure 2 and we are using the rationale previously described. We are identifying the nature and number of a person's subsets regarding television programs and the standards most meaningfully employed in his decisions. This technique can be used among students in the classrooms, or they can employ the method as a take-home assignment in the wider community. In the latter case, they can prepare in the classroom for their interviews by deciding how many titles they wish viewers to compare at a time and planning what other advance instructions they will give interviewees.

Students will find that not all persons reveal exactly the same system of structuring programs into subtests. As patterns do emerge, however, we can begin to cluster the standards into sets; and in this way we can isolate and define criteria actually employed in evaluating broadcasts.

Suggested Discussion Questions and Activities

1. **DISCUSSION** Concerned with an excess of vicarious experience through television, Stengel believes "It makes little difference . . . if we as a result feel no emotional reaction or are not changed." Does this emotional reaction have to occur during or immediately after a viewing experience? Can you think of a personal delayed reaction? What can the English teacher do to promote "a creative response to television"?

2. **ACTIVITY** Coffey's article illustrates some ways commercial television can be utilized in the classroom. Make a list of ways an English teacher can know *well* in advance what programs are to be aired on commercial stations, so videotaping can be arranged and/or recommendations can be made to students. (One excellent source is Television Information Office, 745 Fifth Avenue, New York 10022.)

3. **DISCUSSION** Having read Meadow's article, identify some basic tenets of his philosophy of education. In what ways do the activities he describes facilitate his philosophy? Can you recommend others that would be consistent with his beliefs?

4. **DISCUSSION** What is your reaction to Monaghan's "new way to evaluate programs"? Do you know of any other systems of evaluation? Should everyone have his own system? What is your personal procedure for evaluating TV offerings? Are you able to put it into words or print? Try.

SECTION EIGHT

Film and Filmmaking

From Grabowski's "Film Study Is Here To Stay" to Sheratsky's "Freaking Around with Films," the message is clear: film is in!

STANLEY M. GRABOWSKI

"Students are able to distinguish the worthwhile from the trivial . . . get insights into their own experiences . . . experience an aesthetic enjoyment . . . "

JOHN M. CULKIN

"Each person sees his own film. This paradox is merely the reaffirmation in a new context of the thesis of individual differences, and selective perception. The same film on the screen washes over each viewer as an individual, with individual past experiences, hopes, loves, fears, needs, and intelligence."

AUGUST FRANZA

"We anticipate the prospect of a student request for a film-making course. The questions have already been raised in a minor key and our scouts have informed us that some individualistic senior has been making 8 mm shots on his own. We intend to give him his day in the course and when we do, we will have begun to take the next step."

FRED SILVA

"The chief purpose of film study—no matter who presents it—should be to enhance the student's visual experience by showing him *what* is there."

FRANK DAVID MARTARELLA

"And perhaps in time, when it not only has a message to convey but also possesses a style that is of importance on its own account, the animated film will become the most potent of all media of expression. . . . "

PAUL CARRICO

"In schools where film making is a potential part of every student's experience, teachers note a proliferation, almost an explosion, in other forms of expression, especially poetry."

VIVIAN TILFORD

"If it seems complicated and difficult, it can be. If it sounds like something stimulating and fun for the teachers and students, it is. It seems only fair to warn you, it is very hard to stop when you once get hooked on making films."

RICHARD BUMSTEAD

"The screen educator's task is to help students to employ and respond to the new language as effectively and richly as possible. . . . "

RODNEY E. SHERATSKY

"Introducing students to an awareness of the essentials required for seeing may well be the only realistic, honest, and sensible reason for encouraging students to make films."

Film Study Is Here to Stay

Stanley M. Grabowski

One of the most exciting happenings in education these days is the introduction of film study at all levels of instruction. Educators are recognizing and accepting film as an art form, incorporating it in some way into their curricula.

From Stanley M. Grabowski, "Film Study Is Here to Stay: The Medium Sharpens Students' Vision of Man" *The Clearing House* 42 (December 1967): 253-54. Copyright © 1967 by Fairleigh Dickinson University. Reprinted by permission of the publisher.

Some school administrators are taking film study quite seriously, while others are giving it only token recognition. Film study can mean anything from an occasional film shown to a single class to a full-fledged series of courses. Central High School in Trenton, New Jersey, for example, has purchased $30,000 worth of films as part of its Title I project. This package of films includes documentaries, biographies, social and historical studies, and literary-aesthetic works.

Although most of the schools now engaged in film education are doing it as part of an already existing course like art, English, or the humanities, the important thing is that the film is used for its own sake, as a distinct art form, not merely as a visual aid.

In the past, our schools concentrated on teaching students how to read and write as the basis for communication. The only concession to the visual dimension of communication was the course in drawing or painting.

In an age where we are bombarded by the visual image in magazines, newspapers, television, and highway billboards, it is absolutely necessary to teach students how to "read" visual images.

Even if educators did not see any real art in films worthy of classroom study, they could not bypass films as part of an existing social condition. The statistics are overwhelming. Students spend more time watching television and movies than they do in any other activity except sleeping. A youngster graduating from high school has probably spent two full years in front of the screens, or 50 percent more time than he has spent in school. It would be playing ostrich not to face the fact that more than one-half of the moviegoers in this country are teenagers. If education is supposed to reach the "whole man," then, the educators reasoned, films must be considered as a real factor in the lives of youngsters.

The idea behind using films in the classroom is to expose the student to films of artistic excellence under direction—apart from any formal testing, grading, or evaluation. One of the jobs this can do is to cultivate taste.

Teachers who have used films know the power of the medium in capturing the attention of the students and the way in which the films succeed in communicating attitudes and emotions. More than any other vehicle, the film can sharpen the individual's vision of man—his ideas, his follies, his virtues, and his capacities.

An artistic film, like any work of art, makes us realize that man knows things intuitively and not just through logical thinking. It helps us realize that man moves through a real world, not a dream world; that a man is a many-faceted human being.

For example, *Death of a Salesman* makes us realize how foolish it is to get out of touch with reality, to live in a dream world, to fool oneself. Students seeing this film see this fatal flaw in Willie Loman and ask whether a nonhero such as Willie can be a tragic figure? They can easily see that he is a nonhero because he lacks nobility of spirit. It is only one step further to have them consider whether it isn't a tragedy when any human being fails to reach nobility of spirit. (See "The Dilemma of Modern Man," CH, March 1966, pp. 442-44.)

A simple film like *Marty,* the story of a homely, young-middle-aged, paunchy butcher who falls in love, helps students understand loneliness and the vastness of its empty plains.

In *Treasure of Sierra Madre,* the student realizes how avarice consumes the spirit when it becomes an overwhelming passion.

Many impressive points are made in the *Bridge on the River Kwai.* The two that stand out the most are the indomitable human spirit, and the fact that the letter of the law is not enough to live by.

Caine Mutiny is a film which says loudly that "right is right even if nobody does it, and wrong is wrong even if everybody does it." Here's a film that can be used for cross-media comparision since *Caine Mutiny* originally appeared as a novel, then a stage play, and later a television play.

High Noon, a serious drama dressed in Western clothes, is about one man's courage in the face of opposition.

The mob psychology which plays a part in *High Noon* is even more clearly pronounced in *The Ox-Bow Incident.*

A lyrical Japanese film, *The Island,* emphasizes the nobility of work and the struggle of a family for existence.

The gamut of themes in films can illustrate very dramatically two lines from T. S. Eliot's poems. One of these lines says, "I have measured out my life with coffee spoons," and the students will recognize the truth of this in films that examine the small side of life. Another line says, "This is the way the world ends / Not with a bang, but a whimper." Films which have a bigness about them, with a lot of romantic swoop and flair, will demonstrate this truth.

What else will the students derive from film study? They will be better able to distinguish the worthwhile from the trivial, the shoddy, the tinny, and the sham. They will get insights into their own experiences, becoming aware of how others feel and think. They will develop an understanding of the past and an insight into the present. They will experience an aesthetic enjoyment, and will be exposed to a different presentation of social problems. These and many other benefits will come to the students from a film-study program, depending on the age of the students and the kind of program used.

Film study is here to stay in the schools. Once the big breakthrough in recording movies on tape is made economical (and that is only a few years away), education will be revolutionized. Now is the time to begin preparing for that day by beginning and extending film education.

I Was a Teenage Movie Teacher

John M. Culkin

Teenage movie teachers teach two things: teenagers and movies. Both are fun to work with. Both need working with. Some TMTs put the stress on teaching teenagers and some on teaching movies. The former use films as a way of helping the student to illumine his own experience and to develop a personal point of view. The latter use the student as the audience for a course emphasizing the history and esthetics of film. There is a middle ground to be discovered and defended. And, like all teachers, TMTs teach themselves—their own attitudes, prejudices, likes, and dislikes.

There aren't too many TMTs in captivity, but the number of interested candidates is increasing rapidly. Some teach courses; some teach film units within courses; some organize film clubs. Their work is variously described as "motion picture appreciation," "film study," or, when television is included, "screen education." They are constantly confused with audio-visual specialists whose films deal with the dissection of frogs, or with English teachers who occasionally use a feature film like *Pride and Prejudice* to seduce students into reading the book.

The case for film study in the schools can be put quite simply without invoking the intercession of a long list of respectable experts. We live in a total-information culture, which is being increasingly dominated by the image, both moving and static. By the time the average American student graduates from high school today, he has watched more than 15,000 hours of television and seen more than 500 films. The TV figure is the result of an average of 20 hours of weekly viewing for 15 years; it adds up to two full years of 24 hour-a-day viewing. During this same period, this average student has attended school five hours a day, 180 days a year, for 12 years, to produce a total of 10,800 hours of school time. Only sleeping time surpasses television as the top time-consumer.

Intelligent living within such an environment calls for the development of

From John M. Culkin, "I Was a Teenage Movie Teacher," *Saturday Review,* 16 July 1966, pp. 51-53; 72-73. Copyright © 1966 by Saturday Review, Inc. Reprinted by permission of the publisher and John M. Culkin.

habits of perception, analysis, judgment, and selectivity that are capable of processing the relentless input of such visual data. At a time when so many of our economic, political, and personal decisions are being shaped by the new visual media, we have to organize a posse to outnumber and surround the vidiots in our midst and to replace them with seeing-eye children. And great films and television, like great anything-else, communicate insights about man that we should want to share with each new generation. From here on out, to be liberally educated is to be "cinemate as well as literate." Schools are where the tribe passes on its values to the young. Schools are where film study should be housed.

Old Plato in his analogy of the cave pictured a generation of people whose lives were spent watching shadows on a wall. Later on they rejected the outside world because it didn't correspond to their shadows. (Television, anyone?) The ability to distinguish between shadow and substance must be part of any cultural survival kit.

TMTs want their students to see as many fine films as possible, in much the same way that teachers have always wanted their students to read great books and experience great art. They want to free students from the narrow confines of their own "I, my, me" world in showing them films that widen and deepen their understanding of what it means to be human. They want to equip the student with ways of analyzing and reflecting upon the constant flow of moving images that flood his world. They want to produce an enthusiastic, intelligent, selective, and mature film and television viewer.

What kinds of films are involved? All kinds. Everyone has his own list of classical favorites. Classroom discussions also focus on currently popular films and TV programs like the Bond cycle, *Batman, The Fugitive, Bonanza,* and *The Man from U.N.C.L.E.* Better to help them analyze what they are seeing than to develop critical standards for films or books they may never see or read.

The schools had a go at the movies once before back in the 1930s. The crusade started fast and faded fast since it was built on a negative approach to film. The second spring of the movement is based on a respect for film rather than a fear of film. It regards film as one of the humanities, as one of the liberating arts, and it strives to produce the largest possible audiences for the best possible films. Its methodology is built around the screening, discussion, and analysis of well-made, relevant films. It believes that a lively art demands lively teaching and it is, therefore, opposed to a pedanticism that would stifle the spontaneity and enthusiasm most of us bring to films. It maintains that in an image-saturated culture *all* students should become their own TV and movie critics.

At present the movement is but a cloud on the horizon, no larger than a man's hand, but it will inevitably grow because it is both wanted and needed. To speak in cinematic terms, we can consider the film study movement at three focal lengths: a *long shot* on its cultural context, a *medium shot* on the changing student, and a *closeup* on the role of the schools.

First a *long shot* of our changing culture. Marshall McLuhan, who has emerged as the oracle of mass culture and the darling of the magazine writers, has been telling us, for a long while and in his own obscure fashion, that we live in a postliterate world. Not *illiterate,* although that has often been suggested too, but *postliterate*—a world in which print no longer has a monopoly of communication either within the culture or within the schools. The new environment created by the electronic media has formed a free-flow, total-information ecology within which people receive their communication through a great variety of media and at a pace not within the control of the established and traditional mediators of culture—the family, the church, and the school. We can get some idea of both the extent and rapidity of this change by imagining the effects of a month-long national experiment in which we would be deprived of all the communications media developed and mass-produced within our own century. Goodbye TV, movies, telephones, recordplayers, radios, and a whole way of life stitched together by the new media.

The brief for some kind of media study within the schools normally follows either of two lines of argument: (a) make the media seem so *respectable* that the schools have to recognize them as worthy of inclusion within the curriculum; or (b) make their impact seem so *lethal* that the schools feel forced to deal with them as a tactic of survival.

Walt Whitman said: "To have great poets there must be a great audience." Great audiences for any art form are not born; they are made. They are created by an exposure to and an analysis of excellence within the medium. Some people are distracted because the movies are "mere entertainment" (as though that were a bad thing in itself). The same tag once kept Elizabethan drama, the novel, and vernacular literature out of the schools. Others stress the number of worthless or tasteless films. The piffle index, however, is high for any medium, and the percentage of poor films is probably about the same as the percentage of poor work in print, paint, and other media. The best within the film medium deserves the same attention to content and style that we accord to the traditional arts.

Although the fancy talk about film as an art form is true enough and suasive enough, it is not without its dangers. There is a Steinbeck quote which is to the point: "Culture is a lousy word to describe what mankind is all about." Too often we let talk about art substitute for the experience of art. Once a false mystique about art gets into the air, people begin to become insecure about their own instincts and to react to the expectations of the high priests of art rather than to their own honest reactions. This is especially lamentable in a nice friendly field like the movies where everyone has for so long presumed that he is an expert.

If Whitman's thesis about the relation of art and audience is true for poems which can be written on the backs of old envelopes by a production staff of one, it holds with multiplied validity for the motion picture and television, which are wild combinations of art, technology, and commerce. The traditional interplay of artist and patron has to be rethought for each of the new media. Numbers have a great deal to do with what can be communicated through any of the media that involve large financial investments. Both risk and success are measured by increasingly large numbers as one moves from print to stage to film and to television. A hardbound book hits the best seller lists when it sells 20,000 copies; a Broadway play starts making money after the first 100,000 tickets; a commercial film has to have roughly two and a half patrons for every dollar invested before it breaks even—with the result that a million-dollar movie needs two and a half million patrons; and in television, which is the massest of mass media, a series in prime time needs a continuing audience of approximately 25,000,000 viewers to stay on the air. Last season, for instance, *East Side/West Side* went off the air with a sustaining audience of 14,000,000 regular viewers—an audience that would be astronomical for any of the other media but which is too esoteric to be served by television.

In the commercial media the name of the game is numbers. The one-to-one relationship between de Medici and Michelangelo has given way to a complicated feedback system between the public and the network or the studio. The public is the patron and, distasteful as this may be to the elitists, this numerical approach to taste is the fact of media life. It has its obvious problems. What most want is not what all should get. And just because people take what they get doesn't necessarily mean that they are getting what they want. The public doesn't know what it wants until it gets it and then they may only be accepting what they appear to want. What we need are more choices and more people qualified to make wise choices. Since the quality of films and television depends on the quality of the audience, we should be at pains to improve the quality of that audience. That is what film study is all about.

Second, a *medium shot* of the changing student. It has been said that if Booth Tarkington were writing *Seventeen* today he would have to call it *Twelve*. The mass media have something to do with those five years which we have lost or gained, depending on your point of view. The schools are no longer dealing with the student of 1900 whose sources of information were limited to the home, church, school, and neighborhood gang. Today's student comes equipped with a vast reservoir of facts and vicarious experiences gleaned from the new media. All the analogies comparing the mind to a blank page or an empty bucket died with Edison. The teacher is now in competition with a host of rival communicators, most of whom are smarter, richer, and considerably more efficient. Relevance and competence are educational tactics against which students have not devised a defense.

It is almost sacrilegious to find fault with Bel Kaufman's *Up the Down Staircase* because it is so human and so in sympathy with our own loves and hates. But the lady made me sad on page 198. "I don't think I got through to them, in spite of all my careful paper-plans . . . The trouble is their utter lack of background. 'I never read a book in my life, and I ain't starting now,' a boy informed me."

Honest, Bel, they've got background; it's the one thing we're sure they do have. It may not look much like your background and my background and it isn't spangled with titles from the great books of the Western world. But it's there. We know for sure that it is well-stocked with plenty of TV material just waiting to be tapped with probing questions about phoniness and realness, winners and losers, style and *schmaltz*—all the new ways of talking about the old ideas of the true, the good, and the beautiful. If the school is in business to communicate with these students, it is up to the school to get plugged in to their background. Whatever the eventual goal may be, there is only one place to start and that is—where they *are*.

Teachers have seldom felt more alienated from the kids; yet it has seldom been easier to make contact with their world. We communicate with people by having something in common with them. One thing we can all have in common is the mass media. TV and film help to shape the dreams of today's students. Students often have a kind of defenseless, direct, but interested approach to the media. They love to talk about TV programs and movies. They don't realize how much they're talking about themselves in the process. If the teacher doesn't watch these programs and if he never discusses them with the kids, he's missing the easiest way to wiretrap their private world. This is why all this elite versus popular culture business is so important. The snobs pride themselves on not watching television. Too bad. What happens when this culturally deprived teacher starts waxing lyrical about Elizabethan poetry? Not much. The kids have some polite teacher-talk which they dish out dutifully so that the teacher thinks something is going on in the class. If they like the teacher, they are very generous in keeping the truth from him. If they don't like him they still have enough fear for the sanction of the report card to go along with the game. They seldom say what they really think. Nobody wants to hear it, except, of course, the great teacher, who is by definition the relevant person, the one who understands, communicates, gets through.

Third, a *closeup shot* of our changing education. Stanley Kauffmann said it: "The film in this country is possibly the one art form that is *wanted.*" Television may or may not be an art form, but it is wanted too. Why not start where the action is?

Teenage movie teachers have all kinds of options in their approach to film. My own prejudice at the high school level is for keeping as close as possible to what Robert Warshow has called "the immediate experience." For me this means the vertical interaction between the student and the screen and the horizontal interaction between students who have seen and discussed the same film. Ancillary knowledge about film is less relevant here and is perhaps more appropriate for the specialist or for more advanced programs. A great deal of snobbery takes over once some people learn how to pronounce the names of all the foreign film directors and can recite in chronological order the titles of all 9½ of Fellini's films.

If I had my choice in the schools, I would like to have each student go through a unit on film and television for about 30 hours in his freshman year and then see and discuss one feature film each month during his four years of high school. A modest amount of time compared to the actual viewing hours that he is clocking. The whole process can be broken down into four approaches to films: show them, discuss them, teach about them, and make them.

SHOW THEM

The success of literature teachers can be legitimately measured by the number of books their students read. Same for TMT. A film per month for four years would add up to 40 films. The celluloid syllabus should include both American and foreign films, 16 mm in-school screenings and 35 mm theater screenings, and a generous blend of feature, documentary, and animated films. From time to time it should include a dishonest or pretentious film and occasionally there might be a second screening of a film to check out insights or arguments that arose in the discussion of the film. What is important is that the films be well-made, relevant, and representative. Although most of the films should have the texture of reality about them, a steady diet of grim film gets depressing. Musicals and comedies belong in the series.

DISCUSS THEM

When a TMT is asked whether he is just sitting around showing films and talking about them with the kids, the prescribed answer is: "Yup." This is where the fun begins. When students are given a free forum to discuss films, they are also invited to discuss themselves. This type of viewer-centered, free-flow discussion is built into the nature of the film medium. Film is literally an other-directed medium. Both the sequence and the pace of the communication are determined by the director. There is no chance to pause, reflect, and relate as there is with a book. In the darkness of the theater the viewer's attention is riveted on the screen and he is swept along by the succession of sights and sounds that impinge on his eye and ear. This primarily sensory experience leaves the viewer with a stack of unsorted images. A group discussion is a great way to interpret and relate these images, and to discover their structure.

This physical and psychological context explains why the same film can affect different individuals in different ways. Each person sees his own film. This paradox is merely the reaffirmation in a new context of the thesis of individual differences, and selective perception. The same film on the screen washes over each viewer as an individual, with individual past experiences, hopes, loves, fears, needs, and intelligence. The psychological mechanisms of identification and projection come into play. We empathize with some character on the screen. For a while we become who he is, and we will fill out the experience by reading our own emotions into the character. The result is a variety of responses to the same stimulus. It is normally not a solipsistic kind of irresponsible and indeterminate variety, but usually a range of responses hovering around the central theme of the film.

If the teacher can resist the temptation to reward and punish "correct" answers (this usually means his own subjective interpretation) and can create a climate in which all opinions are respected, these free-winging sessions can dredge up some memorable moments. My winters are warmed by memories of some Job Corpsmen debating the meaning of what it meant to be a winner or a loser in *The Hustler,* of the understanding that resulted from a group of parents and students who had seen and separately discussed the rebellion of Colin Smith in *The Loneliness of the Long Distance Runner,* of ten minutes of sheer poetry in a Harlem basement by a teacher commenting on Terry Molloy's care for his pigeons in *On the Waterfront,* of 200 girls discussing the loneliness and purpose of Zampano and Gelsomina in *La Strada,* of the ten-year-old girl in New York whose favorite scene in *Raisin in the Sun* was "when the movin' man came, 'cause that meant they were gettin' out." Nice things happen in film discussions. Some teachers find that they are talking less and that the kids are learning more.

As the students build up a background of shared experiences, they can then use these films and discussions as reference points for making sense out of their own lives or for communicating with each other. The phrase, "He's a real loser," says everything to someone who has seen and discussed *The Hustler.* The better we know each other, the shorter the sentences we can use.

TEACH ABOUT THEM

Not everything that *can* be known about film and television *should* be known about them.

Each TMT has to make his own way in deciding how much the student should know about film history, techniques, production, and economics. It is important, however, that students get a feel for what is proper to the film medium; that they experience how the tone, rhythm, pace, style, and point of view of a film are determined by the use of editing, sound, lighting, color, perspective, and composition. The making of a film is a highly selective process. The best advice for the teacher is to play it loose and to start with the film-as-experienced. By some people's standards this will be a sloppy and subjective approach, but it is better to recognize and work with the subjectivity than to impose an arbitrary set of objective standards. The approach should be inductive. The standards should grow out of the experience and not be imposed on the experience. We can do without abstract lists of criteria that begin: "A great movie is one which fulfils the following requirements . . ." People know what they like. Those who spend their time telling people that they *shouldn't* like what they *do* like have discovered a first-class way of getting tuned out. Pulling rank won't change taste. Lively analysis in a fair game may do it.

MAKE THEM

The study of film inevitably leads students to a desire to try their hand at making a film. The results are wondrous to behold. In England films are now being made by eight and nine year olds. There are tenative beginnings of such a development in this country under pioneering teachers like George Bouwman of

Horace Mann in New York, Zane Rodriguez of Fordham Prep, Sister Bede Sullivan of Lillis High in Kansas City, and Rodger Larson who has been working with New York's Neighborhood Youth Corps in Harlem.

There are many and varied film projects just beginning around the country. All kinds of respectable organizations and teachers are getting into the act. Within ten years we will wonder what all the fuss was about and will have transcended the need for developing a rationale.

Meanwhile, it is well to remember that to be a TMT, enthusiasm and a pocketful of theater stubs aren't enough. The idea will be as good as the people who make it happen—the teachers who teach it and the people who develop the printed and filmed teaching materials. There is a degree of competence needed which falls between the highly specialized demands of the film purists and the "anybody-can-do-it" school. A summer program would do it. There are books to be read. There are films to be seen. There are people to be consulted—great TMTs like Tony Hodgkinson of Boston University, David Mallery of the National Association of Independent Schools, and Sister Rosalie of Pittsburgh. Opinions on current films can be found by reading good critics. And anyone can get started by getting a buzz session going on *I Spy*. Great movements deserve modest beginnings.

On the national level the movement can get moving through a consortium of talent drawn from the schools and the studios. The medium itself has been called "a shotgun marriage of culture and commerce," and any movement based on the medium will have to talk to both partners. The dialogue must be enlarged among the many groups that are active in the field. The National Council on the Arts, which is blessed by the presence and hard work of director George Stevens and actor Gregory Peck, could be the prime mover in bringing this idea to the schools both through its own activities and those of the long-proposed American Film Institute, which is currently under study. The use of educational television is a natural for an idea that is visual in nature and short on teachers. To my mind the greatest single resource is the creative talent of the directors, writers, actors, art directors, cameramen, and editors who are the real craftsmen within the media. They and their knowledge should be more directly in touch with the audience. Most of them are eager for such contact. A little money and a little organization can make it happen.

And as more and more teachers get involved at the high school level, it becomes increasingly obvious that the idea should be pushed in the elementary grades, almost as soon as the students become steady consumers of television.

Expensive media like films and television cannot get too far ahead of their audience. They have to rely on public acceptance. Americans have spent a lot of time and energy in the past 30 years complaining about the producers of films and television. Much of the energy would have been better utilized in working with the audience. It's not too late to begin.

The Liveliest Art in the Classroom

August Franza

Motion pictures have been influencing and persuading me most of my life. When I was twelve, *The Phantom of the Opera* made me sick to my stomach (although my mother still says it was the virus). When I was 34, *Repulsion* left me psychologically queasy. In between, I discovered foreign films at the Astor Theater in Brooklyn where I realized I had been snared by the medium. I have loved it ever since, but have been abused by it as well. The advent of television made abuse of a mass audience—as far as this English teacher was concerned—a stimulus to action.

Any school failing to incorporate the mass media in its curriculum belongs, in my opinion, in another century. To be contemporary, a school must plug into the networks and media outlets. Thus, what I'm about to describe about film should be viewed in a context of teaching the mass media, not as an isolated phenomenon. A film course should be one piece of a large pie, the other pieces being television, advertising, semantics, magazines, and the book.

The course that Ed Jones and I teach at Syosset High, called "World Films," requires about $1,000 per semester, a couple of automatic projectors, a big screen, a large room that can be turned pitch black at a moment's notice, walls that can absorb loud sound tracks, and 90 minute periods. Or better yet, large flexible blocks of time that can be used in many ways. These are essential ingredients and there's no getting around them with impunity. A film costs anywhere from $20 to $65 to rent for one showing. If the course is going to be more than a print course full of theories about moviemaking and anecdotes about stars, then at least two feature films a week should be shown, which would leave, under normal scheduling conditions, three periods for discussion. In our course, we scheduled 34 films from September to January and about the same number for the spring semester.

Currently, our course is available to seniors and juniors on an elective basis and is given during period eight and after school. When we have a movie to

From August Franza, "The Liveliest Art in the Classroom," *English Journal* 58 (November 1969): 1233-37. Copyright © 1969 by the National Council of Teachers of English. Reprinted by permission of the publisher and August Franza.

show—and that's twice a week—the students stay on to its conclusion. The discussion days are just single periods. Nevertheless, the arrangement is a poor one and fails to attract those many students who have busy extracurricular schedules. Our plan for next year is to arrange two double periods a week within the eight-period schedule that will dignify the course and attract more students.

"World Films" has few ground rules: see the movies, comment on them freely in discussion periods, and keep a movie journal. We are also experimenting with the paperback *The Cinema as Art* (Penguin Books, 1965) by Debrix and Stephenson as required reading for the term, but we're not so sure we need reading materials. The films carry their own momentum and what we have to do is capitalize on it.

The goals of the course are broad and general: to enlarge and deepen film experience; to understand the propaganda value of films; to develop analytical tools and sharpen critical attitudes; to understand film techniques and the process of moviemaking. The achievement of these goals depends on the interaction, in what we would call an existential manner, of teachers, students, and the immediate impact of the films. We present no, or very few, preliminary facts at the course's opening. The course begins with a film, not a lecture or discussion on film. We continue this procedure through the semester. All that students know about the films are the title, the date released, and the director's name (we studiously ignore announcing the stars, if any, to emphasize the director's role). Either immediately after or the day following the film, discussion begins with such questions as: What did you like and dislike about the film? Were there any good shots you would like to see again? Memorable scenes? What was good about them? Did you notice the musical background? How did it improve or weaken the film? Was the camera doing interesting things? Could the director have improved any particular scene? From here in, it's playing strictly by ear, building on comments, emphasizing a technical point, getting an argument going, introducing a germane concept, raising a controversial question, or suggesting a book for further study.

It was the sixth week of the course and we were showing propaganda films. We started out with *Guadalcanal Diary*, following it with *Storm over Asia, The Victors, Potemkin, The Cranes Are Flying,* and *The Bridge.* The last time Ed Jones and I had seen *Guadalcanal Diary* we were just climbing out of knickers into pimples, and World War II was at its heights. What were our students going to say after having seen *The Seven Samurai*? When the reactions came, they were a babble of negative criticism and angry questions: How come they never show Americans bleed? How come an American soldier never screams when he's shot? Is it true that all American soldiers do with their spare time on board ship is dance with one another and sing spirituals? Why are there no dissenters among the Americans? Why are they all depicted as peace-loving, clowning, dancing, singing innocents with a deep respect for religion? Why did Lloyd Nolan say to a soldier afraid to kill, "That's all right. Japs ain't human, anyway"? On the technical side they said the film was dull, antiseptic, the battle scenes too orderly looking. There was no panic, no dirt, no filth, no blood.

The Victors, full of antiheroics, was a much more familiar film for them, leaving us more time to discuss technique: the editing, the use of newsreels, the musical score, the best and worst scenes, and the best and worst shots.

The three Russian films stunned them for various reasons. *The Cranes Are Flying* was so moving it brought many of them to tears. Some said it was so effective and human, it went beyond propaganda. As to *Storm over Asia* and *Potemkin,* the students were impressed by the fact that film making had become sophisticated so early in movie history. Previously, they had thought that 1925 was the movie equivalent of the Middle Ages. It was interesting to watch them change their minds. Yes, the tempo of the films failed, the prints were imperfect, the characterizations were stereotyped, and the messages blunt communist propaganda, but they could not ignore the touching and dramatic closeups, the exciting camera angles, and the orchestration of the editing. It quickly became clear that the redeeming features of these films were the functions of technique and not storytelling. And when they saw the Odessa Steps sequence in *Potemkin,* they knew the differences between art and kitsch. No one had to tell them anything. All they had to do was look with their own eyes.

In a certain sense, we handle each film irreverently; that is, since some of our goals are to stimulate awareness and develop analytical tools that finally will encourage greater appreciation, we want students to know film for what it really is: thousands of feet of edited images tied in with a sound track to create predetermined effects on an audience. To make sure their critical faculties are always working, we will stop a film at a tense moment and ask a question, or rerun a sequence; we might kill the sound track to see the difference the music makes, or one of us will shout during a searing moment: "Remember, it's only a movie," or "Watch that camera."

Of course students sometimes rebel at these inconveniences and illusion-breaking actions, but we keep hammering away at the fact that the movies are not being shown for their entertainment; the local Bijou supplies that need stunningly. Here we're trying to understand how the persuasiveness is achieved. While we do not completely ignore students' protests (How can we these days!) nor try to ruin someone else's cinematic work, we do know that some wrenching away from illusion is absolutely necessary. And furthermore, if all of this is done with some urbanity, good humor, and sensitivity, it finally does work.

During our discussion periods, we often read reviews of recent movies and compare them with the full-page *New York Times'* ads. This comparison causes much amusement and gets in a few sideswipes at advertising. If one of our films causes a great enough stir (as *The Pumpkin Eater* did), we ask the librarian to dig up seven or eight reviews which we read and discuss in class. After a bit of this, students begin to doubt the judgment, intelligence, and accuracy of some reviewers and the whole question of what a reviewer's job is comes into the foreground. Further, we begin to make distinctions between reviewing and criticism and generally end up slamming the reviewers for failure to give film technique proper emphasis.

Then new questions arise: What should a good newspaper review of a movie contain? What should a good critical article contain? By this time, students are aware of the trap and receive their assignment to write a newspaper review based on the class' criteria with a certain amount of acceptance, if not glee or tranquility.

Besides class discussion, students communicate their ideas and feelings about each film in their movie journals. We require them to buy a 29-cent notebook in which to keep a record of each movie as well as any TV or theater film they wish to make entries about. Once a month, we collect the journals, read, and comment on them. All we ask the students to do is express their real opinions about whatever facets of the film appeal to or disturb them. After they've begun, our job is to help them interpret their progress or lack of it, pose questions, suggest directions, and generally encourage the journal keeping process.

Following are some journal entries for the films discussed here.

GUADALCANAL DIARY

Oh, Boy. This wasn't even good propaganda. It was the *Daily News* retelling of WW II, or else it was my father's.

Awful. Lousy plot. How the brave, moral, superior Americans beat the cunning, inferior (nonhuman?) immoral Japs.

It makes me feel sick and ashamed that people really took movies like this seriously . . .

While claiming realism, I could detect very little. The Japs were all small, myopic, and treacherous, while the Americans were good guys, clean, with hairless chests, and shaved armpits. If they were obese, they wore shirts. Sex was nonexistent. The only one to refer to it had a Spanish accent. The only Jew had no build, a big nose . . . The Americans all died gracefully: no blood, no noise. They never got muddy and always sang in four-part harmony.

. . . Nothing more than a "killing is fun doctrine" and a "dying is not so bad" manifesto . . . According to this film, war is a comic book game and only those who make wrong moral choices get killed. War takes boys and makes them men. Killing is the bar mitzvah of of fair-haired Protestants.

THE VICTORS

. . . And the good clean healthy Americans like George Hamilton don't always win. And the American soldiers don't wile away their time writing home to mother. Superior officers aren't so superior, and sergeants belch in the presence of ladies. Kind of different from the soldiers of *Guadalcanal Diary*.

POTEMKIN

The thing that impressed me the most about the film was the amount of motion in it. The screen never contained anything dull; there was always something to look at: masses of swarming people, swinging tables, a ship's engines, soldiers' feet ... I think that every single frame of this movie is an artistic study of balance, people, objects. I remember a scene shown several times, of two stairways, a street and a bridge, all swarming with people all on different levels. It really stuck in my mind. If I could draw I would still be able to draw this scene from memory.

The ship-coming-into-harbor-scenes were good ... the foggy atmosphere, vague shapes, slow-moving ships ... really created a mood ... which prevailed up to the viewing of the martyr's body. Very funereal. The streaming of the people to see the body was wild. I would like to see more of the director's work.

Besides improving the course scheduling, where do we want to go with the course? Right now, we want to sit back and refine it and worry about its survival. Besides the district's generosity, we got a $300 grant from the New York State Council on the Performing Arts. But what of the future? We anticipate the prospect of a student request for a film making course. The questions have already been raised in a minor key and our scouts have informed us that some individualistic senior has been making 8 mm shots on his own. We intend to give him his day in the course and when we do, we will have begun to take the next step.

Further, there is the whole unexplored matter of the use of film on TV. How does the editing of film on Huntley-Brinkley and Walter Cronkite influence the meanings we take away to supper with us? Which leads us full circle back to the opening remarks in this article: the film elective should be only one part of a larger effort to expose the mass media to educational study.

THE FILMS

	*Citizen Kane	1940	US
	One-Eyed Jacks	1961	US
Western	High Noon	1952	US
	Shane	1953	US
	The Seven Samurai	1954	Japan
	Sons and Lovers	1959	British
	The Catered Affair	1956	US
Family	Cry, The Beloved Country	1952	British
	The Magnificent Ambersons	1942	US
	The Pumpkin Eater	1963	British
	Guadalcanal Diary	1943	US
	Storm Over Asia	1928	USSR
War and	The Victors	1963	US
Propaganda	Potemkin	1925	USSR
	The Cranes Are Flying	1957	USSR
	The Bridge	1959	West Germany
	Zero For Conduct	1933	France
Comedy	Duck Soup	1933	US
	Big Deal on Madonna St.	1960	Italy

	Critic and Film Series		British Film Institute
	Crossfire	1947	US
	The Goddess	1957	US
Social	*I Am a Fugitive from a*	1933	US
Commentary	*Chain Gang*		
	All the King's Men	1949	US
	Treasure of Sierra Madre	1948	US
	La Strada	1954	Italy
	Lilith	1963	US
	M	1930	Germany
	El	1952	Mexico
Psychological	*Gaslight*	1944	US
	The Seventh Seal	1956	Sweden
	Exterminating Angel	1962	Spain
	Wild Strawberries	1957	Sweden
	* *Citizen Kane*		

* The course will begin and end with the showing of *Citizen Kane*. The purpose of the two showings is to help students asses their own progress by comparing their first impressions with their last ones.

To Look Or to See: Film Study in the English Curriculum

Fred Silva

The constant reminder that we are now a media civilization has shifted the once controversial discussion of film study from issues of relevance to questions of materials and personnel. In fact, an ad in a current issue of *The English Record* promotes "16 mm English literature," a catalogue of "movies that matter" and lists the renter's supply of films based on works by writers from Cooper to Crane to Eugene O'Neill. This automatic equating of film and literature, however, creates several unattractive, half-hearted replies to the demand for film study in secondary schools.

That most movies have characters, plot, development, language, and related literary devices not only reinforces the film's parallels to literature, but transforms "16 mm English literature" and "movies that matter" into an A-V

From Fred Silva, "To Look or to See: Film Study in the English Curriculum," *The English Record* 20 (October 1969): 38-45. Reprinted by permission of the publisher and Fred Silva.

support for literature. The teacher can now relate literature to the students' lives with moving *Classic Comics*, while apparently overlooking the implicit condescension that the masses cannot handle literature without film aid. A variant of this sugar-coated solution is the library display of books made into current films. Almost apologetically the library invites its patrons: see the film, read the book. But a subtle shift has occurred: the library is the tie-in to the film. A third possibility of this uneasy connection between film and literature develops when a movie generates a "cultural event." Hamlet, let's say, is rented not only for the English class concerned with Shakespeare's play but for the entire school community—or at least as many as will sit still. Though this may be hopefully a passing phenomenon the A-V cultural treatment can kill film as effectively as literature has been harmed by removing it from its proper setting and separating it from its inherent function.

Aside from these probably baroque fears of conditions from a hopefully passing era, certainly no sensible reason exists why the secondary school should not use the film. Because of the acknowledged similarities between film and fictional literary forms, the English teacher is an obvious candidate to handle a film course or unit. Beyond this simple connection, however, the English teacher is a logical candidate for film teaching by reason of his training and the long-range objectives and possibilities of screen education:

1. The English teacher works daily with a language system which communicates ideas and emotions through symbol. Explaining literary language, the English teacher helps the student understand the effects and goals of a variety of poems, short stories, novels, and plays. Because the relationship between symbol and meaning is somewhat similar in literature and film, the English teacher using cinematic vocabulary of shot, angle, sequence, etc., can help the student understand the more visual, more mobile film form. The close analysis of a shot pattern or a montage rhythm calls for as rigorous an effort as does the close reading of prose and poetry. One of the great needs of film study is for students who can carefully and clearly explicate a passage of film as film.

2. The English teacher, acquainted with academic criticism, understands the rigor that must be applied to all critical work, a need particularly important now in film. Up to recently film study has been spotty, too often very enthusiastic gushing or very esoteric or idiosyncratic commentary and theorizing. While some of this has been valuable and necessary, the time has arrived for a more systematic study of film. The new criticism and the broader survey approaches commonly used by the English teacher can be carefully applied to film.

3. The English teacher has a humanities orientation which enables him to employ a variety of information and disciplines to the understanding of an individual film. The synthetic nature of film, which depends for its being on technology, literature, art, and society, requires a uniquely broad, interdisciplinary background for its fullest appreciation. The student, once he has a secure grasp of the art form, ideally should be able to comment on a film from as many angles possible. The serious film student or critic needs a truly broad gauge awareness.

4. The English teacher reaches a great bulk of a population who will be increasingly exposed to film and who will need to have some way of absorbing intelligently the variety of films and their techniques. The amount of TV viewing has been extensively publicized and speaks for itself. Not every individual will become a professional critic, but in his everyday contact with film, he should bring with him a practical sense of what film does. This, after all, is the same hope that prompts us to teach students how to read imaginative literature.

Assuming then that the English teacher is as good as, if not better than, most faculty to handle the film course, or unit, what then does he do with it? First, and most important, he must carefully locate the area of his study. In addition to the literary connections film has equally valid associations with history, sociology, or psychology. The seemingly objective and realistic photographic characteristics of film make it particularly useful for revealing contemporary life or encouraging the study of various human relationships. But one must resist the attraction to use film as an easy way to discuss what we are, where we have been, or why we are what we seem to be. The art of the film is the only sensible material at the core of any beginning cinema study.

In order to prepare a film course the English teacher does not have to know or present everything about movies. He need not know the history of the film—the growth of the Hollywood industry, the rise of the star system, the general development of directorial style, the rise and fall of German, Swedish, or French film industries. He can do without lists of great films, commentaries on film as mass media, and considerations of censorship and morality. There are other matters beyond the English teachers' immediate concern, but he must know how a film achieves its objectives.

Considering the nature of film, we conclude that it depends like literature upon the familiar form and content interrelationship. We see further that technique shapes the form: shots build into sequences which combine into the over-all shape of the film, a process often called montage. To illustrate briefly the nature of cinematic analysis we note that a short (one interrupted lens opening) consists of subject, composition, angle, duration, and movement. Content can be pure (abstract light and shape), realistic (documentary), fictional, (staged), or naturally a combination of these. Obviously the student being introduced to the complexity of film should not be distracted by films used as versions of great literature or as legitimate supplements for other disciplines but should concentrate on the basic artistic techniques of film.

An initial and somewhat unique problem in film teaching is materials. The writing teacher has his grammar book and essay reader; the literature instructor has his anthology or vast selection of paperbacks; but the film teacher can logically work only with films which are neither readily available nor cheaply rented. The problem of low cost film availability will probably prove to be one of the central limitations of solid film study until a satisfactory system is worked out by the rental agencies, the school administrators, and the teachers, each of whom will have to surrender part of his self interest. But that is not our concern here.

One easily available but ultimately unsatisfactory solution to the materials problem is the published film script, of which presently about three dozen are in print, ranging from James Agee preshooting scripts of *African Queen* and others to well-illustrated scripts of such modern and classic films as *Tom Jones, Last Year at Marienbad, Alphaville, Grand Illusion,* and *Potemkin* produced by Grove Press and Simon and Schuster. Undoubtedly other titles are imminent. The temptation to use these film substitutes is particularly strong if the script is of a literary work translated to the screen as in the case of Agee's translation of Stephen Crane's *The Blue Hotel* and *The Bride Comes to Yellow Sky.* The printed script's inadequacy becomes apparent when one recognizes that film is not, after all, a literary expression. Even the most complete script barely suggests the importance of the purely visual elements of film: movement, angle, composition. The script is even less satisfactory as a representation of the film than a printed play is a suggestion of a theater performance largely because the play uses language much more extensively than the film, whose dialogue is often cryptic without the accompanying picture. The film, dependent for its various effects on the moving image, gets lost on the page. Scripts, however, are extremely useful as a postscreening device, particularly if they are well-illustrated and have some cinematic detail. Since the film's visuals tend to fade quickly after a viewing, a good script enables the students to recall more easily what they have seen.

The feature film, usually a more mature and complex expression than the short film, should ideally be the basic viewing experience in film teaching. But the ideal situation may be difficult to obtain because the 90-120-minute feature film is simply too cumbersome a form to be used effectively in the prescribed time periods of the normal class. To show a feature in widely spaced sessions is not recommended because unlike a novel a film is designed to be taken in at one sitting, the recent two part *War and Peace* not withstanding. Ways probably could be developed to circumvent this. Double (or triple) periods or after school/evening screenings are possible. But even so, in a three- or four-week unit, which is more likely to exist in a school situation, much more can be done with a variety of short films. In addition to the growing variety of forms and subjects another advantage of the short film is that a class can see it at least twice in a normal class period. The value of a film increases if a class sees the film, discusses its cinematic values, then sees it again. The short film also moves the student away from the idea that film is only photographed literature since he can view a number of types: animation, experimental, underground, and documentary. Also, frequently the short film contains good imaginative examples of film technique, which can be studied more easily here than in a feature. The quick cut style of editing, for example, which can be somewhat disturbing in a feature such as Richard Lester's *Petulia* has an almost immediate acceptance and can be more readily analyzed in the brief documentary or social comment film. Visual collage effects created by editing pieces of film from documentaries, cartoons, or other short films seem more digestible in the brief effort than in the longer work. One notes in passing the ease with which viewers have come to accept the jarring visual juxtapositions within TV commercials with little qualm—probably because of brevity and lack of narrative.

Whether film study is to be a full term course or a unit within a course, a worthwhile instructional pattern could take the following more or less sequential shape: instruction to film as a visual, nonliterary art form; establishment of a basic film vocabulary; development of an awareness of film style; consideration of similarities and differences between film and older analogous literary forms. This movement clearly avoids the history, sociology, psychology, economics, and archeology of the films. This course plan removes the film from literary comparison to a consideration of the film's own composition/grammar/syntax areas and then returns it to literature but with new awareness of the basic aesthetic issues involved.

The student should first see films which have no literal meaning whatever or films whose narrative content is presented in uniquely cinematic ways. A number of short films are essentially explorations of the basic properties of film: the way to use space, the way to convey movement without shifting the camera, the way to explore the unique possibilities of light and form. These are short enough so that several can be shown in a class period to indicate the visual excitement of non-narrative film. The impressive variety of approach in these films could be demonstrated by the abstract animations of Normal McLaren, the computer based films of Stan Vanderbeek, and the collage films of Bruce Connor among others. The student could also view films that express either storyline or social comment in uniquely film ways. Roman Polanski's *Two Men and a Wardrobe,* an enigmatic absurd parable of modern man, and Carter Davidson's *Help! My Snowman's Burning,* a surrealistic comment on modern lack of privacy, are examples of expression that could be done only on film. A fair number of short more explicit social comment films use cinematic techniques effectively: jump cuts, zooms into and out of details, juxtapositions. Two excellent examples are *Very Nice* and *12-12-42.* In this last a girl's voice speaks meanderingly about the first 20 years of her life as pictures, film clips, and art representations of the world in the years 1942-65 are flashed on the screen. The film excites visual interest in the cuts and apparently random selection of pictures and expresses a social point of view in the contrast between those and the girl's often cruelly vapid comments.

As a student is being introduced to these film genre, he can be taught the vocabulary and fundamental characteristics of film, including both nomenclature and more elaborate considerations such as film's time and space capabilities. More than lists of terminology—shot, sequence, angle, fade out, dissolve, cut, montage—need to be considered: the frame and its possibilities; lens and focal problems; camera point of view and movement within the frame, color vs. black and white; editing for rhythm and shape. The effects achieved by each of these techniques should be imaginatively explored so that watching films doesn't become as sterile a practice as scanning verse lines can be. The question should always be why this angle, this cut, this movement. Not that such questions can or should always be answered, but at least they are raised. An awareness of technique, including its difficulties, enhances appreciation of a performance be it a ballet or TV commercial. If a sentence means more to a student who comprehends its structure, so a film yields more to a student who transcends content. The overriding objective is to teach the student to see more clearly than he has before, to see at least partially without reference to content or intention, to admire a well-executed shot or well-planned sequence for its own sake and not necessarily as a vehicle for any kind of message. This naturally is not to say that this is the only end, but before meaning can be fully appreciated, the medium must be understood.

The student can next begin to apply this awareness of visual effects to developing a sense of an individual director's visual style, that combination of angles, lighting, film stock, and so forth that clearly indicate an individual cinematic vision. What makes a Bergman, a Godard, a Welles, or a Fellini movie exciting and unique simply to look at, even before one considers the themes or subjects of the films? Or to put it another way: what makes a Godard film as easy to spot as a Hemingway short story? Here, of course, where taste becomes the paramount issue and real sophistication is required, the task of the individual student to perceive and distinguish among visual patterns sharpens his understanding of film vocabulary.

One successful way to develop the idea of a director's style is to present a series of significant films representing various directors, periods, and even nationalities. Sergei Eisenstein's *October* (1928) shows a silent film master using one type of montage to describe the Russian Revolution; Orson Welles' *Citizen Kane* (1941) records the great director expanding film's visual and audio possibilities to dissect an American publisher's career; Michaelangelo Antonioni's *L'Avventura* (1960) documents a contemporary director's successful exploration of the cinematic expression of psychological nuance among a group of bored Italians, Jean-Luc Godard's *Masculine Feminine* illustrates a New Wave director's use of a modern elliptical film style to evoke the ambience of Paris of 1965. Films of this quality combined with the short films similar to the ones mentioned above should provide a solid basis for establishing the student's sense of visuals and visual style as applied to narrative features.

Quite naturally the student could now investigate the area of literature into cinema transformation. What happens when a serious director becomes involved with the transfer of say an O'Neill play to the screen? Does it become the well-scrubbed empty *Desire Under the Elms,* or does it become the rich and powerful *Long Day's Journey Into Night*? Does the difference between these two films grow only out of the sensibilities of two different directors, or is there something inherent in film and drama that accounts for the differences? This question defines the important area of relationships between literature and film and raises a host of issues in fiction as well as drama. What happens to point of view in a film based on a first person story or novel? Can one really express cinematically the internal psychological conditions found in fiction? Are there certain kinds of novels better suited to film adaptation than others? How much of the original dialogue of a play needs to be retained? How much should a play be "opened up?" Does the mobility of the camera affect the playwright's work? All these questions, and many others, are complicated once again by the impact of the director's style, but then style may be the key to successful transformation of literature into cinema.

Some excellent examples of strongly directed literature-based films would be very appropriate here and could include Roberto Enrico's adaptation of the Ambrose Bierce short stories "An Occurrence at Owl Creek Bridge," "The Mockingbird," and "Chickamaugua"; Tony Richardson's version of Alan Sillitoe's *The Loneliness of the Long Distance Runner*; Charles Laughton's presentation of Davis Grubb's *The Night of the Hunter*; John Huston's reworking of Crane's *The Red Badge of Courage*; William Wyler's film of Lillian Hellman's *The Little Foxes*; or Orson Welles' experiments with Shakespeare's *Macbeth* or *Othello*. These are only a few of the possibilities; enough important films are available that a teacher need never resort to second rate films. In no sense are these films to be treated as A-V supplements but rather as serious works of film art whose origins happen to be literary, a factor which enables serious comparative discussion. Although these issues may never be touched in the secondary school course, here, as in the section on directorial style, the student undertakes some of the most stimulating investigation of cinema, for what is required is a solid sense of both literature and film.

Once the student develops this general grounding in film as an art form, he can move more confidently in the direction of history, sociology, or whatever else may catch his now opened eye. Toward this end some attention could be directed in a fully developed program to matters other than strictly visual. The student, for example, should be aware of such matters as key works in cinema theory, history, and biography, various landmark films, as well as the work of contemporary film critics. In addition, the student might supplement his viewing experience by keeping screen diaries, preparing scenarios, or composing short critical review articles.

Something should be said about production which has become a very publicized feature of film study. The chief argument in favor of production is almost irresistible: one learns about an art by working with its materials. Add to that a general fascination with gadgetry as institutionalized in the do-it-yourself movement as well as published statements about film production as panacea and one easily understands the popularity of the idea. To me the argument against production is more convincing. Film making is so complex and time consuming an undertaking that to provide an experience which leads a person to believe that a loaded Super 8 transforms anyone into a "film maker" is to do the art and the individual an ultimate disservice. If there is time for shooting and editing and money for the proper equipment in a full semester course or a strong extracurricular program, then by all means production deserves support. If the student can spend a number of periods on camera operation and script development, this is fine. But anything less than that is very misleading. In addition to which few nontrained people have sufficient understanding of such technology as filters, lens, film stock, to be of much use to the true novice.

Additionally, if current trends continue, well-equipped colleges and universities will provide a meaningful instruction in film production.

The chief purpose of film study—no matter who presents it—should be to enhance the student's visual experience by showing him *what* is there. The general suggestions in this essay are directed largely toward that end, but also partly to prevent a condition ruefully predicted by Pauline Kael closing a lecture about the power of film among modern youth: "If you think you can't kill movies, you underestimate the power of education." I know Miss Kael would like us to prove her inaccurate.

Animated Cinema: Cartoons

Frank David Martarella

Cartoons are "too childish," says an 11 year old, Loren Franza, in a protest letter to the *New York Times.* Untrue! Cartoons are not a bit childish. They are unfortunately being mass produced, however, from a childish point of view. Today, the cartoon and its counterpart, the puppet film, hold little esteem, and moviegoers tend to view the animated cinema as the little sister of the live-action cinema of Elizabeth Taylor and Rock Hudson. The reason for this is historical in nature and yet a great deal more than historical.

From the beginning of time, man has enjoyed animating—giving life to something that is lifeless. Cavemen drew pictures of bison showing them running along and devouring plants and animals alike. Greek artists depicted somersaulting acrobats on a vase. (Read John Keats' "Ode To A Grecian Urn.") Early nineteenty-century pioneers in the film industry invented machines in which a series of still pictures of consecutive actions simulated live action when viewed on a recording disc. These were the first animations.

This progress in the field of animation came to a sudden halt, however, when the photographed film came into being. The early film makers, being scientists and not artists, thought the photographed film to be an advance over the animated film, not realizing that the distinction between the motion of the live action film, and that of the animated film made them two entirely different

From Frank David Martarella, "Animated Cinema: Cartoons, as a separate art form, should not imitate live action films," *America* (March 8, 1969), pp. 271-73. Copyright ©by America Press, Inc. Reprinted by permission of the publisher.

mediums. The animated film thus became tied down to photography: the pictures of a cartoon were no longer drawn directly on film but were drawn first on another medium and then photographed onto celluloid.

Animation, however, is not live action, and its subjection to the influence of this foreign medium has always been its pitfall. The movement of the cartoon and the puppet film is not the movement of the real world, but is hand-made movement subject to the creative whim of the animator, not to the physical properties of the world around us. Although photography is now an invariable part of the process of animation, it should only provide a convenient means for the animator to copy and show what he has made by hand. Never should an animator be forced to comply with the techniques of the photographed film—the long shot, closeup, medium shot, tracking shot, pan shot, camera angles, zoom, etc.—for in an animation (most especially in a cartoon) these techniques are unnatural almost to the point of being unmeaningful. The sweep of the live-action film needed to give meaning to photographic techniques is missing in the animated film, and thus these techniques appear artificial.

The world of the animated cinema is free from the world of reality, and the animator is limited only by the medium in which he draws or models, or by the structure of the work itself, and by his own imagination. Any listing of the techniques available to the animator would be incomplete and more than a bit superfluous, since techniques grow out of the artist's material. Switches, for example, can be accomplished in a cartoon by the conventions of graphic art: characters can stay where they are on the screen, and the background can change around them. Emotional states can be indicated by changing color. Indeed, cartoon and puppet films are less limited than live-action films, and the compulsion to make the animated film deliberately limited by imposing the techniques of the live-action cinema upon it has kept it from fulfilling its infinite potential. It is this compulsion that has caused it to be considered the little sister of the live-action film.

But what has obstructed the maturing of this medium's subject matter is something much more complicated. A large majority of animated films made within the last five years have been geared toward a child's intelligence. The one person who is to blame for this is Walt Disney, a man whose pseudo-animations have dominated the entire industry since their birth. Disney was not an animator, but a technician. The animated film industry will always remember him for the brilliant and subtle effects he achieved in his films through experimentation with various scientific processes that up until his time had not been utilized. His animations—homely cartoons founded on the resemblance between the animal world and the human—were, however, in opposition to the medium in which he worked. Their stories excluded violence, sex, cruelty, sadness, and for the most part wit and satire, while preaching a message of unbelievable optimism to the average American.

Disney's style was literary. It was not based on the nature of the cartoon medium, but on a reproduction in cartoon form of a story told somewhat in the idiom of the live-action cinema and based on the real world. What he created was not so much a surface copy of reality as a rational world of fantasy in which things existed, characters moved about and events occurred as in a real world, not as in a world of paper, pencil, and paints. My objection is this: why take all the trouble to create an animation that duplicates the live-action cinema, when one could just as easily work in live action? The true animator (like France's Paul Grimault, for instance), in working with cartoon characters that physically resemble human beings, adapts these characters to the animated world, employing not false realism or over-stylization to bring them to life, but a deep feeling for the joy and sadness of human existence.

Even in his animated techniques, Disney worked against the nature of the cartoon medium, for instead of creating depth through artistic perception, he used a cel division technique in which the cels on which different parts of the scene were drawn were photographed with gaps between them instead of being superimposed, thus giving his final product a "real" depth, as opposed to an illusion of depth, which is the very basis of three-dimensional painting. As a result, Disney's works were false both in their banal optimism and their naturalization of the cartoon medium.

Disney's films proved successful, however, for during the period in which he first worked (the late 1920s and early 1930s) the world was in a state of utter depression, and viewers were more than willing to accept his optimistic banalities. Disney's films were so successful, in fact, that studios began to mass produce them. Thus for years Disney and his imitators (Walter Lantz, Hanna and Barbera, to name a few) dominated the animated film industry, and the media of the cartoon film and puppet film underwent a period of senility before fully maturing.

The negative effect of the Disney phenomenon can be seen even today in Heinz Edelmann's film *The Yellow Submarine,* one of the most talked about cartoons since *Snow White and the Seven Dwarfs.* This film is one of the few feature-length animations that had the courage to try all sorts of new visual innovations that echo the pop art developments of the 1960s. The visual texture of the film is rich in flickering visual puns and transformations, which restore the pleasure of being constantly surprised, something that has always been the trademark of a good animation.

Vivid images rapidly flash on the screen to illustrate the lyrics of the Beatles' songs; words appear on the screen and are fitted into a series of sentences and phrases whose meanings are quickly being shifted, much in the same way that the phrase "It's not how long you make it" is changed into "It's how you make it long" in those cigarette commercials on television. There is even one sequence, which I call the "Lucy in the Sky With Diamonds" episode, which comes close to being a stunning use of stylized human figures—something I thought I would never appreciate in animated films. But while the film deliberately strives to break away from the visual conventions of those undistinguishable Disneylike cartoons, it has aggregated its pop flourish and inventiveness into the literary structure that plagued the Disney films.

The narrative, which could have been written by a four year old, has to do with the Beatles saving the people of Pepperland from the Blue Meanies, their weapons being love and music. Although the world of *The Yellow Submarine* is a bit more like the world of the animated film, which allows for flowers budding from people and huge hands appearing from the sides of the screen, it is still too much like the world of the live action film, with animals displaying their cruel teeth in the most humanistic way imaginable, and its message about loneliness, stupidity, cruelty, and, most especially, love cloys, turning the film into another animated spectacle reminiscent of Walt Disney at his worst.

While *The Yellow Submarine* does present a problem, in that it might revive the precedent set by Disney almost 40 years ago, it will perhaps prove helpful in increasing the interest in feature-length animations not only among the viewing audience but also among film makers and producers, making it easier for animators to have their works produced. Furthermore, the faltering start that the animated film has already made in the realm of satire of adult expression will be extended. More films like Jiri Trnka's *The Hand*, Josef Kabrt's *Iron Helmet*, and Vladimir Lehkly's *Odd Birds*, which present us with a savage humor and tragic intensity missing in live action films, will be produced, as will more profound surreal-abstract animations like Walerian Borowcyk's *Les Jeux des Anges*, depicting the horror of the concentration camp through abstract symbolism. Such films have been emerging in all parts of the world, thus developing a new genre of film.

In recent years, there seems to be a trend in animated films moving toward semi- or total abstraction. John Hubley's *Moonbird*, the most classic of animations, for instance, is semi-abstract in its style. In this film, the very concrete story of two charming young boys who wander about in the moonlight, hunting a great, gaunt moonbird, is enveloped in a mysteriously lyrical and penumbral mood, evoked by loose brushstrokes of blues and greens as translucent and fluid as moonlight itself.

Even more abstract are the works of Len Lye, Norman McLaren, and Niko, animators who create films of moving patterns of form and color, offering purely visual experiences and demanding to be judged as mobiles of graphic art or plastic composition and not as a dramatic or literary form. All these animators I have mentioned draw directly on celluloid, ignoring the frame divisions that are part of the technique of photography. These films are sensual experiences communicating emotions, feelings, and sensations through color and rhythmic movements of lines, dots, and swiggles in direct counterpoint to music.

There are still other possibilities for the animated film involving combinations of different art media. For years we have had animated titles introducing live-action films such as *Walk on the Wild Side* and *Prudence and the Pill*. But now the animated film is being integrated into the body of the live-action film. Tony Richardson, for instance, used a series of exquisite cartoons based upon satirical lampoons of the Victorian period to provide narrative links and social comment in his film *The Charge of the Light Brigade*. Also there have been attempts to combine the animated film with live drama, the most memorable being the insertion of Dick Williams' animated sequence in Jerry Bock's and

Sheldon Harnick's play *The Apple Tree* to reinforce the dramatic effect while commenting on a different level. Undoubtedly, more combinations of these types will appear in the future, and it is also quite possible that there will emerge a blending of live-action with animation within the same frame, as in *Koko the Clown* and *Mary Poppins,* which used this effect to extend the dramatic action to the bizarre.

Is it childish? I think not. New scientific methods such as animograph, which creates the "in between" phases of movement, and technanimation, which transfers drawings to celluloid by xerography, continue to improve the rich texture of the graphic artist and reduce the expense in making animations. And perhaps in time, when it not only has a message to convey but also possesses a style that is of importance on its own account, the animated film will become the most potent of all media of expression, capable of saying far more than sculpture, and at the same time able to intensify its meaning with resources of movement and color richer than those of the live-action film.

Student Filmmaking
Why and How

Paul Carrico

When most people think of movie making, a dense image fallout bombards their minds: the big Hollywood feature, underground movies, news footage on TV, home movies. They rarely think of film making as a part of the ordinary academic experience of thousands of students, and if they did, their response might be "So what?" or "Why?" But regardless of anyone's reaction, students assisted by sensitive teachers have discovered film making as a whole new way of seeing and of telling about the world around them. Dozens of student film festivals regularly draw dozens to hundreds of youthful film makers, their films, and their teachers. A lot of excitement and mutual critical respect is generated by these meetings. Beyond the incandescent enthusiasm and the long sessions of looking at badly exposed and fuzzily focused images to find significant scenes or films, thoughtful educators are asking each other what it all means.

With the exception of a few schools, film making is the newest baby in the media-in-education family. Like any new baby it is fawned over by some, not

From Paul Carrico, "Student Filmmaking Why and How: Giving Students a New Way of Seeing," *Media and Methods* 6 (November 1969): 41-45, 72-74. Copyright © by Media and Methods Institute, Inc. Reprinted by permission of the publisher and Paul Carrico.

taken seriously by others, and the object of intense jealousy by a few. But the questions about its purpose and its parentage come and must be dealt with if progressive teachers are to avoid administrated infanticide or filmic birth control. A cynical question: "Since local TV stations have shown an interest, is film making simply a device to rescue a few teachers and students from the gray world of the classroom to the grayed world of commercial TV?" A serious question: "Is it a glory-road copout for teachers who have failed to come up with a viable consumer rather than a creator-oriented film study program?" (After all, film study is more difficult and more valid than film production!) Two pragmatic questions: "Doesn't it take valuable study time away from the 'hard'(and therefore important) subjects that students must take? Where will all the money come from?" A silly question and the one I encountered at Notre Dame High School: "What about all those kids who 'sneak back' into school to edit their films; after all, they're spending entirely too much time in the building!" My own reaction was that if schools are to have problems, this is the kind of problem they should have.

These questions remain; new ones will be invented. The best answer to them is to be found in the films themselves and in what happens in the students who make them. Heightened awareness expressed in a creative act transcends nit-picking and even serious questions. What follows here may serve as an answer or at least an approach to answers to some admittedly valid questions as well as a guide to getting started.

Even with a scant five years of production experience behind me (I am therefore a "pioneer"), I have often wondered why making films has not always been a normal part of the student experience instead of a marginal activity for a few. Hardware problems, the usual scapegoat, have never been a real no-no. Unfortunately, however, education is a conservative institution, and only recently has the establishment been able to recover from the abortive attempts at film education based on moral indignation in the forties and recognize and treat intelligently the film as an artful and occasionally artistic form of communication. The best student films I have seen have grown out of imaginatively conceived and well-executed film study programs. A friend once noted, "If you teach people to read, some of them will want to write." Teach students to "read" films and the same fortuitous problem will appear. Thus, lack of imaginative film study programs has dampened activity in film making.

At first the desire to make films is amorphous and young film makers conceive their first efforts on the scale of something as grand and daring as the sequel to *The Ten Commandments.* But with well-sequenced exposure to the short film form, they find there the proper idiom for expressing their view of the world. Occasionally well-made student films are produced in relative cinematic isolation since some teachers are fearful that too much exposure to the work of others can be too formative and a hindrance to the purity of the individual's expression. No matter. Under the guidance of a competent teacher, either the saturation or the starvation philosophy can be successful, depending on the visual sophistication and motivation of both student and teacher.

ROLE OF THE TEACHER

The film teacher is nearly always a producer-critic, not a creator. The average teacher (even the average film teacher) has had his once-glimpsed creativity either educated or "production-lined" out of his system and is "dead at the top." Despite tutorial fantasies, film making is an area in which most students are clearly superior to their print-oriented teacher. Such superiority in a creative venture does not eliminate the teacher but it does modify his role.

A teacher-producer knows the creative process but rarely participates in it. His job is to assemble people and materials and to assure the proper atmosphere for creative people to work. The critic assesses the final product. Students rarely need their teacher for this role, since by the time they finish the film, it has been screened so often that they know exactly what is wrong with it. But students are not arrogant and often appreciate someone's telling them what is right with their work.

I have long been convinced that creativity and criticism are separate functions; at the end of the second semester I used to take a band of young film makers and their films around to other schools, PTA's or to any group who would consent to be an audience. Such exposure provided the response and the feedback that every incipient artist needs and took care of the critical function experientially.

Creativity cannot be taught but only given a chance to grow and to be channelled. The most perennially successful film teachers try to avoid "inspiration" as such and set up as neutral a creative situation as possible. Active inspiration is "hot" and puts the teacher's trademark on student work. Unless the appeal comes from the medium itself and the student's own need for self-expression, then his movie is not worth doing in the first place and becomes the same sterile exercise as the traditional term paper or as teacher-stamped as a yearbook. The "cool" film teacher perceives himself primarily as an adult advisor, hardware expert, or the one who makes film stock, camera, editing equipment, and production facilities available and leaves the student censor-free to deal with reality around him as best he can.

Freedom from censorship implies that students should also solve their own creative problems such as scripting, sound selection, movement, and pacing with the teacher refraining from any but technical advice. Students have the right to make their own mistakes. A sign of success in this "hands off" pedagogical method is not only the quality of the production (sometimes rough but really honest) but especially the fact that the name of the teacher is almost always omitted from the screen credits, so much do the students see the film as completely their own.

A few teachers, notably David McKendall, formerly at New Trier High School in Wilmette, Illinois, have employed the "apprentice" method, whereby the teacher controls every aspect of a film that is primarily his own. Students assist the teacher in the production and experience all the skills, thrills, and frustrations of having participated in a well-made film. Such an approach tends to be craft-orientated but the rare creative teacher who employs it can usually deter students from a preoccupation with hardware, a problem that becomes acute in the case of some industry technicians. Such a technique is used more usually with small highly-selected classes devoted almost exclusively to production.

Other teachers see themselves in the role of carefully guiding the student step by step through the maze of mechanical skills involved in successful film making before permitting the student to express himself fully on film. This approach is very much like teaching grammar as a way of helping a student learn to write. Exercises in the use of the camera—the ability to choose the right lenses for a particular shooting situation, panning correctly, tracking, hand-holding a camera, photographing for texture and effect—are carefully outlined for the student. Often professional film makers are employed to criticize each student attempt. Other aspects of film making are just as carefully organized and orchestrated to teach basic skills. The most highly publicized program of this type is a federally financed experiment in Demarest, New Jersey, run by teacher, Rodney Sheratsky.

A variation was used by the author at Notre Dame High School in Niles, Illinois. In an elective course for students who completed at least a semester in film criticism, young film makers were required to submit four projects. The first was a film made without a camera-abstract figures drawn on raw 16 mm film stock with magic markers or aniline dyes. The second was a student-conceived exercise in animation using solid objects such as toys, balls, clay, etc., paper and string, or line drawings. The third was the automatic discipline of a mini-film (a film exactly one minute long) or a commercial, a form that students know well. The fourth project was a film which constituted the major work of the semester; here there were no restrictions whatever. This method put the emphasis on the medium as a self-disciplining form rather than on the teacher as guide. Students quickly discover the limitations of the medium and of themselves; rarely do they need a businessman-producer, a censor, or a teacher to tell them what they cannot do.

Other teachers such as Bob Johnson at Sir Francis Drake High School, San Anselmo, California and David Coynik at Notre Dame High School, Niles, Illinois, use a completely free-wheeling approach, adopting whatever method is suitable to the students they have. Both are competent film makers in their own right and know how to respect the independence of their students.

More important than the attitude that a film teacher takes toward the young film maker, is the attitude of the school officials and the other teachers. Outside of extracurricular activities such as sports, the school play, or an engaging music program, students rarely are involved in any experiential way in academic life. Film makers—especially during the editing phase—often forget to call parents, to eat, or to be overly concerned about the next morning's algebra assignment. The more creative students tend to be mercurial and forget the school structure. Ideal weather conditions sometimes lure them from the school corridor to the street, camera in hand. Authoritarian schools find such activity intolerable and respond in a repressive way; modern schools are more flexible regarding individual differences.

Worse than repression is the penchant of some administrators to exploit students (and their film teacher) to make "useful" promotional films for the school. Such films turn out to be dry, stilted, and "talky" since the subject matter is not suited to the film medium. The only exception I have seen to this is a film made by David Coynik's students, entitled *A Thousand Days*. The students were subsidized by Notre Dame High School but left free to choose "cinematic" material and to "tell it like it was." *A Thousand Days* is one of the most honest (and best) promotional films I have ever seen because it tries hard to be truthful rather than to impress.

A film can successfully be made by a class. Sister Bede Sullivan formerly at Lillis High School in Kansas City, Missouri, divided a class into teams in order to make a long film about student leisure. But for a school administration to use a film class as a self-conscious adjunct to its public relations program is downright unfair. Film production succeeds best when it is used as a free authentic vehicle of student expression.

Finally, administrators and academic counsellors who demand measurable results find the classroom film experience impossible to understand. But some of their questions are valid. Does film override or replace traditionally accepted forms of student expression? Is there a carryover of enthusiasm when a student is confronted with more pedestrian but necessary academic courses. Do ACT or CEEB test results improve? Unfortunately the only guide to answering these questions at present is human judgment.

In schools where film making is a potential part of every student's experience, teachers note a proliferation, almost an explosion, in other forms of expression, especially poetry. Such a release of energy comes with discovery. Through film making many students come to terms with their own vast viewing experience. Such personal "structuring" frees them from the amorphous, and hence poisonous effect of previous media intake and releases fantastic psychic energy.

There is as yet no empirical way to measure carryover but often students find information-centered classes boring after a bout with film. Modern educators agree that no course need ever be one in which "the tedium is the message." "Turned-on" students demand more of teachers; any teacher who can respond need never fear the stimulating effect of a film making or film criticism course. Indeed, at many schools, teachers in sociology and religion classes are accepting the "term film" along with the traditional term paper.

Testing programs, extrinsic to the school, have not caught up to the film student as yet; tests would be geared to subject matter deemed academically respectable by college entrance committees. To date no one has suggested that students excited about learning score lower on "objective," corporation-administered tests.

THE CONTENT AND FORM OF STUDENT FILMS

Generalizations cannot be photographed and unlike research term papers, student films are made out of bits of the film maker's own world. In inner-city schools the films tend to be about people, interacting with other people. Affluent students make more abstract films replete with alienation and protest. Although student films make general statements about human relationships, violence, or the hypocrisy of organized religion, such statements are formed out of the stuff of the photographable real world. Still shots lifted from magazines and images from TV are often incorporated into environmental and action shots to render an experience or to make a statement.

The films are rarely humorous. Heavy-handed contrast editing (a plush suburban church juxtaposed with a mangy dog in a ghetto street) suggest the blatant irony of many student films. Many are lyrical and impressionistic, evoking experiences rather than narrating them. Most narrative films demand action-matching the shots in a scene, a form of editing students find technically too sophisticated. Financial considerations demand that the films be limited to 10 or 15 minutes; a student film longer than 30 minutes is rare. Screen humor, especially purely visual humor, requires sophistication, split-second timing, and a certain emotional distance; hence it is not too surprising to find such humor almost totally absent from student films. Besides, the world they see is painfully close to Benjamin's in *The Graduate*: full of adult phoniness at home, war abroad, and ready for revolution everywhere. Student preoccupation with alienation, death, authenticity, and sober involvement may shock demure adults, but to an educator such concerns are quite understandable.

What Camera To Buy

An evaluation of super 8 mm cameras appeared in the January 1969 issue of *M&M*, pp. 52-54. Criteria for selecting a camera, specific camera models, prices, and specifications were given. While the super 8 cameras market has changed somewhat since then, this guide is still a valuable starting point for teachers and students just getting into film making.

Film Stock. The cost, size and often the quality of film equipment is determined by film stock width, measured in millimeters. Sixteen millimeter stock, especially since the rise of silver prices in March 1968, has made production in this format almost prohibitively expensive for the average school. A typical price for a 100-foot roll of black-and-white 16 mm film including processing is almost $8.00. At "sound" speed (24 frames per second) 100 feet will last about 3.2 minutes. Good color film stock with processing varies from $12.00 to $14.00 a roll.

So it comes as no surprise that students usually stay away from 16 mm film and favor much less expensive 8 mm or super 8 mm film stock. Black-and-white film in these sizes is hard to come by since the market demand has traditionally been for color, but most professional film laboratories stock it. Unlike the price differential in 16 mm film stocks, the price of color film is very close to that of black and white. A typical price for 50 feet of ordinary 8 mm film with processing is $3.25; $3.75 for a super 8 mm cartridge of film. At "silent" speed (16 or 18 frames per second) 50 feet is equivalent to 4 or 4.5 minutes of screen time. These prices can represent quite a saving over 16 mm film. Often stock can be bought more cheaply than the above mentioned prices, but let the buyer beware! Sometimes bargain film is full of splices, is flawed, or overage. Our intention here is not to discuss the wide variety of film stocks available. Any reputable laboratory, camera store, or film manufacturer can supply all the technical information necessary.

The advantage of 16 mm is the extremely sharp projected image. The stronger light source in 16 mm projectors also permits the film to be projected under marginal blackout conditions which would "wash out" anything in 8 mm. The individual frame size is also 400 percent larger than standard 8 mm (twice as high and twice as wide). Editing is therefore easier and it is possible to recognize each frame without running it through a viewer magnifier each time, a necessity with small size film. The difference between standard 8 mm and super 8 mm film stock is not in the width of the film but in the size and spacing of the sprocket holes, which permits an image 56 percent larger than the one on 8 mm film. Under similar conditions, super 8 will project a larger, less grainy picture.

The advantage of super 8 over ordinary 8 mm is not only in the projected image but in the ease involved in the shooting process. Almost all super 8 film is packaged in cartridges and easily inserted in the camera, thus eliminating the need to thread the film through the camera shuttle and attach it to another reel. As soon as the film is inserted, the ASA speed of the film (a chemical speed that indicates the film's sensitivity to light) is automatically locked in with the photoelectrical mechanism in "electric eye" cameras. These features make the average super 8 camera virtually foolproof to operate.

The disadvantages are not so obvious since the industry rarely mentions them. American-made film cartridges, as pioneered by Kodak, allow the film to run in one direction only, a feature which eliminates the possibility of "in camera" addition of lap-dissolves and superimpositions, a procedure possible in many reel-to-reel cameras. Reel-to-reel super 8 cameras are made by only a few companies and are generally very expensive. Some foreign-made cartridges, particularly the Fujica, permit the film to be reversed but must be used only with the Fujica system and not in cameras designed for the American-style cartridge. While the American-style cartridge is not a disadvantage to the occasional camera user, it can be inhibiting for a student who needs dissolves or superimpositions in his movie.

Over-all considerations dictate the super 8 route for most film classes. Standard 8 mm is becoming obsolete but if the production and editing equipment is available at a really low price it should not be rejected. Super 8 is here to stay, is easy for even the slowest student to use, and more economical than 16 mm. As manufacturers become more sensitive to the student market, improvements will be made in equipment and lab services. Local film labs are becoming somewhat responsive to the needs of the student film maker, and in general it is safer to do business with a competent local lab rather than an unknown processor in another part of the country.

Shooting Equipment. The basic hardware of film making is divided into two categories: shooting (or production), and editing. Besides properly chosen film stock, a camera, lights, tripod, and a meter for measuring light intensity are basic tools for a film maker to get images on the film.

Cameras in every style and price range superabound. Some teachers whose schools make cameras available to students prefer having a lot of low-priced cameras to one or two expensive models. While it is true that great instruments by themselves do not make great artists, a better grade of camera can enhance young talent. Desirable qualities for any camera are: *simplicity, durability,* and *versatility.* Cameras in a school will receive rough usage, so delicate knobs and fragile bodies are not generally "student proof." Simplicity of operation is necessary, especially for a student with a viable idea for a movie but hampered by a "hardware hangup." This seems to be especially true of female film makers, though not limited exclusively to them. A camera should be versatile enough to allow the advanced student to do virtually anything his imagination might suggest. Ease of maintenance is also an important consideration.

Valuable features include (1) a zoom lens, (2) a variety of speed changes (frames per second), (3) a photoelectrically operated iris or diaphragm, (4) a stop frame mechanism for animation, and (5) reflex viewing.

A *zoom lens* is a lens with a variable focal length, which in effect means that the viewing angle can be changed. If one looks through a piece of water pipe only one inch long, he can see a lot of world, but the same pipe eight inches long will narrow his view of the same world. A zoom lens has the same effect but is in addition variable over its given range. At its narrowest angle or "zoom in" position, the lens also tends to compress distance; at its widest angle or "pull back" position it tends to expand distance. At the 25 mm (one inch) stop the lens will "see" subjects in relation to each other pretty much as the eye sees them.

The zoom lens has a bad reputation because of its abuse by home movie makers. The world is a mighty disappointing place as seen through the viewfinder and the amateur film maker tries to compensate by excessive panning and zooming. The effect on a viewer is irritation and cinematic seasickness. If students can learn to use the infinite framing capabilities of a zoom lens and to choose details with discrimination, it will prove a valuable tool and eliminate numerous camera setups.

Slow motion and *accelerated motion,* too often used as gimmicks, should be available to a film maker. Professional cameras have a great range of speeds from just a few frames per second to sometimes several thousand. For students, a range close to the camera's normal speed is usually adequate. Closely related to this feature is the ability to expose one frame at a time, essential for animation.

The *photoelectrically operated iris* which controls the amount of light that reaches the sensitive film is useful where light conditions are even. But because the photoelectric cell "reads" the most intense or "hottest"light available, a device for overriding the photoelectric cell for marginal or special lighting conditions is desirable. In such an instance a light meter, either the one built into the camera or one specially designed for the purpose can be used. Good photography is the art of painting with light and a little care here can save the frustration of overexposured or underexposed footage. Light meters are inexpensive and easy to learn how to read, a sometimes necessary tool for any film maker.

When selecting an "electric eye" camera, the buyer should make sure it has the capability of accepting many different sensitivities as measured by ASA speeds. The cheaper cameras have a much more limited range. ASA speeds should range from 40 for Kodachrome II to at least 160 for Tri-X Reversal. New films coming out (Four-X, for example) will demand even wider ranges.

These films will allow students to shoot scenes at night, in subways, and in other areas where heretofore there just was not enough light to get an exposure.

Interior lighting is the most serious technical flaw common to almost all student-made films. Camera mounted lights are rarely of any value, yet these are the ones—called "sun guns" or light bars—most often supplied or recommended by manufacturers. Most student "sets" can adequately be lighted with three well-placed and inexpensive photoflood lamps. Some schools find it within their budget to purchase a kit of Quartz-iodine combination flood-spotlights. Advice on lighting setups and the proper choice of bulbs of the correct color temperature (measured in degrees Kelvin) is available from film manufacturers, cinema labs, or local professionals. Adequate lighting can be learned by anyone in a relatively short time and is as important to a good production as rhetoric is to a good theme paper.

Reflex viewing means that the camera operator sees through the camera lens itself instead of an optical system parallel to it. The photographer literally sees what the camera sees. This feature is especially valuable on close work such as titles where faulty framing is extremely annoying. Reflex viewing automatically eliminates the problem of faulty framing as well as the problems of fuzzy focus or a finger in front of the lens. The operator is enabled to positively select focus between subjects in the foreground or background. Some directors today use a shift of focus as an effective substitution for cutting.

Few people can hold a camera steady while shooting, especially if the bulk of the weight is behind the camera grip. Unsteadiness or jiggling is particularly noticeable to a viewer on long shots. Professional cameramen as a rule use a tripod whenever possible. A tripod should be chosen which is sturdy and designed specifically for a movie camera. Tripods for still cameras are generally too flimsy and do not allow the operator to pan smoothly. The camera must be held rigid when shooting animation; there is no substitute for a tripod here.

Editing Equipment. To anyone conversant with the film medium, it is all too obvious that editing is the most important aspect of film making. On the editing table discrete scraps of film are transformed into statement; it is the part of film making students find most rewarding. The necessary pieces of equipment include at least one projector, pairs of rewinds, a viewer-magnifier, and a splicing block with film cement or splicing tape. Alternate equipment might include extra takeup reels and a synchronizer complete with a pair of long-shaft rewinds (16 mm only).

A projector is listed as a piece of editing equipment because every film maker makes his final decisions whether to cut or not to cut on the basis of how the film will look on the screen. For some film makers the process of editing is endless and they will nibble away at their creations long after the films are in release. This is especially true of students who change their films almost every time it is screened for a live audience. The editing projector should be one that the student loads and threads manually. Automatic or "self-threaders" and splices rarely mix. A "freeze" or "stop" frame mechanism and when possible a manually operated film advance clutch is useful for analyzing individual frames and necessary for accurate timing and sound synchronizing . . . .

Rewinds are simple crank-operated mechanisms for transferring film from one reel to another. Motor-driven rewinding is possible on almost every projector but a separate pair mounted on the editing table or on either end of a wide board is a necessity. Between a pair of rewinds most of the actual cutting is done. A viewer-magnifier through which the film can be pulled by the rewinds is necessary, especially during the initial stages when the pieces of film are seen for the first time. Some manufacturers incorporate a pair of rewinds into the viewer mechanism itself but these tend to be fragile and unable to withstand constant use. Professional editing equipment, designed for day-after-day usage, is definitely preferable for a school.

The splicing block should, when possible, be mounted between the rewinds for easy access and for the protection of the block. Blocks employing either liquid cement or mylar splicing tape are available. Students find tape easier to use with standard 8 mm or super 8 mm. Applied with care it provides an adequate bond. The block should feature a straight cut parallel to the frame line of the film instead of a curved cut popular on some home movie units.

Synchronizers and their associated long-shaft rewinds are for use only with 16 mm film at the present time. Using this equipment means that the student can on the editing table add fades, dissolves, and superimpositions to his film, but the equipment is relatively sophisticated for young film makers.

After the film has been cut into pieces, it should be labelled and stored safely while editing proceeds. The preferred way is to hang the film by one end on a "clothesline" or on a light rack built over a bin or a drum lined with a plastic bag. The soft lining along with careful handling prevents scratching. Egg crates can also be used to store the tiny rolls of film where preferred storage is not available.

After the film is edited, it can be returned to the lab for splice-free printing. If a print is not planned the film should be inspected for faulty splices and cleaned with a linen cloth moistened with film cleaner before projection. In most student productions, the many steps in the film assembly process are omitted for economic reasons and the original footage becomes the work print, the answer print, and the release print.

The most important service a school can provide the student is free and easy access to equipment, especially editing material. It is difficult for anyone to create "on cue," and school structure should not for a film class become stricture.

Sound Equipment. An apparent deprivation, the technical inability to tightly synchronize sound and picture, becomes a negative but important advantage for both teacher and student. Even with the most sophisticated equipment, adding sound is tedious. Sound, too, is so fascinating for young film makers that their creations might well become a series of highly verbal set pieces accompanied by pictures "in synch." At present, there are on the market several camera-tape recorder combinations which can be electronically locked together during shooting. On the surface these combinations look like an instant solution to the sound hangup but they present problems in editing. The freedom to edit film is basic to film making and a freedom that a film maker should never relinquish. Any salesman should be required to demonstrate the advertised ease of editing. Of the two systems for interlocking—optical or magnetic—magnetic is presently preferable. The optical system now in distribution requires separate meticulous steps to remove a scene. The magnetic system is also complicated but simpler and more flexible than the optical system.

Separate recording units can be used, but nonprofessional tape recorders and projectors rarely "track" at the same speed every time, thus making simultaneous sound difficult to achieve. Sound such as music or voice-over narrations is then used to underline or reinforce the visuals. During the screening the projector speed can usually be manipulated to slow down or speed up the film to permit closer synch. However, the lack of any easy way to add simultaneous sound in student films puts emphasis on the proper aspect of film making, the *visual.*

An encouraging new development is a new line of super 8 projectors which permits recording directly on a magnetic strip chemically bonded to the edge of the film. This feature has long been available in 16 mm but the excessive cost of the projectors and mediocre sales promotion has kept these units out of the average schools. While this system is not always suitable for the tight "lip synch" sound of the speaking face, it does assure exact "as recorded" synch during projection-playback. When audio-visual budgets are drawn up it is advisable to order one projector that can record the sound—these are relatively expensive—and one or more less expensive projection-playback units . . . .

CONCLUSION

Why permit or even encourage students to make their own movies? If the purpose is to turn out junior size film technicians, the activity is not worth serious academic attention. Students can acquire these skills more effectively at a professional cinema school or on the job in the industry. Nor should film making be used as a substitute for a film study or appreciation (a *verboten* word in academic circles) course that failed because of teacher inadequacy. But used in conjunction with such a course, it is an invaluable way to give the student a new way of seeing that's more important than what they see and a real feel for the medium.

Few films, even ones made by great film artists, are ever realized perfectly. Sometimes a film never gets off the ground. A group of my students (marginal kids with long hair, a beat-up convertible [jointly owned], and levis), back in the days before those things became quasi-fashionable, decided to make a film about Chicago's vertical slums, or "public housing." After dozens of interviews, runaround from politicians, and harassment from gangs, they decided that the movie was impossible to make. A teacher dedicated to education-as-product rather than process might have given them a failing mark. I gave them an "A" for all they learned about sociology, government, politics, each other, and goodness knows what else. Film making courses are one of the few places students can succeed through failure.

Some final precautions: not everyone is capable of making a film, no more than everyone is capable of writing a good poem or short story. To force it on the half-willing student as an assignment is a sure way to kill its vitality and richness. A few students, too, find film such a personal medium that they almost literally pour out their souls. Such outpouring can approach psychodrama, and while there is undoubtedly a great deal to be said about the value of channeling one's amorphous subconscious into an intelligent and disciplined form, a great deal of psychological harm can result when a teacher becomes inordinately fascinated with self-revelation. Often such revelation is not apparent either to the creator or to other students; he simply feels that he has "gotten something out of his system" and an adult with critical insight will frequently find it necessary to keep such insights a professional secret. Film making, like any other humanizing activity, has its prudential as well as its financial limits.

Sing Sweetly
of My Many Bruises

Vivian Tilford

I stood in the corner watching. Paul held the light. James raised the kitchen knife and waited to be told when to start the action. As soon as James looked up, I asked, "Ready?" He nodded, and I gave Mark the signal to start. He began bringing down the knife in quick strokes as if he were stabbing someone. He was really very good, and then I remembered that this boy had been separated from his parents because he had once tried to kill his father. I believe it was then that movie making in the classroom seemed even more important to me than it had before.

This wasn't our first film, and it will be followed by many more, but I thought I saw a change in Mark after he made this film. Not a big change, of course, but a closeness between the two of us and also a willingness to talk to his classmates and participate more in group activities.

There have been other students that have been shy and withdrawn. Fred had been in my English class as a freshman and again as a junior. He had probably never said more than a few words to me and I could hardly remember his name when I saw him in the hall. He was placed in a special class called Basic Communications that I teach. The class decided it would like to try movie making. They were all low achievers in that class and Fred was selected to be the star of one movie. He was very serious about his part in the film and his acting was quite good. I think everyone was a little surprised at the talent he displayed. Fred's confidence grew as we filmed and I felt I could see some improvement in his personality. I certainly never again forgot his name.

The scriptwriter was a boy who was absent a great deal of the time. He wanted to learn to operate the camera and I, of course, encouraged him to do so. His interest in making the film and using the camera seemed to spark his interest in school enough to make his attendance record much better for the rest of that year.

I have been able to see important changes in students after they became involved in a film. Shy students who have never been noticed in a classroom

From Vivian Tilford, "Sing Sweetly of My Many Bruises," *Arizona English Bulletin* 12 (February 1970): 51-54. Reprinted by permission of the publisher.

become aware of their talents, and other students may become aware of the special beauty of an individual when his face fills the screen with a warm smile. What better way can there be to show the worth of an individual?

Our latest 8 mm film was called "Love, Speed, and Thrills" and was presented to an auditorium filled with parents and students who had come to see an original one-act play and movies that had been written and produced by the students at Chandler High School. The purpose was not only to entertain but also to make money for additional film and equipment to enable additional students to participate in film making.

Movie making seems to get in the blood of a few more students each year. It all begins in the classroom. If movie making seems to have no practical value for students other than the few who might make a career out of TV or cinema, stop to consider the diminishing work week for everyone. What will our students do with all the free time that is theirs now and theirs to come? Young men whose days are filled with football or track will not be able to carry this with them into their future, but photography is much less expensive than many of our programs and develops the creative individual to a much greater degree.

There are many ways that the production can be handled, and the encouraging thing is that anything that works seems to be the right way. I like to begin by looking at all the footage that my classes in previous years have made. Before I had this visual library I would use commercial films and some of my personal rolls that I felt would help students know what they might expect from the medium.

The next step is to ask students for a script. These have come from individuals or a group effort. I suggest you not be too particular about the script and form of writing. I have seen exceptionally good films come from students who had great difficulty getting their ideas down on paper but could visualize them well. After all, the movie is their message—not their script. Some students may like to try a storyboard which is a comic strip type of description of what they want to shoot. It makes it very easy to see what they have in mind.

When one script is ready, start casting and gathering properties. Unless it is a comedy, try to use real places and things and little makeup. I ask students to keep in mind when they are writing that we must shoot the movie at school and the props must be easy to find or inexpensive to buy. I have found the administration to be very helpful about allowing me to take my class to various spots around the campus to shoot as long as I am willing to keep up with the students and don't lose a few along the way. When just a few students are involved it might be best to shoot after school or on Saturday. I also tried to make the classroom the location for as many shots as possible to make it easier to keep up with students who like to wander off "location."

If the problem of equipment is causing concern, there are several ways this might be handled. I bought a regular 8 mm Cannon with a zoom lens and a rewind feature for fades and dissolves for $90 about five years ago and have allowed students to use it with a tripod for three years and it is still working well. My one rule is—I go where the camera goes. (Some have asked to borrow it and shoot a roll on their own. I offer to go with them on a Saturday or Sunday to shoot.) Another necessary piece of equipment is a good tripod. A sun gun or movie light will handle the light for indoor pictures. Light might be borrowed from a student or use your own. Keep extension cords handy. Take advantage of the sunlight from the windows by placing your actors in front of the windows and using the movie light to help flood their faces. Use a lot of closeups to make sure you catch all the expression in the face. If you have plenty of lights set them up in a triangle with one light near the camera and one off to the right. The other one will be to the left of the camera. When taking movies outside choose a covered walkway or a shaded area. The light will be better on the faces than in the bright sunlight.

Another important point is how to pay for the film. Some teachers have the students buy their own. It has worked better for me to buy the film when I was just beginning and these films then belong to me. I felt that way that I could edit them as much as I liked. If the student buys his film then it is his film and I feel it should be given to him at the end of the production. It is also difficult to put rolls together for one production if the film belongs to many different people unless they are all willing to donate it to the school.

When my classes began using a great deal of film and it was becoming rather costly, I asked for a loan from the student council of $50.

Our real money maker has been the Cinematographers Club—a group of students who have more than an average interest in filming. The club has shown completed films to interested parents and students at night and made enough to be able to continue filming. Last year we had built up our Cinematographers fund to $150. We have bought a good tripod, a record of silent movies music, and a Blackhawk film from our fund. We will continue to have a showing each year of the completed films. Our last performance combined films and an original one-act play entitled "The Happy Journey of Bonnie and Clyde." It was a financial success.

Students who become interested in filming can do a great deal completely on their own or with little supervision once the basics have been mastered. One group wrote the script and gathered actors together in class but used their own equipment, bought all their own film, and did all the shooting on their own time. They estimated their 30-minute movie cost them about $25, which they didn't make back on their showing only because they were not able to advertise properly. Their production was quite good and they want to make more movies. This is, after all, the most important criteria for judging the success of their project. From my observations in class, the group worked hard on their project and learned to know each other much better by getting together outside of class and working on something that was important to them.

When the rolls of films start coming back, show them in class but point out all the good things you can see. Every bit of acting that seems natural and appropriate should be called to the attention of the class. Compliment the cameraman by pointing out good closeup shots that are in focus and any other angles that show the action well. These kinds of things are difficult to teach, so never let an opportunity go by. This is the time when the teacher probably has the greatest impact. The students will probably be laughing at all the mistakes and some may be going through agony waiting and wondering what will happen next. But remind them, the mistakes can be taken out and reshot if necessary and, after all, this is a time to all learn together.

Editing can be very long and time consuming. Allow plenty of time for it. I have done most of it, but if students can be taught to do it for you, it will probably be better for them and you. It is possible to do a great deal with the film at this point. Everyone seems to develop their own way of doing it. Cutting the film into various pieces, labeling each piece in a jar, glass, envelope, or box and putting it back together to say what you want it to is basically what editing means. The most important rule is to try to keep the film clean and to learn to make good splices that will hold. This isn't too difficult. The A-V man can probably show you in about five minutes or he might edit the film for you if you prefer it that way. Keep looking at the film after you have it all together for additional places when scenes can be shortened or cut out. When you get it down to the point you want it, a sound track on tape will help add excitement. Maybe a group of students could work on this that were not as involved in the earlier part of the production as you had wanted them to be. It really takes hours of listening and picking out bits of music or sound effects for each part of the movie. They will need a stop watch to time each part of the film so that they will know how many seconds of sound will be needed. This will not be known until all the editing is done, of course, but music can be gathered and timed and planned for specific scenes.

For equipment they will probably need one tape recorder and two record players. Or better than that, one record player and two tape recorders. Direct jacks leading from the tape recorder to the record players are important too. If narration is used it seems to work out best to put the narration on one tape, stopping to make corrections as you go along and then adding this with music to another tape through a sound mixer if this is available.

If it seems complicated and difficult, it can be. If it sounds like something stimulating and fun for the teacher and students, it is. It seems only fair to warn you, it is very hard to stop once you get hooked on making films.

Can They Picture Themselves Better with Movies?

Richard Bumstead

> Students in a screen education course gain self-awareness say the directors of a $78,000, two-year pilot project in North Reading, Mass., but a flaw in research design may taint conclusions.

Today's high school diploma represents about 11,000 hours of seat-warming from first grade to graduation. During this same period, and on his own time, a high school graduate has stared at his television set for 15,000 hours (75 percent of the material shown is filmed) and sat through 500 full-length feature films at the local theater. Statistics like these are enough to stop the eye, if not freeze it into a glassy stare.

Hence, argues the American Film Institute and a small but enthusiastic band of screen educators in the U.S., courses in screen education deserve a place in the curriculum of colleges, universities and secondary schools, not as a peripheral activity, but as an integral part of the humanities program. Film and television are such powerful media, they say, that young people should develop some discrimination about their grammar and content.

Screen education has established a base on campus through film societies and courses in film history and film production which AFI says are "invariably oversubscribed." But screen education has not yet broken into the more structured high school curriculum, despite the experimentation in many schools with cameras, tape recorders, TV monitors, and other paraphernalia of the new media.

Screen educators are now in the process of legitimizing their discipline—making it palatable to high school faculty traditionalists and conservatives on the school board. When a group of educators gathered at Waltham, Massachusetts one year ago to define what screen education for grades K-12 should be, they said:

Film and television constitute a special kind of language or mode of communication, consisting of projected moving images accompanied by sounds. This language ("screen") can be seen as a distinctive and particularly eloquent ingredient of the multimedia forms in which artists are currently attempting a total sensory involvement of the individual in the medium-message complex.

The screen educator's task is to help students to employ and respond to the new language as effectively and richly as possible, both to increase the students' understanding of themselves and of others, and to explore and enjoy this new mode of expression.

This is all very well for people who can cut through McLuhanese, but not much of a guide for a teacher assigned the task—probably by a desperate principal willing to try anything—of making an educational experience out of 15 inarticulate, restless sophomores, five super 8 movie cameras, 1,000 feet of film, one splicer, and an exposure meter that doesn't work.

How does one avoid a lot of tomfoolery (a good old-fashioned word sure to be on the tongues of sceptical school committeemen)? How is a course in screen education lifted above the level of entertainment and playing with gadgets, a degeneration to which it is peculiarly susceptible?

$78,000 TO TEST A PROGRAM

Demonstrating the potential of screen education within a high school routine is the purpose of a $78,000, two-year project in North Reading, Massachusetts. The U.S. Office of Education is funding this research and demonstration grant under Title VII, Part A (Research and experimentation in media for educational purposes) of the National Education Defense Act.

An interim report on the first year's experience (1967-68) has recently been released by the head of the project, Anthony Hodgkinson, both a professor at Boston University and a leading screen educator, and his on-site project directory, Dave Powell. These men come from Great Britain, where educational authorities are a step ahead of the U.S. in the pedagogical use of film. Their findings, titled "A Descriptive Report of Some of the First Year's Activities," can be obtained from David J. Powell, North Reading High School, North Reading, Mass. 01864. Mr. Powell taught in a comprehensive high school in London before joining the English department at North Reading High School three years ago. "I never worked on any commercial films," Mr. Powell said. "My interest in the medium has always been its educational possibilities." His full beard, slightly mod clothes, and vigorous British-accented speech project the image of a man who could merge easily into a film production crew.

North Reading, an outlying suburb of Boston, has a population of about 11,000—composed mostly of technicians who work in the electronic plants on Route 128 and junior executive family types who are filling up acres of old Yankee farm country with their homes. About 1,650 students attend the new junior and senior high schools, situated side by side in the center of a large campus.

The school administration appears receptive to staff ideas for curriculum changes. In addition to a go-ahead for Powell's screen education project, the English and social studies departments were allowed to develop courses on subjects wanted to study.

About 210 students (13 percent of the school population) are now enrolled in screen education courses taught by Powell and two other faculty members, Robert Ball and Charles McVinney. One project aim, according to Powell, is to determine what kind of course will be best suited for students at specific grade levels, in terms of content and activities. Course content, couched in terms of a traditional subject, now follows closely Powell's definition of screen education:

> Just as the student in a traditional English course studies the literature the writer, the grammar of English, and tries his hand at writing, a screen education student will view some of the great film classics, discuss the issues raised, learn production methods and the language of the film and try to communicate an idea through this medium.

The screen education courses taught at the high school level operate within the humanities curriculum. An elective course program operates in the English and social studies departments, using the semester (half-year) as a basic length for each course. Each student in grade 10-12 elects his program with the one requisite that at the end of the three years his six electives shall constitute a fair balance of literature and language.

The screen education courses are as follows:

Screen Fundamentals

(Sophomore level, one semester, prerequisite for junior and senior courses)

An exploration of visual perceptions and the "language" of the visual and aural media. Designed to promote greater understanding of the media and develop skills in their expressive modes (i.e., use of the movie camera). English credit.

Communications

(Junior level, two semesters)

A study of the major modern media and their uses—film, television, radio, newspapers, and advertising. This course has a very practical emphasis in student production of film, tape, etc. English credit.

Screen and Society

(Senior level, two semesters)

A study of current and recurrent social problems and issues i.e., Race and Prejudice, The American Dream, War, The Individual and Society. The format includes the showing of major feature-length films and short films, classroom discussion, project work, relevant reading and work with the modern media as expressive modes. English or social studies credit.

Although many schools will possess the most basic tools required for a screen education program, there are a number of additional pieces of equipment that may be needed, especially if a film making program is to be included. In many cases students will possess some of the equipment themselves, particularly tape recorders and cameras.

One of the most important decisions is the size format to be used in movie making. After all the pros and cons have been weighed, super 8 comes out as being the most flexible and economical. Equipment of varying complexities is available in this format, allowing the initial budget to be kept low.

A class of 25 students might use the following kinds and quantities of equipment. All such quantities and prices are approximate, and should not be regarded as either definitive or exhaustive in scope:

1	16 mm projector	$ 800.00
*1	super 8 projector	100.00
1	carousel slide projector	115.00
*5	simple super 8 cameras	200.00
*1	tripod	20.00
1	light meter	30.00
*1	set Photo floods	10.00
5	simple cameras (slide)	50.00
*2	movie editors	90.00
*3	splicers super 8	35.00
1	tape recorder	120.00
1	portable tape recorder	60.00
3	slide sorters	12.00
		$1,642.00
* Super 8 only		$ 455.00

Note: School with 16 mm projector, slide projector, and tape recorder $607 only.

APPRECIATE, EMULATE, ORIGINATE

This progression—from analysis to production to communication—is the principle on which Powell has organized graded courses for the past school year. Sophomores study the language of visual and aural media by screening films and listening to radio tapes and examining productions in other media. Juniors produce films and tapes, and learn the grammar of the media. Seniors use different media to examine society in near-journalism style.

All students are expected to work with still or motion picture cameras and tape recorders. Since film is considered the medium that subsumes the rest, it is emphasized. As a student takes the sophomore, junior, and senior courses he hopefully becomes so proficient in the use of equipment that he can concentrate on structure and style in his senior year project and not remain tangled in production details.

Hands-on training early in the course helps the student understand a medium. One teacher made the mistake in an elementary course of screening a professional film to spark class discussion of film techniques. Instead, the students became so engrossed in the plot that they paid no attention to directorial style.

In the production phase of each course, Powell follows the classic educational prescription of moving from the immediate to the remote, from the simple to the complex, in organizing exercises and projects. In the sophomore screen fundamentals class, for example, the first assignment is this: using a still camera (usually a Polaroid Land camera for its immediate feedback feature), take a portrait of yourself that reveals your basic personality trait—studious, athletic, boisterous, happy-go-lucky, or whatever.

By the end of the term, sophomores are expected to serve on a film crew to help in producing a three-minute narrative or documentary film in the super 8 format with tape-recorded sound. Advanced students, who frequently tackle more complex subjects, often go off-campus into North Reading or other communities in the greater Boston area.

What kinds of films do students produce? Prospective screen educators had better steel themselves to bathroom sex and biff-bang-bop violence.

FEMME FATALE WITH SHOCK APPEAL?

One impertinent sophomore unveiled her self-portrait for the criticism of Powell and the class. She had posed, gangster-moll fashion, with one hand on her hip and the other resting on a deliberately visible sanitary-napkin dispenser. A cigarette dangled from her lips. How should a teacher react to this kind of photograph? "You must treat it simply as a photograph—this was a good shot by the way," Powell conceded. "Don't, for godsakes, take the bait and discuss it as an idea, which is what they want you to do."

Powell can anticipate his students' propensity to portray dramatic conflict in violent terms. Since he knows he will get it anyhow, sophomores are asked to record the cause, event, and conclusion of some kind of conflict in four or five still photographs. He receives something like: girl steals purse, other girl hits purse-stealer, gets purse back. The aim is to stimulate class thinking around story lines that hold a series of photographs or a film together.

Perhaps the word "violence" is unfair. Powell seeks dramatic conflict having a beginning, middle, and end. A good guy vs. bad guy plot comes easily to the 15- and 16-year-old mind, trained by hours at the TV screen.

The freshmen section, for example, produced a super 8 film called "Foiled Revenge," in which a bored class bombards its teacher with balls of foil until the teacher begins to return the fire.

"Fitzie's Flunkies" was a junior class venture in super 8—the comic misadventures of a gang of "Hell's Angels" motorcyclists. So much for group efforts.

LONERS TACKLE SERIOUS SUBJECTS

The students who worked alone on projects tackled serious subjects. One boy filmed a draft resistance rally on the Boston Commons in documentary style. Another recorded the high school girls' gymnastics competition. An impressionistic film-and-sound tape about the town and its school was made by one boy for a hospitalized basketball player. Powell described this film maker as a "slow and somewhat timid worker who dragged the project out and tended to withdraw himself from the class group in order to finish it."

Although Powell definitely prefers group projects, film making seems a highly individualistic effort. The students go about their work, occasionally consulting Powell, usually about the availability of some piece of equipment. His role, if he follows the prescription of the Waltham conference, is that of "participant, an advisor and an authority on little else than the hardware . . ."

The report of the conference continues: "Advice on choice of material or treatment more often than not becomes an adult intrusion."

Following this hands-off attitude on story ideas, Powell grades student productions on whether the film worked as the students intended it to—not on the correctness or propriety of the idea. If, for example, a crew intended to shoot a comic sequence, does the edited film version garner smiles from the audience?

He also puts a high value on student involvement in a project. There is a tactical reason for this. For one thing, students fool around less if their grade depends on involvement in the group. Powell, however, sees a far greater motive for seeking involvement—it increases a student's self-knowledge or self-realization.

Two graduate students at Boston University are attempting to test Mr. Powell's theory that the film course improves student self-awareness. At the beginning of the term, students in the film course and a random selection of other students completed the Catell Junior-Senior Personality Questionnaire.

This questionnaire is intended to measure 14 factors of personality, such as general intelligence, emotional maturity, anxiety level, superego strength, and extroversion. In addition, the B.U. graduate students administered a questionnaire posing straightforward elicitations of the student's own view of himself.

Agreement between the direct questionnaire and the more subtle Cattell results will, according to those conducting the investigation, reveal high self-awareness. Discrepancy between the two, it is reasoned, will infer low self-awareness. At the end of the screen education course, both experimental and control groups will again take the direct questionnaire. If the screen education students move their self-image closer to the Cattell on the second try than control students, this will be regarded as evidence that the course better advances self-awareness than a random selection of high school courses.

LAUDABLE, PERHAPS FAULTY STUDY

Apparently the graduate students have failed to take into account that there may be something different about kids who have enrolled in the course, since there is no evident attempt to control this factor. Whatever the study results, they will contain unascertainable error on this count, a rather widespread defect of educational research. The graduate students are to be saluted, however, for their courage in trying to design a valid instrument for measuring self-awareness by the bootstrap method of asking different kinds of questions of the same person.

It is curious that Powell and his colleagues have chosen this ground to defend the value of screen education. Most school courses are judged on the basis of what a student produces: a term paper, a science project, a score on a national math test. One assumes that if these products are "good"—and the criteria for judging them have been well established over the years—then the process, the sweat, and struggle a student goes through are presumed educational.

Powell, on the other hand, asks that adults view student films uncritically, much as a father would view his child's scraggly drawing. The fact that students put together a film at all is a source of some wonder. Powell said that despite introductory exercises, getting kids to suggest suitable story ideas for a film was "like pulling hen's teeth." One applauds the very existence of a film under such circumstances, and probably this is how people view the student efforts at a public screening. But when the federal grant runs out, Powell is unlikely to bolster his arguments for continuing screen education courses at North Reading High School by showing the school committee "Fitzies Flunkies."

The difficulty with stressing increased "self-awareness" as a prime educational value is that one could argue that this derives from a student's being on a basketball team, in the choir, or joining in almost any purposeful group activity in a school. What makes screen education so special in building self-awareness? Unless this question is answered, screen education will likely end up on the periphery of the high school curriculum.

Let's grant its legitimacy for the moment. Where should screen education fit into the high school organization? Not in the A-V department, Powell insists. "The A-V specialist is more oriented towards presenting information with A-V equipment than he is in having students use this equipment to express themselves."

Instead, Powell is arguing for the amorphous state of "project" because this label hints that screen education is developmental, constantly changing, and that this fluidity and nonstructure will not threaten established academic departments. (His insistence that screen education be alloted its own budget may be threatening, however, since the faculty competes for discretionary funds.) He hopes that faculty members in the traditional departments will not hesitate to contribute to or benefit from the activities going on in screen education. He notes that social studies and English teachers are already making more frequent use of films in their classrooms.

Powell set one precedent that has endeared him to his faculty colleagues. As the students tackled more complex film projects, the school and campus became too confining, so Powell fought for and received permission for the student camera crews to shoot around town—without the supervision of a teacher. Now other departments have sent out unsupervised research teams. It was an extension of regulations that he regretted in one instance.

One student crew, making a slide-film narrative, staged a scene in a local cemetery. The story line was this: bad guys knocks down tombstone, sheriff and deputies arrest him and hang him from the limb of the nearest tree. A typical sophomoric plot, blood-thirsty but innocent. That particular day, however, a camera crew from the local educational TV station filmed the students at work, and the story ran on the evening's newscast. A member of North Reading's Commission of Cemeteries happened to catch the show and next day he demanded an apology for the "frivolous and irreverent use of cemeteries."

Powell soon found himself explaining the details of this particular exercise to the school committee and making amends to the complaining officer. "I had no idea there was such a commission," he said. "And I'll wager half the town didn't either."

COURSE ATTRACTS NONVERBAL STUDENTS

His current success in establishing a place for screen education in the school curriculum, other than on the periphery along with driver training and industrial arts, may be measured by the kind of students who enroll in his courses. He reports that students with below-average skill in verbalization are the ones who have been attracted to screen education. These are students who end their education with a high school degree. They usually see little relevance in traditional English courses and welcome a term away from books and papers. (They are in for quite a surprise, since Powell demands considerable writing as part of their work in screen education.) This is the group, the nonacademic or terminal student, that would benefit most from screen education, according to a third of the faculty who answered a questionnaire on the project.

Few college-prep students enrolled, because they worry about screen education credits being accepted for college admission. Powell said he has queried four college admission officers on this point, and was told that if high schools granted course credit they would honor them.

Despite this willingness to go along (and these admission officers spoke only for themselves), Mr. Powell and his fellow screen educators may have a difficult task convincing college-bound students, and their parents, to favor a course in screen education over a course in one of the traditional subjects. If they succeed, it will assure the subject's respectability.

Once the novelty pales it may also prove difficult to sustain the notion that nonverbal students should spend valuable school time "communicating" through film when they have not mastered the discipline of speaking or writing correctly, the more traditional and far more functional means of getting one's ideas across.

A FILM LIBRARY

Agee, James. *Agee on Film.* Boston: Beacon Press.*
Alpert, Hollis. *The Dreams and the Dreamers.* New York: Macmillan.
Arnheim, Rudolph. *Film As Art.* Berkeley and Los Angeles: University of California Press.*
Bazin, Andre. *What is Cinema?* Hugh Gray, trans. Berkeley and Los Angeles: University of California Press.
Carmen, Ira H. *Movies, Censorship and the Law.* Ann Arbor: University of Michigan Press.
Crowther, Bosley. "Movies and Censorship," Public Affairs Committee, 22 East 38 Street, New York, New York 10016. 25 cents.*
Eisenstein, Sergei. *Film Form and The Film Sense.* Meridan Press.*
Fulton, A. R. Motion *Pictures.* University of Oklahoma Press.
Griffith, Richard and Mayer, Arthur. *The Movies.* New York: Simon & Schuster.
Houston, Penelope. *The Contemporary Cinema.* Baltimore: Penguin Books.*
Jacobs, Lewis, ed., *Introduction to the Art of Movies.* Noonday Press.*
Kael, Pauline. *I Lost It at the Movies.* New York: Bantam.*
Kauffman, Stanley. *A World on Film.* Delta.*
Knight, Arthur. *The Liveliest Art.* Mentor.*
Kracauer, Siegfried. *Theory of Film.* New York: Oxford University Press.*
Lawson, John Howard. *Film: The Creative Process.* Hill and Wang.
MacGowen, Kenneth. *Behind the Screen: The History and Techniques of the Motion Picture.* New York: Delacorte Press.
McCann, Richard Dyer. *Film: A Montage of Theories.* New York: Dutton.*
Schickel, Richard. *Movies.* New York: Basic Books.
Talbot, Daniel, ed., *Film, An Anthology.* New York: Simon & Schuster.
Warshow, Robert. *The Immediate Experience.* New York: Doubleday.*
* Available in paperback

Freaking Around with Films

Rodney E. Sheratsky

Film, we have been assured by four writers under 30, is The Art That Matters.[1] Educators impressed with the truth of this and desperate to turn their

From Rodney E. Sheratsky, "Freaking Around with Films," *Media and Methods* 7 (November 1970): 40-42, 54. Copyright ©1970 by Media and Methods Institute, Inc. Reprinted by permission of *Media and Methods* and Rodney E. Sheratsky.

students on, bought it. They announced curricula made relevant through film.

Film study and film making are becoming endemic. The American Film Institute, which in part exists to foster screen education and film making, lists more than 1,000 teachers on its current roster.[2] Presumably, these are the Film Teachers. There are thousands more who are only film teachers. Moreover, 73 members listed in the directory advised AFI that their institutions are sponsoring film-making activities. . . . The question, obviously, is not how many, but how effectively, how intelligently and skillfully are these teachers using film and making film? One way of finding out is to examine the views of students themselves.

Why do students want to make films? Stefan Kanfer, film critic of *Time,* has reported some of the reasons: "Everybody's making a movie . . . ,"[3] [It's] a form of artistic expression . . . ,"[4] ". . . film is the most vital modern art form."[5] Where will all this burst of creativity lead? "In the long run . . . the contemporary enthusiasm for student films is likely to turn out a far greater number of enlightened appreciators than new creators. That in itself could be a boon to movies; whether cinema grows as an art form depends largely upon whether film-educated audiences demand better things of it."[6]

Fortunately, Mr. Kanfer's article acknowledges that, because of the limitations of certain equipment and the talents of some students, not all films are excellent, imaginative, or worthy of an audience. If one doubts the notion that film "is the medium of youth"—and it is a notion that could be challenged—he should ask students why teenagers should *not* make films. After studying film production for four months, two high school seniors expressed it this way:

> Too many students want to major in film making after their initial exposure to the medium. Although these students' first films might be excellent, only a handful of people in the world will ever become renowned for their films. Film making is a terribly expensive interest; as such, it is a fine diversion for the rich.[7]
>
> Isn't it more important for students to become involved with techniques and ideas which are absolutely essential? Frankly, making films is not essential. The majority of students could spend their time much more profitably reading about the history of man and thinking about what he has done to cause the horrible dilemmas we face. The "film freaks" I know are "freaks" because they know nothing about the history of ideas; all they know is the method necessary to achieve certain effects with their cameras.[8]

Who can reject either statement, particularly the last in which one student has implied why so many student films are failures? Without respect for the tradition of ideas, a film maker can think only of technique.

But, no matter how many argue against teaching students to make films, some are still going to insist that students have a right to "use" *their* medium to foster their "creative expression," even if they have nothing worth expressing. There are at least 11 types of students who should not make films. The types, by the way, were compiled by high school seniors who completed the first half of a two semester course, film production. Who should not study film making? Students:

1. Who are not willing to admit their films do not have even adequate photography and lighting;
2. Who habitually announce projects they are not intellectually capable of fulfilling;
3. Who cannot work alone. ("Much of what is good in a student's film is the result of working alone, during those periods in a project when the work is tedious," cautioned one senior.);
4. Who insist that a good film can be made only after a committee of seven, eight, or more designs and approves every phase on the project;
5. Who are irresponsible, lazy, and undisciplined;
6. Who do not respect the equipment (cameras, editor-viewers, lights, and exposure meters) and budgets they have been permitted to use;
7. Who want to make films because they cannot read or write;
8. Who think they have become "expert" film makers just because they have learned the elementary techniques of film making;
9. Who cannot realize that their films are hopelessly inept, boring, and banal;
10. Who want to make films because film making is "in";
11. Who do not have an appreciation and a feeling for life. [9]

There is a very practical reason to discourage students from making films. The reason was suggested by a poet, working on a screenplay for Warner Brothers:

The question remains: how many will get a chance? A person can become a great poet in the privacy of his home, accumulate 20 or 30 years worth of manuscripts and bitterness, and, perhaps, finally have his day. A film maker without the machinery for making films can accumulate only 20 or 30 years of bitterness. It is a conceit of the successful that talent will out. However, as there are always so many incompetents among the successful, it seems clear that there are no doubt many gifted people among the failures. "You have to sell yourself," says Steven Gaines. "In the end, it's luck," says Jeff Young. [10]

The writer, of course, referred to those who hope to work in the film industry. What about those who want to work independently? Or those who insist on making their films their way, The Establishment be damned? Or those independents, members of the American underground whose work has the look of home movies rather than "real" movies?

There are still other practical questions to answer before a high school encourages students to make films. Who will teach film making—the English teacher who has never made a film? The art teacher who has been trained in the visual arts; Graduate students of film schools? (Because professional film makers do not have the time to teach on a regular daily or weekly basis, graduate students could be trained to teach high school students. This is a suggestion the American Film Institute could explore. If those who have no training in film decide they are capable of teaching film making, a fad of the sixties will pass into oblivion during the seventies.)

Is there, then, no reason to teach high school students to make films? Yes, there is, but it does not pertain to any of the dramatic, fashionable, grandiose reasons cited and questioned previously. Indeed, the reasons for teaching film making are so basic, they might seem blatantly obvious. Still, it might refresh teachers to analyze the obvious before they announce the grandiose. A giant of early documentary cinema can help us.

At the summary session of the 1969 Robert Flaherty Film Seminar, Mrs. Frances Flaherty, a woman dedicated to preserving her husband's memory and passing on to a younger generation the heritage of her husband's art, reminded 75 film makers, teachers, librarians, and students of Pudovkin's charge, "The basic aim of cinema is to teach people to see all things new." [11] Later, she quoted the French philosopher de Chardin, "To see more is to become more. Deeper seeing is closer union . . . to see or to perish is man's condition." [12]

In the remarkable study film for *Louisiana Story*, Mrs. Flaherty reminisces, "Bob always used to say that the camera is a seeing machine. And the job of the director is to help the viewer discover and explore for himself." Robert Flaherty's idea is striking. Yet, the documentarian's point raises some complex questions. If the camera is a seeing machine, whose sight is more crucial—the operator's or the viewer's? If it is the camera's operator who is seeing, then how can we be certain that his seeing machine will work if he does not have Flaherty's confidence in an audience astute and willing enough to want to discover and explore? If the camera is a seeing machine, should the photographer and director record every reality they feel the audience should see? And what about the camera and the functions we have expected art to fulfill—namely, to communicate ideas and emotions? To organize life into meaningful patterns? To make order out of chaos? To reveal universal truths through the self-imposed individuality of the artist? What becomes the function of the seeing machine when one renounces these traditional beliefs about art's functions? Suppose one accepts, instead, composer John Cage's argument that art is meaningful only when it is born of chance and indeterminacy? Cage believes the artist must work to make discoveries in his daily life. Only chance will open to us possibilities we could never realize if we accepted only another person's notions of life and art. [13]

But what about students and the seeing machine? In too many of our high schools, students will graduate without ever having been taught how to see. That is deplorable. Rightfully, we train our students how to read, write, think, listen, and speak. Although our more aware schools encourage students to use reading machines, tape recorders, slide, overhead and movie projectors, too many neglect to cultivate their student's visual perception. By the time they have been graduated from high schools, too many students are visually illiterate. Many of our students look, yet do not see. Work with high school seniors who have just begun film projects and you will understand why the old saying, "They have eyes, yet see not," is a cliché. It's a cliché because it's true for so many people in so many places. Unless students have been made aware of the process of visual perception, how can they help their audiences to see the phenomena they have arranged to have projected on the screen?

We have seen how today's magazines report the development of high school film making activities throughout the country. Some educators claim that, when students have convincingly demonstrated throughout their high school years that the book and pens they have been using are purposeless, a camera might help unsatisfied students to develop images of themselves that will increase their self respect. Or, to state it another way, because film is supposed to "turn kids on," it is instant panacea. This justification for film making should be questioned by all who deplore the use of any art form as a device to "save" people. Rodger Larson, Jr., with his students in New York City's ghettoes, would be the first to admit that his students do not make films for therapy. They make films because they are so committed to the art that they are willing to work ten hours for each minute of film that is eventually projected on the screen. The students, whose films project unbelievably vital reactions to life, are fiercely dedicated. They want their films screened not because they reflect people whose lives have been saved by film. They want their films screened because they are valid, important works which have become so because of the talent, intelligence, and stamina necessary for their creation.

Others believe that the camera provides us with a machine that can cultivate, sharpen, and deepen our powers of seeing. When students have cultivated these powers, then they can help to fulfill the Flaherty ideal: helping viewers discover and explore. In addition to helping students learn how to see, a film making program can help students to make patterns. The intelligent making of patterns depends upon one's intelligent manipulation of materials to express the patterns.

What about the patterns in student-made films? What assignments can students be given which will help them to cultivate visual awareness and make patterns which connect with ideas and points in the film?

After they have been taught and shown why it is important to care for and clean their cameras, as well as projectors and other pieces of equipment, students might shoot the following assignments. The assignments are basic; they're also necessary if students are going to approach their work with care, thought, and discipline. Each assignment is for one roll of film:

1. Select an area with definite boundaries (a room, a house, a street, a field). With images and lighting, capture the atmosphere of that space. Emphasize good lighting, sharp focus, and meaningful framing. Keep the camera stationary. Use a tripod. Do not pan, tilt, or zoom.
2. Return to the area used for the first assignment. In addition to shooting for the same specifications, use such camera movements as the pan, tilt, or zoom.
3. Shoot a person leaving for and arriving at his destination. Stress continuity and character motivation so the audience understands how and why the individual travels from point to point.
4. Edit the exercise in continuity.

5. Shoot two persons conversing. Do not rely on recorded sound, obvious signals, or titles. Rely, instead, on significant gestures so the audience understands the topic of the conversation.
6. Edit the conversation exercise.
7. Shoot a one-minute commercial. Rely on striking images, sounds, and lighting to "sell" the product.
8. Select a composer whose last name begins with B (Bach, Beatles, Beethoven, Bernstein, Brubeck, etc.). Choreograph and edit the movement of the images to the music of the composer.

During the remaining weeks of the course, students may work on "longer" projects (about 10-20 minutes). After students have selected the ideas for their films, they may submit treatments, scripts, or storyboards before they shoot. (Incidentally, the technical crew should have no more than a director, cameraman, and editor. If too many students are assigned to a project, those who are not actively involved will lose interest.) Ask students to screen their unedited rushes so others may comment about the quality of the shooting and the possibilities for final editing.

Instant success and recognition cannot be promised to anyone who makes films; indeed, the teacher who promises and expects instant rewards contributes to one of the more generic deficiencies of the under-25 generation.

Robert Flaherty did not use his seeing machine for instant purposes. During a 30-year career as a film maker, Flaherty made only four feature-length films. Today, *Nanook of the North, Moana, Man of Aran,* and *Louisiana Story* still seem in advance of their day. A man committed to the ideal that a film maker must help the audience to discover phenomena, he knew one does not learn how to see instantly. One learns how to see after much careful and thoughtful work with his camera. The goals of a film-making program—to help students see and encourage them to make meaningful patterns—are modest. And yet, properly realized, these are goals one can spend a lifetime trying to fulfill.

Introducing students to an awareness of the essentials required for seeing may well be the only realistic, honest, and sensible reason for encouraging students to make films. On the high school level, all one can—and should—do is introduce students to an awareness of the essentials required for seeing. A high school film-making program should not become a professional film making school. Why? Most public schools cannot compete with the facilities many colleges and university film departments offer their students. If a high school teacher encourages his students to think they are film makers on the basis of one course in film making, he's as dishonest as his colleague who tells a child, "My! Only someone with your rare talent could have made this work of art," when the work of "art" was thoughtlessly conceived and artlessly completed. During the sixties we have witnessed the damage done by such dishonest, though well intentioned, teachers who were more concerned with protecting the child's ego than with cultivating his intellect and artistic talent. Film critic Pauline Kael has questioned the results: "Did anyone guess or foresee what narcissistic confidence this generation would develop in its banal 'creativity?' Now we're surrounded, inundated by artists. And a staggering number of them wish to be or already call themselves 'film makers'." [14]

NOTES

1. "The Art That Matters—A Look at Today's Film Scene by the Under-Thirties," *Saturday Review,* 27 December 1969, p. 7.
2. The American Film Institute, *Educational Membership Directory 69,* Introduction.
3. Stefan Kanfer, "The Student Movie-Makers," *Film 68/69* (New York: Simon and Schuster, 1969), p. 247.
4. Ibid., p. 248.
5. Op.cit.
6. Ibid., p. 252.
7. A survey, "Why High School Students Should Not Study Film Making," conducted at the Center for Film Production, Northern Valley Regional High School at Demarest, Demarest, New Jersey.
8. Ibid.
9. Ibid.
10. R. J. Monaco, "You're Only As Young As They Think You Are," *Saturday Review,* 27 December 1969, p. 17.
11. Robert Flaherty Film Seminar, August 26-September 2, 1969, The Hotchkiss School, Lakeville, Connecticut. Remarks made September 2, 1969.
12. Op. cit.
13. John Cage, "45' For A Speaker," *Silence* (Cambridge, Mass.: The M.I.T. Press, 1967), pp. 146-193.
14. Pauline Kael, "Movie Brutalities," *Kiss Kiss Bang Bang* (Boston: Little, Brown and Co., 1968), p. 17.

Suggested Discussion Questions and Activities

1. **DISCUSSION** There are many methods and beliefs expressed in these articles. With which do you agree, question, or find fault? Why?

2. **ACTIVITY** Assume you have just been assigned to secondary school X and asked to design a course or a series of activities in film study and film making. Outline the steps you would take to get such a project underway.

3. **ACTIVITY** All film programs cost money, usually more than is allocated for the regular English budget, and not every school is able to secure a federal grant for a film project. Believing, as Culkin comments, "Great moments deserve modest beginnings":

   (a) Identify all of the resources you might approach or tap for support and all of the schemes you might employ to sponsor a film program. (Don't forget to enlist the aid of students; they have great ideas and even better schemes.)

   (b) Investigate the cost of film purchase and rental, local movie showings for classes, equipment costs and rental fees; look into a variety of sources as a dollar or two will make a large difference when all of the costs are totaled.